GOD'S FRONTIERSMEN
The Scots-Irish Epic

To John on his Special Birthday

from Joan & Oliver

NOSURRENDER

GOD'S FRONTIERSMEN

The Scots-Irish Epic

RORY FITZPATRICK

Photography by
KENNETH McNALLY

PERIBO
PUBLISHERS OF FINE BOOKS

For Peter

ENDPAPERS *'Where there are drumlins, there are drums', said the geographer Estyn Evans. The rich hillocks or drumlins, left by the Ice Age in Ulster, were usually occupied by Protestant settlers and echoed in the summer months to Orange music.*

FRONTISPIECE *William III, not the historical figure, nor even an expression of religious bigotry, but a piece of folk magic – an amulet to protect his people.*

First published in Australia in 1989 by
Peribo Pty Limited
9 Gibbes Street, Chatswood, NSW 2067

First published in Great Britain in 1989 by
George Weidenfeld & Nicolson Ltd

ISBN 1–86322–000–3

Designed by Joy FitzSimmons

Printed and bound in Great Britain by
Butler & Tanner Ltd, Frome and London

CONTENTS

Maps

ACKNOWLEDGMENTS

I would like to acknowledge the generous assistance and advice of many scholars and writers on both sides of the Atlantic, particularly: Kathleen Brown, Woodrow Wilson Centre, Staunton, Va.; Tyler Blethen, University of Western Carolina; Denis Clark, Philadelphia; W. H. Crawford, Ulster Folk Museum; Jan Davidson, University of Western Carolina; David N. Doyle, University College, Dublin; George MacDonald Fraser, novelist and historian; Alan Gailey, Ulster Folk Museum; Raymond Gillespie, Dept. of Finance, Dublin; Finlay Holmes, Queen's University, Belfast; Cecil J. Houston, University of Toronto; Ed Knowlin, Westmoreland County Historical Society, Pa.; Richard McMaster, Bluffton College, Ohio; Denis McNeice, Ulster-American Folk Park, Omagh, Northern Ireland; Grady McWhiney, Texas Christian University, Fort Worth; W. A. Maguire, Ulster Museum, Belfast; David Miller, Carnegie-Mellon University, Pittsburgh; Kerby Miller, University of Missouri; Bobby G. Moss, Gaffney, S.C.; Noel Nesbitt, Ulster Museum, Belfast; Deane Root, University of Pittsburgh; William J. Smyth, St Patrick's College, Maynooth, Ireland; John Speers, Newark, New Jersey; A. T. Q. Stewart, Queen's University, Belfast; Charles Stoner, Chambersburg, Pa.; George Thompson, former director of Ulster Folk Museum; Brian Trainor, former director of Public Record Office of Northern Ireland; Brian M. Walker, Queen's University, Belfast; John Winter, Ulster-American Folk Park; Curtis Wood, University of Western Carolina.

I would also like to thank many museums, historical societies and other institutions including: Kittochtinny Historical Society, Pa.; Westmoreland County Historical Society, Pa.; Valley Forge National Park; Virginia Military Institute, Lexington; The Hermitage, Tennessee; Tinkling Spring Presbyterian Church, Va.; Donegal Presbyterian Church, Pa.; National Park Service, U.S.A.; Public Record Office of Northern Ireland; Ulster-American Folk Park; Ulster Folk Park.

My especial thanks to Tim McIvor, now of the New Zealand Civil Service, for his painstaking research into the Scots–Irish story in Australia and New Zealand and for his cataloguing of research material for the whole project, to my editor Martha Caute for her patience and advice during the months while I was struggling simultaneously to write the book and produce the television series and to my secretary Ruth Davis for the skill with which she interpreted my handwriting and for the immaculate typescript which resulted.

R.F.

INTRODUCTION

THE POPULAR IMAGE of the Ulster Protestant purveyed by much of the world's press and television and by the authors of instant studies of the Irish question is that of a red-faced man, his features contorted, beating a large drum. This simple visual cliché has been used repeatedly to convey violence, intransigence and bigotry, neat labels under which, in the high speed information world of today, a busy journalist can package an entire people. Each television documentary or book on the Ulster troubles offers a history of the so-called native or Catholic Irish but usually nothing on the background of the Protestant people. It is almost as if they were destitute of features, emotions or even intelligent life, without existence in time, a monolith whose only purpose is to be the granite against which the national aspirations of an Irish people are dashed. The intention of this book is to explode that myth.

The ancestors of the Protestant population of Ulster arrived there in a series of immigrations during the seventeenth century, coming from the Scottish Lowlands and Borders and to a lesser extent from various parts of England, as far apart as Lancashire, Norfolk and Devon. Within a hundred years they had transformed the north of Ireland from a land composed largely of woods and swamps, interspersed with small areas of modest cultivation, into a province with roads, market towns and ports, supported by an increasingly arable system of farming, a thriving cattle trade and a domestic textile industry. Into a country where Catholic medieval values and an indolent pastoral economy pervaded, they brought Calvinistic Protestantism and a stern work ethic.

Although they came into what was an English colony and many of them were originally part of the official settlement of Ulster by the English Crown, the Scots so predominated in numbers, in the toughness of their culture and in the determination with which they acquired land, that the whole Plantation enterprise took on Scottish characteristics and the name 'Ulster Scots' came in time to be applied to the entire non-Irish population of the Province which included large numbers of English, much smaller numbers of Welsh and some refugee French Protestants. In America the term 'Scotch-Irish', which had originally been used by Ulster students training for the Presbyterian ministry at Scottish universities, was applied to the Protestant immigrants from Ulster to distinguish them from the Catholic Irish who arrived later. For the purposes of this book, the terms Ulster Scots and Scots- or Scotch-Irish are regarded as interchangeable; they are also applied for the sake of identification in chapters dealing with Canada, Australia and New Zealand, lands where these terms would not have been known.

From the early years of the eighteenth century, thousands of Ulster Scots emigrated to the Colonies of British North America, first to New England and then in much larger numbers to Pennsylvania. From thence they went southwards through the Great Valley, east of the Appalachian Mountains, into the Shenandoah Valley of Virginia and on to the Piedmont of North and South Carolina. Within three generations the line of the Appalachian range, from New England to Georgia was dotted with settlements of Ulster origin.

This was the beginning of the American Old West and the Scots-Irish people provided most of its pioneers; the archetypal frontiersman, Davy Crockett, was the son of an immigrant from County Derry. They also left in the Appalachian region a rich heritage of material culture – the masonry skills of the Ulster Scot can be traced from the bawns, or defensive walls, of Plantation Ulster to the stone houses of Kentucky – a story-telling tradition and a legacy of music and dance which was the basis of Appalachian mountain culture.

In the American War of Independence the Scots-Irish contribution was twofold. A large proportion of the political activists, particularly in Pennsylvania and the Carolinas, were Scots-Irish and the Presbyterian congregations, composed very largely of first, second and third generation Ulster people, provided the conduits for revolutionary philosophy. One contemporary summed up the whole revolution as 'an Irish-Scotch Presbyterian Rebellion'.

During the actual fighting, the Ulster communities, steeled by years of spasmodic warfare against the Indians, provided both guerilla fighters and regular troops for Washington's army. The famous Pennsylvania Line, the so-called 'Line of Ireland', had regiments composed of Scots-Irish, like Col. William Thompson's Second Regiment – frontier riflemen who could kill British redcoats at twice the accepted range of the military musket. It was the guerilla fighters from the Ulster mountain communities who turned the tide of war against the British in the southern colonies. At this early stage they were already Americans; they 'formed the nucleus of the American army, absolutely loyal to the American cause and knowing no fatherland but the wilderness'.

The nineteenth century was a period of immense achievement in politics and business for the Scots-Irish in America. They provided the United States with ten Presidents, two of whom, Andrew Jackson and Woodrow Wilson, were among the greatest chief executives to occupy the White House. Jackson, first of the Scots-Irish Presidential line, had the ideal combination of opinions and experience for his period – radical politics, anti-colonialist soldiering and frontiersmanship. Wilson, at the end of the line, seemed the epitome of the Scots-Irish legend as a thinker and an achiever. God-fearing, individualistic and determined, he was, as leading architect of the Versailles Treaty at the end of the First World War, for a brief period the arbiter of the world. The rest of the Presidents were a mixed bunch: Andrew Johnston was capable but unfortunate; Ulysses Grant drank too much; one or two were downright mediocre.

Shrewdness, a Presbyterian devotion to hard work, and good political connections enabled hundreds of Scots-Irish to be successful small and middle-grade businessmen, but the apex of the group's commercial success came with the banking Mellons and oil-rich Gettys; Thomas Mellon, from County Tyrone, created what is probably the greatest business dynasty the world has seen. In education, in state politics, particularly in the South, and in evangelism, descendants of the Ulster pioneers contributed largely to the nineteenth-century development of American life.

On each succeeding frontier to the Rocky Mountains, the Scots-Irish were prominent, either as groups or as individuals. They spearheaded the first thrusts through the Appalachians into Western Pennsylvania, Kentucky and Tennessee; theirs were among the first settlements in Ohio, Illinois and Indiana; they were aboard the prairie schooners which crossed the heart of the continent to the 'grass states' where their traditional herding skills met the challenge of spaces undreamed of in Ireland or even Carolina. The Rockies brought out the individual greatness in Scots-Irish like Kit Carson, John Colter and Robert Campbell.

In the nineteenth century the Ulster Scots diaspora took new directions. Between 1820 and 1840, Protestant immigrants from the north of Ireland colonized the wilderness of Upper Canada, leap-frogging the Canadian Loyalist settlements along the shores of the St Lawrence and penetrating northwards through the woods of Ontario to the Laurentian Shield. By mid-century some Ulster farmers were acquiring huge tracts of land in the outback of New South Wales and Victoria and becoming part of the Australian millionaire 'squattocracy'. In both Australia and New Zealand educated Ulster Scots were providing a remarkable proportion of the professional people – doctors, lawyers, engineers – on which the new colonial societies were to be built.

When, in the summer of 1798, twelve-year-old James Thompson watched an Ulster rebel army marching to meet British troops in battle, he knew they were Ulster-Scots Presbyterians because they wore their Sunday clothes. Nothing could have been more revealing; the occasion was a challenge to tyrannical authority and, in their minds, it had the truth, the dignity, and the solemnity of the Sabbath.

The rebellion had come, not only as the culmination of decades of increasing radicalism among Ulster Presbyterians but also as an outcome of their evolution as a distinct racial group. Caught in the natural geographic unit of Ulster between an aristocratic land-owning class, largely English in origin and allegiance and Episcopalian in religion, and a Catholic native Irish who feared and resented them, the Calvinist settlers had become a self-reliant people strongly conscious and proud of their cultural heritage and confident enough to state in arms that they no longer depended on English masters.

One of the most harmful myths about the Ulster Scots is that they are an immobile people entrenched in a rampart of ancient prejudice; Scots-Irish history, as a whole, offers a completely antithetical viewpoint. 'A people who in many ways were the epitome of mobility and change': the verdict drawn by two modern American scholars from their study of Ulster migrations to southern Appalachia could be applied in both the physical and psychological sense to the entire Scots-Irish experience.

1 • THE ROOTS OF A PEOPLE

'They christen without the cross, marry without a ring ... die without repentance and bury without divine service.'

A Perfect Description of the People and Country of Scotland, 1617

'John Tenender, session officer, shall have his red staff in the kirk on Sabbath-days, therewith to wauken sleepers and to remove greeting bairns furth of the kirk.'

Perth Kirk Session Record, 1616

TO UNDERSTAND the Scots-Irish it is necessary to meet them in their first homeland, the Scottish Lowlands and Borders in that dynamic period of the seventeenth century when they were preparing for their first emigrations. Scotland was then a land of poverty, violence and intolerance but at the same time Scottish society possessed a degree of religious democracy remarkable for the period, an immense thirst for education and a pentecostal vision which was comparable to that of the early Christians. From this paradoxical situation a remarkable people emerged, a people who bear to this day the psychological imprint of their Scottish experience.

The landscape of Lowland Scotland in the seventeenth century was bare and treeless, much of it marshy and uncultivated. Dotting the countryside were 'farmtouns' – groups of houses with mud walls, roofs of branches and sods, a hole in the centre of the roof serving as a chimney and small unglazed windows, with one solid unpretentious, stone-built house, the home of the principal tenant of the farm and perhaps, a mill and a church. The farmland surrounding the 'toun' was divided into strips of arable and pastoral, the arable producing barley for beer and oats for the staple peasant foods of porridge and oatcake. The mill, the property of the landlord where his tenants were compelled to grind their corn, represented the oppressive element in this social unit: the Reformed Kirk, where master and servant were, at least in theory, equal, represented its aspirations to liberty.

The Scottish social structure was complex and antiquated. At the top of the pile was a group of powerful, land-owning nobles, arrogant and quarrelsome, barely under Royal control; beneath them a much larger number of country gentlemen or lairds who followed the predatory example of the nobles and were usually involved in feuds and cattle-stealing forays. Next came the tenants of the farmtouns, who were often the equivalent of English yeomen, letting their lands to sub-tenants and employing a variety of shepherds, ploughmen and casual labourers. Each type of individual had his own status and his own duties within the farm organization, all under the jurisdiction of the local baron court over which the laird presided.

This post-feudal order was important because the Scots were then overwhelmingly a rural people, but the Royal burghs, towns like Edinburgh, Aberdeen, Perth, Ayr, with special trading privileges and the right of self-government, exercised an influence out of proportion to their population in shaping the outlook of the Scottish people. They were the nurseries of Protestant religious independence; they provided the opportunities for overseas trade which stimulated Scottish restlessness; they pointed new ways to power through the acquisition of wealth – all three characteristics which were to figure largely in the subsequent history of the Scots-Irish.

The Scottish Reformation brought a new ardour for learning. Scotland, says the Scots-Irish historian, James Leyburn, was 'the first country to inaugurate public education'. The aim of the Kirk, by no means fulfilled, was to provide a primary school for every parish, a grammar school in each burgh and a reformed university system with many more places for students. Before the end of the sixteenth century two new universities, Edinburgh and Aberdeen had joined Glasgow and St Andrews. By the mid-century most parishes had schools and the curriculum, while still religion-orientated, had broadened to include such secular subjects as arithmetic. The Reformed Kirk even showed a social conscience, giving an indication in its early enthusiastic days that it was prepared to bring about a new era of social justice based on the teachings of Christ.

But for all this apparent enlightenment, Scotland was still 'full of barbarity, feuds and oppressions'. Women, in particular, were victims. There were frequent abductions, the richer girls to be forcibly married for the sake of their dowries, the poor to be raped. Robert Napier, a gentleman's son took away eleven-year-old Elizabeth Turnbull after seeing her while at dinner in her father's home. Katherine Weir, aged fourteen, was snatched by William Geddes at the head of a party of men who arrived with 'swords, gauntlets, steel bonnets and plait sleeves'.

Women who gossiped, like Bessie Tailiefeir from Cannongate in Edinburgh, were 'branked' – their heads enclosed in iron frames with spikes thrust into their mouths. Male fear of female sexuality was extreme; the Kirk Session of Perth forbade two unmarried sisters to live together in the same house under pain of banishment. An English traveller observed that the women of the Scottish upper classes were 'kept like lions in iron grates', and in Aberdeen, 'following the example of other weel reformit congregations', wives were ordered to sit in the centre of the church where they could be watched.

The execution fire that burned steadily on the Castle Hill in Edinburgh (on 15 October 1656 five people were burned) usually claimed women accused of sorcery:

> Some women were ta'en as witches and being put to ane assize and convict, albeit they persevered constant in their denial to the end, yet they burnt quick [alive] in sic

LEFT *Though the Scottish Calvinists were among the most ferocious witch-hunters in Europe, their Presbyterian cousins in Ulster treated witchcraft with intelligence, and its supposed adherents with mercy.*

BELOW *This nineteenth-century engraving of Scottish Border reivers attacking a castle shows the romantic influence of the novels of Walter Scott.*

> ane cruel manner that some of them diet in dispair, renuncand and blasphemand, and others, half burnt, brak out of the fire and were cast in quick into it again while [until] they were burnt to the died [to death].

Margaret Barclay of Irvine, in Ayrshire, was remorselessly tortured until she confessed that her lapdog was, in fact, the devil and, though she recanted when the torture stopped, was sent to the stake. Some of the women who died were merely herbalists or other types of amateur healers. Margaret Wallace, who cured people by hypnotism, was sentenced to be 'worried at the stake and burnt'. A mariner sailing into his native Dundee after years at sea saw the fire in which his mother was burning. Gipsies and homosexuals proved easy targets for Scottish zealots, both lay and clerical. When the extreme wing of the Calvinist party was dominant, homosexuals were vigorously prosecuted. 'Culprits of all ages from boys to old men . . . burnt on the Castle Hill . . . sometimes two together'. 'Egyptians' or gipsies were banished from the country; in 1624 eight who had failed to comply with orders to leave the country were hanged and their wives and children deported. Twelve years later the Privy Council, complaining that it was 'troublesome and burdenable' to keep a group of gipsies in jail at Haddington, decreed that 'the men be hangit and the women to be drowned'.

Incest was punished by beheading and the interpretation of the offence was very wide. John Weir was sentenced to death for marrying the widow of his grand-uncle, Alexander Blair for marrying his first wife's half-brother's daughter. Henry Dick lost his head because of an unspecified sexual encounter with his wife's sister, and Janet Imrie, who slept with two brothers, was beheaded in 1643. The High Street in Edinburgh was the scene of constant bloodshed. A laird on his way to the Court of Session met an officer 'with whom he had some slight quarrel', ran him through with his sword and proceeded to court. In June 1685 the son of the Earl of Morton killed a footman of the Laird of Chatto, near St Giles Cathedral, in a dispute over a mongrel dog. The son of the Archbishop of St Andrews murdered the family cook as he was preparing the Archbishop's supper but was able to buy a pardon. Accounts of such violence between relations, neighbours and acquaintances in the Lowlands, or so-called 'civilized' parts of Scotland, fill pages of the Privy Council records. On the sea coasts, plagued by pirates, life was even harsher. A visitor to Leith in July 1610 would have seen twenty-seven buccaneers swinging from a makeshift gibbet on the pier.

Protest in Reformation Scotland was severely punished. In 1597, Francis Tennant, a satirist of Edinburgh was sentenced to 'have his tongue cuttit out at the rute'. A rash Englishman, John Dickson, was hanged for calling the king a bastard. Thomas Ross, who, while studying at Oxford, wrote 'a libel on the Scottish nation', was extradited and in the Scottish capital 'his right hand was first struck off, then he was beheaded and quartered, his head being fixed on a prick at the Nether Bow Port and his hand at the West Port'.

It is ironic that the Calvinist regime should exercise such severity against authors of lampoons when the success of the Reformation itself had depended to a great degree on this type of propaganda. Folk songs with anti-Romanist refrains like 'The Paip, that pagane, full of pride' did more than sermons, however inspiring, to spread the message of the Reformers among the common people. The tradition, despite persecution, did not die and was to surface most notably in the Scots-Irish journalists who were so effective in promoting the radical cause in Revolutionary America.

Religious dissent was tolerated to a greater degree than secular protest. No matter how violent their language towards what they described as the 'Roman Anti-Christ', the Scottish Calvinists were mild in their treatment of Catholics. (This is worth remembering when interpreting anti-Catholic speeches in modern Ulster.) Recusant Papists were punished with fines and imprisonment in cases which, in Catholic or Protestant countries in Europe, would have meant death. The only priest to suffer martyrdom, the Jesuit John Ogilvie, was condemned by Archbishop Spottiswoode, who himself was regarded by extreme Calvinists as 'a traitor ... to the Church of Scotland'. David Mathew, in *Scotland Under Charles the First*, offers the intriguing suggestion that this comparative tolerance was due to the conviction that God in his own good time would deal with Catholics.

Discipline inside the Reformed Kirk was strict. Everyone was compelled under severe penalties to go to church twice on Sundays; in Aberdeen a baillie and two elders went from house to house to catch anyone who stayed at home. The author John Buchan believed that the Reformation destroyed the old 'Merrie Scotland'; certainly it did away with the traditional holidays and countryside customs. The celebration of Christmas was forbidden; midsummer and Hallowe'en bonfires, pilgrimages to holy wells, folk plays – all came under ban. Punishments by the Kirk included ducking in water, shaving of heads, and flogging. The ultimate punishment was excommunication after which the culprit became a non-person, 'given into the hands of Satan and therefore made odious to all men that they should eschew his company'.

The killjoys of Scottish puritanism were also active philistines, 'the bigots of the iron time', in the words of Walter Scott. In 1579, Parliament passed an Act condemning 'ministrels, sangsters, and story-tellers ... vagabond scholars of the universities of St Andrews, Glasgow and Aberdeen'. In the same year two poets were hanged in Edinburgh following the publication of their verses, a practice since discontinued.

The violence of their society had little to do with the decision of thousands of Scots to emigrate to Ireland, but it prepared them for a frontier life extending in time and distance beyond anything the most gifted of their visionary pastors could have foreseen. The other elements of Lowland Scots life, the attitude towards groups like 'Egyptians' whose social behaviour was alien, the sexual guilt complex associated with women, the mercantilist instinct, the zeal for education, became part of the mental luggage of the emigrants.

The stimulus to move was economic. By the beginning of the seventeenth century the country was heavily populated in relation to its resources and technology, and the antiquated system of land tenure had become highly unstable. High inflation in the sixteenth century had changed land ownership and destroyed much of the traditional relationship between landlord and tenant. A period of good returns from agriculture after 1610 led to greatly increased exports of food; 'within the compass of one year there were shipped away from that port [Leith] four score thousand balls of wheat, oats and barley into Spain, France and other foreign parts'. But this prosperity benefitted the land-owning classes to the detriment of the tenants and sub-tenants.

The expectations of the nobles and lairds were raised by the unaccustomed prosperity, expectations enhanced by the living standards they had seen on the Continent; the sons of Scottish gentlemen were great travellers, serving as mercenaries in armies all over Europe or trading as merchants, especially out of the Baltic ports. Locked into a system where much of their rent was paid in kind, by produce or work performed, the landowners were existing by a superior kind of subsistence living. To break free and achieve a more luxurious standard of living they imposed money rents, changing tenancies over to a feuing system, whereby a tenant made an initial payment and thereafter an annual fixed one. The result was that thousands of tenants, unable to meet the new monetary demands, were evicted, 'cast . . . out of their kindly possessions, which their predecessors and they had enjoyed'. The Lowlands, the area with the largest population and the one most affected by social changes, now had a large pool of potential emigrants, people desperate for land or work; 'Scotland, by reason of her populousness being constrained to disburden her selfe (like the painful Bees) did every yeere send forth swarmes', Sir William Alexander noted in 1624.

When James VI of Scotland succeeded his distant cousin Elizabeth to the throne of England, Ireland as a subject kingdom of the English Crown became a potential settlement area for Scots. Ireland had been nominally under the English Crown since the twelfth century but it was only at the end of the sixteenth century that Ulster, the last Irish province to resist, was brought under English military control. In a terrible nine-year war the armies of Elizabeth finally defeated the Ulster chieftains, Hugh O'Neill and Hugh O'Donnell, reducing the province by terror and famine. One English general, Arthur Chichester, summed up their methods when he described an English raid deep into the Irish heartlands, 'We spare none of what quality or sex soever and it hath bred much terror in the people who heard not a drum there or saw a fire of long time'. It was in a land wasted by a scorched earth policy and against a background of genocide that the first Scots settlement was to begin.

Not only did Ireland pose a strategic threat, but her incessant wars soaked up English manpower and money. The verdict of the Venetian ambassador to London could still stand today, 'Ireland is such that it would be better for the king if it did not exist and the sea alone rolled there'. James recognized that his predecessor's subjugation of Ulster was only a temporary expedient. His special mission, he believed, was to provide a self-financing machinery which would not only neutralize the potential Irish menace to English security but would also bring the country into line with Britain in faith and culture: 'The settling of religion, the introducing of civility, order and government among a barbarous and unsubdued people ... is worthy of a Christian Prince.' He recognized that his own land-hungry countrymen, accustomed to hard living conditions and to defending their lands and cattle from forays by neighbouring lairds, were much more likely to make a success of the Ulster Plantation than people from the settled and orderly parishes of the English shires. As the king himself put it, 'The Scots are a middle temper, between the English tender breeding and the Irish rude breeding and are a great deal more likely to adventure to plant Ulster than the English'.

However, James also knew that his fellow Scots, even substantial landowners, were by English standards miserably poor and could not provide the craftsmen, masons, carpenters and blacksmiths needed to build towns, villages and castles and turn Ulster into a proper British province. So English money and English expertise, and therefore English planters, were essential. And, however well suited the Scots were to the job of settling the province, the most cogent reason why there should be English settlers was that Ireland was an English possession, had been conquered by English arms and was ruled by English officials. Scots and English must, therefore, act together as civilizing and proselytizing agents among the Irish.

There had been attempts to create British colonies in Ulster during the reign of Elizabeth but these had come to nothing. From much earlier times gallowglasses – mercenary soldiers from the Scottish Highlands who had come to fight in the Irish clan wars – intermarried with the Irish and remained. And along the coasts of Antrim and Down there were pockets of Scottish settlers – traders and farmers and fugitives (for political or criminal reasons) from Scottish justice.

Though the official Plantation of Ulster was to begin some time later, a curious event in the opening years of the seventeenth century accelerated the immigration process. This involved two dubious Scottish gentlemen and a drunken and virtually bankrupt Irish chief who owned much of the rich northern part of County Down. Sir Hugh Montgomery was an Ayrshire landowner who had served as a mercenary in the French army; his partner in the enterprise was James Hamilton, a Dublin University don who was also a Government spy. The Irish chief was Conn O'Neill, the besotted Lord of Clandeboye, who had been imprisoned in Carrickfergus Castle for rioting. Montgomery engineered his escape in a bizarre episode which included smuggling ropes to the dungeon in a hollowed-out cheese and the old reliable ruse of making love to the jailer's daughter. Montgomery was to have received half of Conn's estates as a reward but the predatory Hamilton who had been waiting in the background came in to claim a share. He was able to enforce this claim because of his connections at the royal court, with the result that Conn's property was divided one-third each between Montgomery, Hamilton and Conn himself.

Later, by adroit chicanery, O'Neill was relieved of most of the rest of his possessions and Hamilton was able to add to his portion of the spoils some further land grants obtained in County Antrim. He and Montgomery began to enlist Scottish settlers for their new estates. They invited lesser lairds and substantial farmers, who in turn brought under-tenants, craftsmen and labourers. The idea of a network of gentlemen-settlers who would act as justices of the peace and military commanders, and who had dependents in the shape of sub-tenants and servants at their command, was to provide a blueprint for the great Plantation of Ulster which followed.

The beginning of the seventeenth century was the beginning of the age of colonialism. Newfoundland had become an English possession in the penultimate decade of the sixteenth century and in 1607 the first English colony on the mainland of America had been established at Jamestown in Virginia. This had been followed by colonies in the Caribbean and in South America, but it was the Jamestown settlement which caught the public imagination. For the surviving spirits of the great Elizabethan age this was an opportunity for adventure and profit. Inevitably, Ulster was compared with Virginia. Some believed that Virginia, because of the small numbers and primitive state of the aboriginal inhabitants, was ripe for profitable exploitation while Ulster meant risk and trouble. Others, like Chichester, lamented that British adventurers were bent on 'the finding out of Virginia, Guiana and other remote and unknown countries' while they ignored the colonial opportunities on their own doorstep.

Despite the excitement in the air it was not easy to persuade English landowners to invest in Ireland, a place with a reputation for fighting, rain and the unreliability of its inhabitants. Thomas Blennerhasset, a Norfolk squire, might write in his pamphlet, aimed at encouraging East Anglian emigration, 'Art thou rich ... use there thy talent, it will be quickly a million', but it was quite another matter getting his fellow landowners or the rich city merchants to put up the necessary capital. And in the City of London it was cajoling and bullying rather than attractive investment brochures, that produced the required result.

Various plans for the settlement of Ulster were discussed during the first decade of the seventeenth century. The will to implement them was there on the part of the king's officials, only the opportunity was lacking. The Ulster chieftains, Hugh O'Neill, Hugh O'Donnell and Conor Maguire, controlled the greater part of the province, and after their defeat in the Elizabethan War they had been allowed to stay on as British subjects, with the title of earl. In 1607 that obstacle was suddenly and unexpectedly removed. Frightened by continual English harassment, the chiefs fled to Europe. James declared them traitors and confiscated their territory, along with the rest of Ulster west of Antrim and Down, and three years after the flight of the Irish earls the king's scheme for the Plantation of Ulster was under way. Large tracts of land were granted to English and Scottish lords described as 'undertakers'; to English army officers serving in Ireland, who were called 'servitors', and to suitable Irish chiefs. A new county was created from the old county of Coleraine and part of County Tyrone; these lands were granted to the London livery companies and called County Londonderry. The Ulster counties were surveyed by the king's officials, strict regulations for the Plantation were laid down and a timetable drawn up. The English and Scottish grantees were required to provide

LEFT *Arthur Chichester – epitome of English cool and pragmatism. After the savage conquest of Ulster, he urged coexistence with the native Irish.*

BELOW *His direct descendant Terence O'Neill (ironically bearing the surname of Chichester's arch-enemy), as Unionist Prime Minister of Ulster, urged the same policy with disastrous results.*

settlers, clear the land of scrub and forest and most important, build a series of castles and fortified houses to keep the potentially rebellious Irish under control: 'Every Undertaker ... shall build thereupon a Castle with a strong Court or Bawne about it.' Throughout the early Plantation years the king interfered continually, sending his officials to check on progress, admonishing and punishing those who fell short of their commitments. 'Wee will give you speedie direction how to proceed sevearly with those who are found to be delinquent', he wrote to the Deputy Lieutenant of Ireland.

As had occurred earlier in Down and Antrim, the undertakers leased their lands to gentlemen and well-to-do farmers who were responsible for recruiting the small farmers, craftsmen and labourers. The English tenants came largely from the counties closest to Ulster – Lancashire and Cheshire – but there were also immigrants from around London, from East Anglia and from Devon. The great mass of the early settlers, however, were Scottish, from Lanark, Ayrshire and the south west and from the Lothians. They gave the Ulster settlement a Scottish flavour which it never lost.

Armstrong, Johnston, Bell, Graham, Scott, Elliot – the names of the reivers, or Riding Families, of the Borders recur through Scots-Irish history from the days of the first emigrations to remote frontiers in America and Australia. For centuries these families had controlled the Borders, living by cattle stealing, kidnapping, blackmail and general looting. On dark nights between two full moons, when there was not even a gleam on a steel bonnet or breastplate to give them away, their war parties rode across the Debateable Lands – that area where both kingdoms claimed jurisdiction but lacked the power to exercise it – into England or into the territory of a neighbouring laird and left behind a trail of burning homes and murdered tenants. From time to time random justice was visited upon them: 'Thomas Armstrang ... taen to the mercat cross of Edinburgh and their his richt hand ... strickin fra his arme and thaireftir ... hanget upoune ane gibbet'. But it was not until James became King of England that the Borders were finally subdued.

James greatly admired the comparatively law-abiding society of his southern kingdom and introduced measures to curb the violence of the Scottish nobles and gentry. Then he turned his attention to the Borders. Here his methods were ruthless and, as he could now police both sides of the Border, highly effective. The reivers were hunted down and the fortified towers from which they had dominated the Borders marches were captured and burned. There were mass executions, sometimes after the most rudimentary trials and often it was enough to be called Graham or Armstrong for the king's officers to hang a man on the spot. If the malefactor was not important enough he was drowned to save the cost of a rope. Ulster offered a chance of escape. A Border outlaw could choose deportation to Ireland as an alternative to the gallows; 'Thom, Jok and Lancie Armestrangis ... sall pass furth of the kingdoms of Scotland and England, and sall not returne....'

Ireland also provided a hiding place and a lucrative market for horses and cattle stolen in the Borders or 'Middle Shires'. The Scottish Privy Council issued a proclamation in 1612 against the 'thevishe and wicked trade', and three years later King James wrote angrily to the Chancellor of Scotland, 'it is almost become ane ordinerie trade to transport goods into Ireland stollin in the middle sheires'. To halt the escape of outlaws and the passage of stolen goods, it was made compulsory for all ships' captains to check on the identity and character of passengers and the ownership of livestock they transported. With the short sea crossing and the large number of entry points on the Irish side, particularly in the deeply indented coast of north Donegal, the Government had insufficient customs men to maintain effective patrols. 'There are many Creaks in Loughswilly ... and no officers or waiters to control them', the Surveyor-General reported in 1637. But this traffic had some advantages for the Scottish authorities, as Dr Perceval-Maxwell points out in his exhaustive study of Scots immigration in James's reign: 'This was a small price to pay for the departure of a very large number of Borderers who would otherwise have had little else to do but create disorder at home.'

The number emigrating, voluntarily or otherwise, from the Borders was small in comparison with those from places like Ayrshire, but their importance in the Scots-Irish story was out of all proportion to their numbers. These Border men were fearless and highly adaptable guerilla fighters and the tradition they gave to the Ulster Scots was to prove invaluable when, one hundred and fifty years later, the Scots-Irish pioneers were in the vanguard of the battle for the American continent. It is also worth noting that the reivers were implacable enemies who neither forgave nor forgot and, whatever can be said of the Scots-Irish down the centuries, they cannot be accused of having short memories.

There was also a strong tradition of folk music and balladry among the Border people. The itinerant ballad maker was a protected person in that violent community, probably because the reiver chiefs wanted their deeds, and particularly the way they met death, whether in battle or on the scaffold, recorded for posterity. Thomas Armstrong from the Debateable Lands had a good exit line when he was about to die for what the Middle Shires would have regarded as a highly praiseworthy act, the killing of a royal warden: 'Goodnight and joy be to ye all.' Themes of blood feud and revenge, as when the little son of Johnnie Armstrong of Gilnockie is made to promise at his father's hanging

> If ever I live to be a man,
> My Father's Death reveng'd shall be

abound in Border narratives. The historian George Macaulay Trevelyan perceived a close parallel between the world of the Border raider and that of the Odyssey: 'Like the Homeric Greeks, they were cruel, coarse savages, slaying each other as the beasts of the forest, and yet they were also poets who could express in the grand style the inexorable fate of the individual man and woman.'

This culture of storytelling with elemental themes, of music that could be tragic or madly gay, was carried to the American frontier where it flourished and diversified, often in situations of physical remoteness and loneliness that were similar to its Scottish birthplace. The Border tendency to admire anti-authoritarian figures, no matter how bloodthirsty, is to be found in scores of native American ballads celebrating outlaws from Jesse James to Bonnie and Clyde.

2 • SAINTS AND HORSE-THIEVES

'Make speede, get thee to Ulster, serve God, be sober.'

Thomas Blennerhasset, 'A Direction for the Plantation of Ulster'

'Going to Ireland was looked on as a miserable mark of a deplorable person.'

Rev. Andrew Stewart

THE SCOTTISH PIONEERS who crossed the narrow channel to Londonderry, to Carrickfergus or to Donaghadee were a motley lot. On twenty-ton sailing ships, such as the *Gift of God* from Glasgow, hard-working tenant farmers jostled with penniless adventurers, who were probably the younger sons of small landowners. Calvinist preachers burning to convert the new land looked suspiciously at rough fellow passengers, guessing from their names that they were horse-thieves from the Scottish Borders and, perhaps, like the Rev. Andrew Stewart, muttered to themselves about 'scum ... fleeing from justice ... hoping to be without the fear of man's justice in a land where there was nothing, or but little yet, of the fear of God'. Up in the ship's prow a Scots lord tried to maintain distance and a specious dignity on an income, probably mortgaged, of less than £150 a year. But from whatever walk of life the passengers came they had all passed through one of the most totally transforming experiences in the history of Western civilization, the Scottish Reformation.

In the last quarter of the sixteenth century the corrupt and disorganized Roman Catholic Church in Scotland had been overturned by the fanatical zeal of Calvinist reformers like Andrew Melville and John Knox, assisted by noblemen who were motivated by a peculiarly Scottish blend of patriotism (Roman Catholicism represented foreign, particularly French, influence), self-righteous piety and plain greed. That Reformation was far more complete than the earlier English one, far more complete than any other national break with Rome. The Mass, statues, religious orders, recognition of Papal authority, all were swept away. But the emotional and psychological change was much deeper, and that was to have a lasting effect on the character of the Scots-Irish people. The sixteenth-century Scot suddenly found himself face to face with his God, with no intermediary priest, no liturgical anaesthetic to relieve the shock of the experience. He began to see himself with a new awareness, as a rational being with powers of choice and decision, and this change was to affect the Scot in everything he did or thought.

The Scots were no more modest about the achievements of their Reformation than they are about anything else. Nor were they willing to see it through other eyes than their own. 'Now, O Scotland, God be thanked, thy name is in the Bible.' The Reformation was far more than a sweeping away of outward forms of worship or a reforming of evil practices. It was, obviously, a return to the primitive purity of Christ's Apostolic Church. Going back further, seventeenth-century Scots saw close comparisons with ancient Israel: 'a very near parallel betwixt Israel and this church, the only two sworn nations to the Lord'. Time and time again, right to the present day, Ulster Unionists have heard this comforting parallel drawn from pulpit or political platform and received it with a fervent singing of the hymn 'O God Our Help in Ages Past'. It is a remarkable fact – almost totally ignored by political commentators – that in this materialistic age so many Ulster Protestants believe that the Old Testament God who brought their sister nation out of the desert will guide them safely through the greatest crisis in their existence. It is also worth asking whether this perceived relationship with the ancient Jewish nation accounts for the lack of anti-Semitism among Ulster Scots. For although anti-Semitism was never very significant in Ireland – there were too few Jews – a strong strain of the virus exists in the Catholic Republican make-up, something vividly illustrated by James Joyce in the citizen episode of *Ulysses*.

The idea of a people sworn or covenanted to God and living according to his rules has been brilliantly expounded down the years by charismatic preachers, first to the Scots and then to the Scots-Irish peoples. To hear Ian Paisley, when he leaves the muddied waters of contemporary Ulster politics and goes back to the pure evangel of his inherited religious philosophy, is a deeply moving experience.

In early seventeenth-century Scotland, alongside the idea of a Covenanted people went the Apocalyptic vision of God's kingdom on earth. To many reformers this kingdom was at hand, soon to be established in the fields and towns of Scotland and perhaps, as S. A. Burrell points out in his article 'The Apocalyptic Vision of the Early Covenanters', also established in Europe by the arms of godly Scottish soldiers. It is true that this vision of God's kingdom was only dimly apprehended by the mass of ordinary people – farmers, weavers, masons, shepherds – but to the few who gave the political and religious lead to Scottish Calvinism, chiefly clerics but also some lawyers, schoolmasters and educated gentlemen, it was a burning reality. It was this vision which engrained in the future Scots-Irish people their hunger for a Promised Land. This land has always remained beyond the next horizon but the words 'Zion', 'the land of Canaan' and 'Eden' have appeared again and again in text and political speech throughout Scots-Irish history, whether in Ulster, on the Pennsylvanian frontier or in the early wilderness of Upper Canada.

The Scottish Reformation brought a third great idea which was to have a profound effect on the politics of the Scots-Irish, and through them, in the second half of the eighteenth century, on the destiny of Britain's American colonies. From the 1570s to the 1630s the Scottish reformers were dismantling the old Roman Catholic system of Church organization – in which the parish priest was appointed by the bishop who in turn was part of a rigid autocratic system leading up to the Pope – and putting in its place a democratic system, with a minister appointed by the congregation and controlled by its chosen representatives, the Kirk Session. Above local level the principle of limited democracy was maintained in the Presbytery, the Synod and the General Assembly in Edinburgh. The ordinary layman felt he was participating in Church government right to the top and at least he believed he knew what was going on. Presbyterianism was born, though the term, or the idea of a separate dissenting Church, did not come until much later.

The shift to a democratic Church did not come easily. Things like the link with Rome and monastic orders went early in the Reformation period. But the system of bishops, which the Crown saw as important to civic government and the existing social structure, continued. Episcopacy received a great boost when James VI of Scotland succeeded his cousin Elizabeth to the throne of England. South of the Border bishops were an important part of the Reformation and staunch supporters of royal power. James and his son, Charles I, recognized their usefulness and determined that episcopal rule should remain not only in the Church of England but in those of Scotland and Ireland. The inevitable clash between this view of how religion should be organized and the emerging Presbyterian one was to have a deep effect on the destiny of the Scots-Irish.

This day-to-day involvement by most educated Lowland Scots in the direction of their religion, which, inevitably, also meant their politics, gave Scots an appetite for political argument and political power which in a favourable climate grew to full-blown radicalism. Nearly two centuries later the descendants of these people, tempered by the Irish experience and embroiled in the American Revolution, were called by an irate British politician, 'the most God-provoking democrats this side of hell'. The fact that, despite long links with the British Conservative Party, grass roots Ulster Unionism is basically anti-authoritarian is a little-recognized factor in the Irish conflict. Irish nationalism, although it may take on labels like 'Republican' and find support among British radicals, is deeply conservative. In fact the first Tories were not British Conservatives but Irish political outlaws, while the term 'Whig', the original label of the Liberal Party, is derived from 'Whiggamore', meaning a Calvinist opponent of royal totalitarianism.

Visions of building God's kingdom in a new land were fine for Sabbath afternoons when the tenant farmer forgot, in the intoxicating rhetoric of his minister, the misery of scraping a living from the exhausted soil. But Ulster had very practical attractions too. Not only was land plentiful and available at a cheap rent; it was also fertile from underusage. Although the native Irish grew some crops, their economy was mainly pastoral and they moved their cattle from summer to winter pasture, thus easing the pressure on the soil. Large areas of hardwood forests were particularly attractive to the Lowland Scots, who had come from an almost treeless land. Fish were plentiful in the rivers and along the coast; salmon was exported to England, and Laud, the tubby little Archbishop of Canterbury, licked his lips over fat Lough Neagh eels. In the woods there was an

The Scots nobles, lairds, clergy and common folk sign the National Covenant in Greyfriars Churchyard, Edinburgh, to defend the Calvinist principles of the Scottish Kirk. The covenant theme in modern times is an essential part of Ulster-Scots realpolitik.

abundance of game, from red deer to rabbits, which provided survival rations for the settlers until they harvested their first crops.

The Montgomery Manuscripts, written at the end of the seventeenth century, give a graphic description of the first days of the settlement in North Down. When the first Scots came in 1606, 'in three parishes could not be found thirty cabins nor any stone walls but roofless churches ... and the stump of an old castle'. In this war-devastated landscape the settlers built temporary shelters with rods and branches of trees. They cleared the scrub which had grown up on land already deforested by the dispossessed Irish. Meanwhile, week by week, and even day by day, shiploads of new settlers came in, with their cattle, sheep and farming tools. Such was the rush of settlers and the demand for places on the ferries plying between Scotland and Ireland that shipowners pushed up fares. In 1610 the Scottish Privy Council imposed fare controls. Not only farmers but masons, carpenters and blacksmiths came over to begin the greatest building boom Ireland – or even Britain – had yet seen. After the first harvests were reaped, the building of towns, like Newtownards in County Down, began. Watermills for grinding cereals were set up and small-scale manufacture of linen and woollen cloth was organized.

Relations between Catholic Irish and Ulster Scots is still Ulster's fundamental problem, so first meetings between them in the early 1600s have their relevance today. What sort of people were the native Irish? Contemporary English writers, visitors or soldiers serving in Ireland are our main sources of information and they, like their twentieth-century counterparts, the men of the media, did not let the facts stand in the way of a good story. Laurence Eachard of Oxford, who wrote *An Exact Description of Ireland*, was in every way unlike the modern don. He was anything but exact, but his writing was terse, vivid and always entertaining. The native Irish were 'of a hotter and moister nature than other nations ... reckoned of quick wit (though besotted to many follies) prodigal and careless of their lives ... given to fleshy lusts ... kind and courteous to strangers ... constant in love... in enmity implacable ... most vehement and passionate.' Of course they had their peccadilloes: 'They are given to idleness above measure ... they count it no shame to commit robberies ... they also suppose that violence and murder are no ways displeasing to God, for if it were a sin he would not present them with that opportunity.' Seventeenth- or twentieth-century logic? Eachard was less a propagandist than a journalist willing to be convinced, but what he wrote was based on then current perceptions of the Irish, and in the culture clash between Protestant and Catholic, Ulster Scot and native Irish, perception is more important than reality. Myths are the volatile fuel of Ulster's present inter-community strife, and those myths have seventeenth-century roots.

Real dangers there were. 'The wolf and the woodkerne were the greatest enemies to the first planters', said one Scots minister. Wolves were plentiful and Eachard wrote that the natives 'pray for wolves and wish them well and then they are not afraid to be hurt by them'. The more practical Scots relied on guns and hounds. Woodkerne were the sons of now landless Irish gentry who lived in bands in the woods and existed by preying

Scots-Irish and English Settlements in Ulster

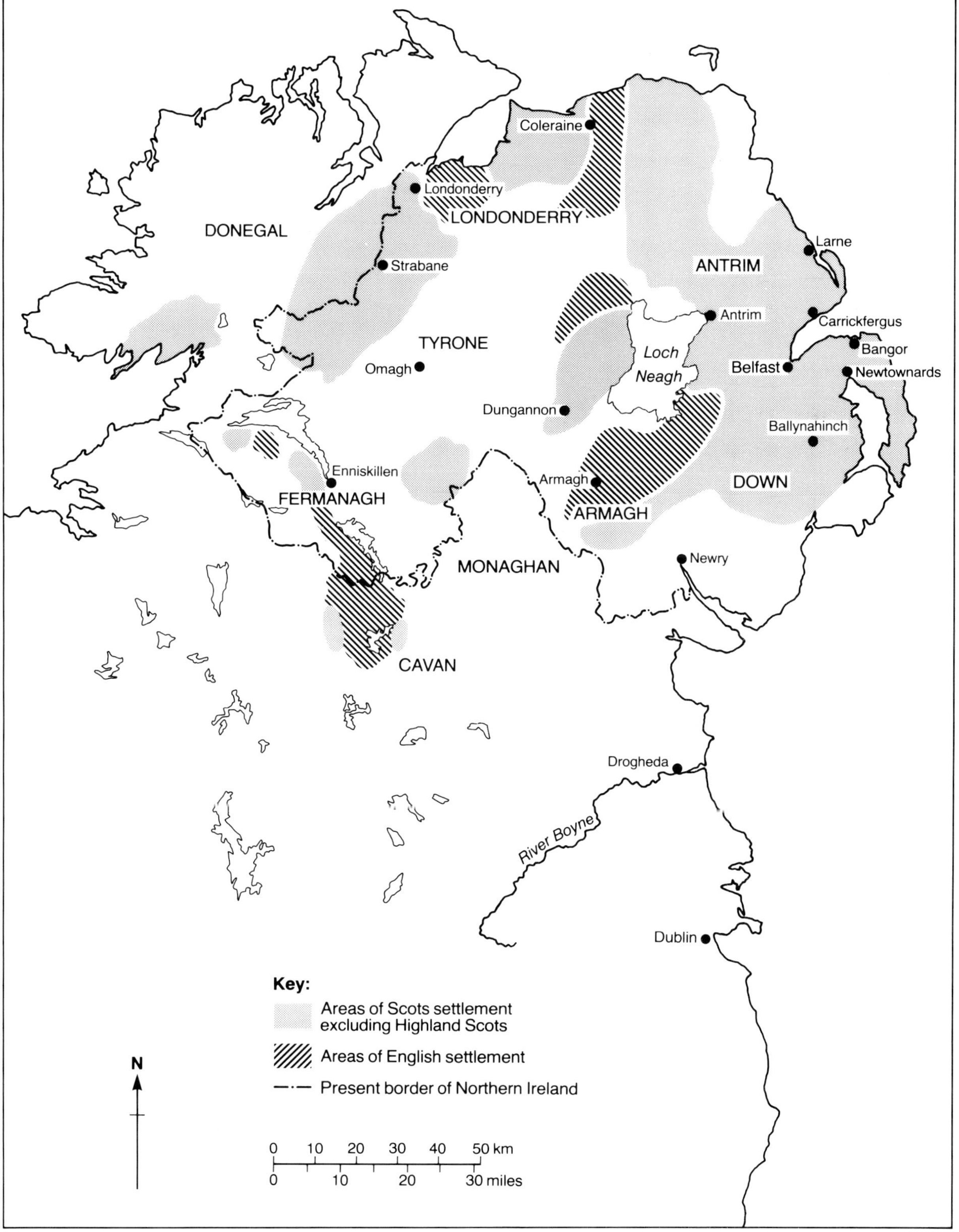

on the newcomers. Contemporary letters and reports are filled with tales of their depredations. Isolated Scots families, like that of John Montgomery near Donaghadee in County Down, were wiped out in midnight raids. The assize records tell of the equally bloody retribution exacted on the outlaws: 'Art McGillechree and Gillese McKerney on the 3rd January, 1614, stole a black gelding worth four pounds – to be executed.' After sentence woodkerne were led round the settlers' village with ropes round their necks, then hanged. Many a Bell or Armstrong from the Scottish Borders must have looked on such a scene and said to himself, "There but for the Grace of the Protestant God ...'.

The Scots arrived in a province where organized religion had almost ceased to exist. Irish Roman Catholicism, cut off by decades of war from a supply of educated priests, was degenerating into something approaching paganism. Eachard found some Irish worshipping the moon. English efforts to introduce Protestantism had a strong element of farce; Protestant ministers were often ex-soldiers, almost totally uneducated and, according to one contemporary writer, more likely to be found in the pub than the pulpit. Large numbers of churches were in ruins and services were rare. Into this religious stagnation the Scots ministers came like a breath of fresh air. They were mobile, earnest and hardworking, 'such men for strict walking and abundant paines with their people, Sabbath day, weekdays, in church and from house to house'.

Robert Blair, who came to Ulster in 1622, was typical of the Calvinist stream of Scots ministers. He was a mixture of spiritual vision and blunt common sense, a man so sure he was right that he found it impossible to see any other point of view. As a student, he chose a haunted room in college so as not to be disturbed by less dedicated fellow students, and when the ghost appeared he chased it around the room with a stick.

Blair had doubts on the voyage to Ireland as to whether he was doing the right thing, but an inner voice, the constant guide of the Scots-Irish, spoke unequivocally, 'Thou fool ... thou must either preach the gospel in Ireland or no where at all'. First impressions in the new land were bad; he met some Irishmen staggering home from the pub, smelling heavily of garlic – presumably a seventeenth-century breath sweetener. But next day he had one of those private spiritual experiences that are the hallmark of Presbyterianism: 'I met unexpectedly so sweet a peace and so great a joy as I behoved to look thereon as my welcome thither and returning to a private place about a mile above Craigfergus I prostrated myself upon the grass to rejoice in the Lord.' Ulster was, after all, the promised Eden.

The certainty that God was watching over them was as strong with the new Scots settlers as with the Israelites of old. Harvests were vital if they were to survive the winter in a hostile, war-devastated, undeveloped land. Storms and heavy rains threatened the cereal crops in the area around Bangor, County Down, where Blair was minister. He set a day of prayer and fasting to avert what would have been a famine. 'That same night He sent a mighty wind, which did fully dry the corns ... and this wind continuing to blow fair for two days, the people ceased neither night nor day till the whole corns were got in.'

ABOVE *The dispossessed Irish chieftain, mourning for a purely imaginary past when he and his peers dined off golden plates to the music of harps, became a figure of fun to his supplanters. As a woodkerne, or outlaw, he was considerably less amusing.*

RIGHT *In the eyes of Scottish Calvinists and English Puritans, the Catholic Irish were a lazy, frivolous people incapable of becoming self-disciplined, prosperous Britons. An element of truth has kept this particular myth alive.*

The wolf and the woodkerne – those displaced Irish who lived as outlaws in the forest – were not the only dangers the settlers encountered. As might be expected in such a heathenish land, diabolical influences were strong and ready to manifest themselves. Satan himself announced that he was coming on Hallowe'en Night to take away one of Blair's parishioners. Blair assembled the people of the village at the man's home and spent the night in prayer, preaching and singing psalms. The sight of a congregation of Ulster Presbyterians in full spate was too much for the devil, who did not venture back to Bangor – at least not until quite recently.

Water, in springs and rivers, has a spiritual and practical significance in the history of the Scots-Irish. Rivers to a restless people were a means of transport or a barrier to progress, but for settlers established for a generation or two they could become a focus of local patriotism, or perhaps *pietas*, as in the Valley of Virginia. Water has the obvious symbolism derived from Revelations: 'Then he showed me the river of the water of life, bright as crystal, flowing from the throne of God.' In the American wilderness springs also provided gathering points for religious worship, places where the thirst of horses and people could be quenched, places where churches would later rise, as at Donegal Springs, Meetinghouse Springs and Tinkling Springs.

The first evangelical river in Ireland was the narrow trout burn called Six Mile Water which winds through the rich farmlands of mid-Antrim. On the banks of this stream Blair and his fellow ministers tackled the problem of ungodliness among their fellow settlers, and their unfitness to build the new Zion. On a summer day four ministers would preach in turn for perhaps two hours each; the endurance of early Presbyterian congregations was phenomenal. But then the whole audience, old and young, was involved in something which was of the utmost importance and often very dramatic. Andrew Stewart attended the Six Mile Water Revival as a boy of eight and heard Blair preach; 'his hearers ... fell into such anxiety and terror of conscience that they looked on themselves as altogether lost and damned ... I have seen them stricken and swoon with the Word – yea a dozen a day carried out of the doors as dead'. This tradition of evangelism is still alive and kicking in the Bible lands of the Southern States, lands to which the Scots-Irish were the first to carry the Christian faith.

Blair was an uncompromising Calvinist, who curtly dismissed the whole structure of Church government which had sustained Christendom for centuries: 'It is not the lording of a prelate over a province, nor a primate over a kingdom ... but the blessing of Christ upon the labours of his pastors that doth perfect the saints.' But it was twenty years yet before the saints, in the shape of the Scottish Covenanting Army, would come marching in. Presbyterianism still lacked a formal Church structure, let alone the musket and sword to enforce its will. With the blessing of the king, a Protestant episcopal system was now being set up, parish by parish, in Ulster. Many Scots ministers, particularly in north Donegal, fitted well enough into the system, and some of the most successful of the new bishops were Scots. Blair and his stiff-necked colleagues, who in typical Scots-Irish fashion made no secret of their revolutionary views, could hardly expect to be

Francis Jobson's early seventeenth-century map of Ulster, with shiploads of settlers approaching the coast, illustrates the colonialist mood of the period.

ABOVE *The starving inhabitants of Derry greet the relief ship* Mountjoy: *the end of a siege, the beginning of a legend.*

RIGHT *King William of Orange has inspired generations of professional banner makers for the Orange Order.*

OVERLEAF *Monea Castle, an imposing stronghold in County Fermanagh, was built in 1618 by Malcolm Hamilton as part of the terms of his land grant from King James I.*

tolerated for ever. They were suspended from their parishes and some fled to Scotland to escape arrest. These early Dissenters made good martyrs, ready with beautifully phrased speeches of justification which would ring down the years to other situations and other martyrs. Robert Cunningham, a gentle and saintly cleric, told the bishop as he was silenced, 'I rather lay downe my ministrie at the feet of my Lord and Saviour than live with ane eivil conscience in frie libertie'. The stage was set for a long-running persecution of Ulster Presbyterians which was to have a profound effect on the future of the Scots-Irish people.

The Scots settled mainly in the east, north and north-west of the province, a semicircle which took in Antrim and Down and bent northwards across County Londonderry to end in Donegal. The corresponding area of English settlement stretched along the Lagan Valley behind Belfast, through Armagh and South Tyrone into Fermanagh. But whatever the areas of distribution, the Scots dominated the settlement from the beginning. Their numbers were greater, and they were better suited by temperament to the task. In the hard early years the whole enterprise would have collapsed if the hard-working Scots had not provided the food supplies. Captain Nicholas Pynnar, one of the king's surveyors, reported that the English were so frightened of the natives that they did not venture into the fields: 'were it not for the Scottish tenants which do plough in many places . . . those Parts may starve'. Even in the lands of the London companies the Scots dominated: 'The Scots are twenty to one to the English and having the prime trade in town and country thrive and grow rich.'

It was the Scots, also, who were the mainstay of the planters' defence. One English settler, John Taylor of Armagh, put it frankly, 'It were good to set this land to Scotsmen for the English will gladly sit down upon the other if the Scots shall be a wall between them and the Irish'. By substituting 'Indians' for 'Irish', this proposition became equally applicable when the Scots-Irish reached the New World.

The Scots-settled areas of Northern Ireland are predominantly Presbyterian, areas of English settlement, Anglican. There is a curious exception in County Fermanagh, where settlers arriving before Presbyterianism had established a separate identity joined the established Episcopal Church, and remained inside that Church because they were too remote from the influence of Scottish Calvinism to be drawn into the Dissenting communities which sprang up in the mid-century. Overall the Episcopal Church in Ulster has taken on a strong Calvinist shading, a tribute to the pervading influence of Presbyterianism. Nor does that influence stop at the boundaries of Protestantism. The degree to which Northern Irish Catholicism has been shaped by interaction with the puritanism of the Nonconformists has yet to be studied in detail.

In agriculture, unlike religion, there were very many similarities between the immigrants from Scotland and the native Irish, though with a much smaller population and a great deal of rough, uncleared land, the Irish depended more on the raising of livestock than the Scots had done in their homeland. Irish wealth was counted in numbers of

ABOVE *Dalway's Bawn, County Antrim, a fortified house constructed in 1609 as a refuge against attacks by the native Irish.*

RIGHT *The pepperpot tower or bartizan of Monea Castle (see also p. 28) shows the Scottish architectural influence in Ulster.*

cattle rather than possession of land, and Irish husbandry was based on a system of moving cattle to mountain pastures in the summer and back to the valleys for wintering, what Arthur Chichester described irritably as, 'runninge up and downe the country with their cattle'. The living quarters of these Irish herdsmen were as temporary as their pastures; they were 'like Nomades removing their dwellings according to the commodity of the pastures for their cows', wrote Fynes Moryson, an English colonial official. They 'sleep under the canopy of heaven . . . they make a fire in the midst . . . and round it they sleep . . . lying all in a circle about the fire with their feet towards it.' (Move on two and a half centuries, change the dress and you are looking at the cattle drovers of Kansas or Texas.) To the Scots none of this was very strange. For them, too, the possession of cattle was a measure of affluence, and much of their time was taken up herding or driving cows to market. A major cause of the lawlessness of their society and the immediacy of their justice was the fact that wealth on the hoof was mobile and marketable and therefore a target for predators.

The arrival of the Scots was a boost to the Celtic droving tradition. Many more cattle and better breeding strains were imported, and the Scots rationalized the Irish marketing system by creating a network of regular markets and fairs. Exports of livestock, as well as beef and hides, from Ulster ports increased dramatically. In the long run the danger and uncertainty of colonial life in Ulster deterred the farmer from over-dependence on crop husbandry and kept the emphasis on cattle for many generations. As the identity of the Scots-Irish people emerged, the cattle droving tradition became part of it.

The turbulent religious politics of seventeenth-century Scotland had a profound effect on Ulster. The struggles of Ulster Scots Calvinists like Blair and Cunningham against their bishops mirrored the greater struggle in Scotland, where King James, and later his son Charles I, with the assistance of the Scottish Episcopal Party, strove to maintain the rule of bishops. Not only Church government but the very nature of Scottish society was in the balance. The Presbyterian fundamentalists set out to destroy the ceremonies, festivals and traditional countryside sites around which Scottish medieval life had been structured, things which to them were 'superstitious, idolatrous . . . and come from hell'. Relics of the Auld Kirk of Rome, such as pilgrimages and sacred shrines, were obvious targets but the prescription was widened to include village dancing, bonfires and travelling entertainers. People were compelled to work on Christmas Day to end any idea of Yuletide as a feast day; for a long time in Ulster the celebration of Christmas was frowned on by stricter congregations. At the heart of this puritan revolution was the strict observance of the Lord's Day. An Act of Parliament in 1656 made Sabbatarianism the law of the land, forbidding all work, travel or any form of enjoyment on Sunday.

The reformers worked at a high emotional pitch and their language was intemperate. The favourite pulpit subject was 'the wrath and fire of God'; prelates were 'Anti-Christ's first born and the first-fruit of his foul womb'. Sometimes their view of the world became trance-like and moved into the realms of poetic expression. The Calvinist divine Samuel

Illustration from Sir John Temple's The Irish Rebellion, *a particularly horrific account of atrocities by Catholics in 1641.*

Rutherford exhorted a friend, 'Why should night-dreams and day shadows and water froth and May flowers run away with your heart.' Such exalted language was to occur later in the sermons of Scots-Irish preachers.

When Charles I and Archbishop Laud attempted to impose the new English Prayer Book, which to Scottish Presbyterian nostrils gave off a whiff of popery as strong as brimstone, the excitement was intense. Scottish nobles, burgesses and ministers met in Greyfriars churchyard in Edinburgh to pledge themselves in the National Covenant to defend the religious practices of the Reformed Church. As war between the king and the Covenanters threatened, the Scottish colonists in Ulster for the first time became objects of suspicion to the British authorities. Nor was that suspicion unjustified. Many Ulster Scots signed the Covenant, and, with the premature arrogance they so often displayed, began to talk openly of the coming destruction of the Episcopal system in Ireland. So alarmed was the Lord Deputy, Thomas Wentworth, that he sent an army to Ulster to enforce a counter-pledge, later to be notorious as the Black Oath, on all males over sixteen swearing them to 'renounce and abjure all Covenants, oaths and bonds whatsoever'. Many thousands fled back to Scotland rather than take the oath.

On Sunday 24 October 1641, when the remaining planter people were still locked in argument about the recent abolition of bishops in Scotland, or the rights and wrongs of signing the Black Oath, the native Irish all over Ulster rose in rebellion. The attack was swift, unexpected and almost totally successful. Plantation strong-points like Tully Castle in Fermanagh, built by Sir John Hume after the style of the impregnable towers of his native Scottish Borders, fell to the rebels. From the precarious safety of a besieged Londonderry, an English settler, William Griffin, wrote to his cousin in Berkshire of 'the most inhumane cruelty and bloody practices that the rebels have inflicted upon poor Protestants here, how they have dealt with our Ministers worse than the Turks do with their mutes and Eunuchs ... how many children they have burnt, taken by the heels and dashed out their brains.' The Scots had a fearsome reputation as fighters and at first the Irish did not venture to attack them. In fact they tried to draw the Scots settlers on to their side, recognizing with some perspicacity the revolutionary streak in the Scotsmen. But success went to Irish heads and the Scots joined the English settlers as legitimate targets. Soon ships packed with refugees were headed for Ayr, Girvan and Portpatrick. The entire settlement seemed to be doomed and the Presbyterian dream of a new Zion perishing in the flames of the Plantation towns. To those who had fled rather than submit to the Black Oath, the massacre was the just judgement of God on 'the fearing and worldly people' who had remained.

The facts of the 1641 Rebellion are hard to establish, despite the volumes of evidence taken from eyewitnesses a decade later, but in a way the myths are more important. For centuries it was believed that up to two hundred thousand Protestants had been slaughtered; the probable truth is that about four thousand died in actual fighting and about twice that figure from disease and hunger. As William Griffin recorded, great cruelty was practised by the rebels. There were mass drownings of Protestants, people were burned alive in their homes and women and children tortured to death. These only confirmed the sixteenth-century view that the Irish believed 'neither violence, robbery or murder is displeasing to God'. But the cruelties perpetrated by the rebels were also greatly exaggerated, and those practised by the victorious Scots and English armies when the tide of war turned were, with the notable exception of the Cromwellian massacre at Drogheda, conveniently forgotten.

It would be appropriate to say that 1641 still haunts the Protestant folk memory just as, immediately after the event, the ghosts of murdered settlers stalked the land. The most spectacular of these apparitions was a woman with burning eyes who rose from the River Bann at the site of a mass drowning. A Catholic priest, with considerable lack of tact, tried to exorcise the ghost. She remained silent. But when a Presbyterian minister asked her what she wanted, she replied in ringing tones 'Revenge'.

3 • THE SWORD OF THE LORD

'God should be cried unto to bless the country with a spiritual ministry and for a blessing to the going out of the army against the Irish'

Rev. Patrick Adair

ON THE MORNING of 10 June 1642, surrounded by the gleaming breastplates and halberds of the New Scots Army, Mr John Baird, chaplain to Colonel Campbell's regiment, preached in the courtyard of the great Norman castle which sits on the edge of the sea at Carrickfergus. His text was taken from the Psalmist, 'Do good in Thy good pleasure unto Zion, build Thou the walls of Jerusalem'. Once again the concept of the new Zion in Ulster was being revived but this time it was backed by an army recently arrived from Scotland.

Although the Scottish colony had been almost destroyed in the rebellion of the previous year, the mood of the Scots, both in the homeland and in Ireland, was far from despondent. Two years earlier the army raised to defend the National Covenant had successfully invaded England, thus ending a century and a half of humiliation at English hands which had begun with the disastrous battle of Flodden. Scottish influence seemed capable of shaping the political destinies of the three kingdoms of the British Isles. In Ulster, before the shock of 1641, the Scottish colonists had begun to reassert their Calvinism, occasionally attacking Episcopalian ministers and making no secret of the fact that they looked to the powerful army in Scotland to impose a Presbyterian reformation in Ireland.

The army of the National Covenant represented the high noon of Presbyterian power. It had something of an international flavour; many of its officers were veterans of the Thirty Years' War and had served under the immortalized leader of the Protestant cause in Europe, Gustavus Adolphus. The Swedish king's immense reputation shed lustre on the arms of the Covenanters. But the Scottish army was also both nationalist and evangelical, 'flying at the Captaine's tent-doore a brave new colour stamped with the Scottish Armes and this ditton "for Christ's Croun and the Covenant"'. The theocratism of Scottish society extended to the army, which was subjected to 'good sermons and prayers, morning and even, under the roof of heaven, to which their drums did call them for bells'.

The idea of a Protestant crusade affected even its commander, the level-headed Alexander Leslie, an experienced professional soldier. He considered invading Europe and destroying the Roman Anti-Christ. In the heady religious atmosphere the extreme Calvinist chaplains, like political commissars, tried to run the army, disastrously as it turned out. Their bloodthirstiness shocked even soldiers hardened in Europe's great sectarian conflict. At the battle of Philiphaugh they led the massacre of all prisoners, including women and children, to the cry of 'Jesus and no quarter'.

Psychologically, as well as actually, the Scottish nation was prepared for war; rumours of prodigies circulated through the country. A tenant farmer in Aberdeenshire saw, 'Ane great army . . . about eight hours in the morning . . . and visibly continued till sunrising; syne vanished away in his sight with noise into ane moss hard beside'. Much mysterious drumming was heard, there was 'horribly uncouth, unkindly weather', and the Rev. Andrew Leitch awoke at midnight to find the sun shining. Unlike his fellow Covenanters, the lawyer Sir Thomas Hope was pessimistic: 'repeated dreams portends some calamity'.

The New Scots force fell far short of the model set by the National Covenant Army, from which it drew its nucleus of 1500 veterans. The rest were levies, often reluctant ones, from the Scottish counties. Some, indeed, had been moved by the plight of their countrymen fleeing from the 1641 Rebellion. They had seen the flood of refugees coming into Ayrshire ports and heard the atrocity stories being hawked from village to village. But the wave of sympathy and anger which swept Scotland was not enough to inspire the rank and file, among whom there was considerable reluctance to serve in Ulster. Desertion became rife and it was necessary to bring in the death penalty to curb it.

Despite these shortcomings, the New Scots Army arrived at Carrickfergus in April 1642 to high expectations on the part of the Ulster Scots, some apprehension on the part of the English and extensive terror in the more vulnerable communities of native Irish; it was fear of just such an invasion which had helped to spark off the Rebellion. Although the English Parliament were sponsoring, and paying for, the Scots as restorers of law and order, they were suspicious of their motives. The Scottish demand to have Londonderry as a port was turned down, and the scheme to have the Scottish soldiers paid with grants of Ulster land was seen as a plot for a total Scottish takeover of the province. The suspicions were largely justified. To the resident and incoming Scots settlers the army was a guarantee of their right not only to exist as a racial group in Ireland but also to take over Ulster as a province modelled on a Covenanted Scotland.

The chaplains of the New Scots Army were as much concerned with the moral rehabilitation of the troops in their charge as with the destruction of heretical enemies. They used their considerable power to bring the backsliders among the officers and men at Carrickfergus and the other garrisons into line with the strict observances of the reformers. 'They found it necessary to choose elders in the regiments for helping them in carrying out discipline in the army', wrote Patrick Adair, one of the Scottish ministers. But these clerical attentions were not always welcomed, especially by the officers, 'no favourers of religion . . . much abhorring the setting up of discipline . . . which might have the power to censure them for their drinking and whoring'.

The geopolitical strategy of the New Scots Army disappointed the many Protestants who hoped for an immediate reversal of the territorial losses of 1641. Even when Alexander Leslie came to take command, he contented himself with raids into Irish-held country. Then, having failed to bring off the overall victory expected of him, he returned to Scotland, leaving his subordinate, General Robert Monro, in command. Monro maintained the same tactics, opting for punitive raids rather than attempting a complete reconquest of the province. He was particularly successful in catching the Irish while they moved their cattle from pasture to pasture, and was soon sending captured cattle back in large numbers to Scotland. With the soldiers inflamed by stories of 1641, the warfare was vicious. Prisoners on surrender were hacked to pieces or later hanged. When the Scots took Newry, 'we entered into an examination of the townsmen if all were Papists'. The result of this military inquisition was that the 'indifferent' were separated from the 'bad whereof 60 with two priests were shot and hanged'. Monro followed the example of Chichester forty years earlier and introduced a policy of starving out the Irish rebels by destroying their food supplies. Grain crops were burnt as they stood, cattle driven off and herdsmen killed. In spite of this, the war dragged on without much indication that the Scots were regaining control.

In the meantime a quieter, but in the long run more important, conquest was going on. Using the Church organization in the army as a basis, the Scots chaplains set up a framework of Presbyterian congregations in the counties of Antrim and Down which was extended when more of Ulster was brought under army control. 'The people were very hungry in receiving the Gospel', Patrick Adair claimed, and this was probably true as it is a recognized phenomenon of deeply troubled times that people turn to religion, often not their own, particularly if the faith on offer is a confident and positive one. Adair saw, 'this wasted church now beginning to rise out of the ashes'. Ministers were brought in from Scotland and they rode from parish to parish 'with a guard of horse', not only preaching and teaching, but demanding the keys of the churches wherever they went. The great linguist and scholar John Livingston, who had been banished from his church at Killinchy in County Down, and who was so beloved by his congregation that afterwards they, twice a year, crossed to Scotland to take communion with him, returned to conduct a campaign of unremitting evangelism, snatching only a few hours' sleep each day. 'The whole of the people ... lifting up hands to God entered into the Solemn League and Covenant.' The ascendancy of the Presbyterian Party in Ireland was destined to be short-lived, but in a few enthusiastic years they laid the foundation of the Irish Presbyterian Church which was to provide the religious and social structure of the Scots-Irish.

The struggle for Ireland, which had begun as a fairly straightforward contest between native and planter, Catholic and Protestant, soon became caught up in the complexities of the English Civil War. Armies representing different interests – Parliamentarian, Royalist, Presbyterian, Catholic Irish – operated in a maelstrom of shifting political and military alliances, all invoking the same God to bless their aims with success. In the confused situation the promised money and supplies from the English Parliament were not forthcoming and the Scots soldiers were reduced to a 'wretched dyet ... sometimes half a pound [of meal] a day with twentie myles marcheing'. When Monro was heavily defeated by the native Irish commander Owen Roe O'Neill at Benburb, the chaplains saw the disaster as the 'Righteous Hand of God' on the 'prodigiously profane' Scots army, but a more down-to-earth view blamed their defeat on the half-starved condition of the soldiers. It was, said one writer, 'well scene at Benbourb when coming to the push of pike they had no power to stand but oppressed by weakness caused by famine dyed by the sword'. There appears also to have been a psychological element at work, a food anxiety that seems still to exist among the Scots and Scots-Irish and manifests itself in the way modern Glaswegians seek comfort in sticky buns as well as whisky and in the great transatlantic culture they so much influenced, where the neon eyes of eating places wink unendingly across the landscape. After the Newry massacre, a chaplain accompanying Monro's lean troopers inspected the Irish dead and wrote indignantly that they 'were so fat that one might have hid their fingers in the lirks of their breasts'. The New Scots had no choice but to live off the countryside, thus creating deep resentment among the people they had come to protect. The 'oppression and insolence of the Scottish army was worse nor the rebellion'. Even the weather was against them. In the month of May Scots soldiers died from exposure due to 'tempestuous nights of hail, rain, cold and excessive wind'.

At this period John Milton, in the course of a religious controversy, issued what might be taken as the standard London view of the Scots-Irish position in Ulster (enduring with some modifications to this day) that they 'being neighbourly admitted ... by the courtsie of England to hold possession in our Province ... have proved ingrateful and treacherous guests'. His master, Oliver Cromwell, subscribed to that view, and, when the New Scots were involved in the Scottish invasion of England in 1648, the Parliamentary commander in Ireland, General Monck, moved against them. Carrickfergus was captured and Monro sent as a prisoner to England. With the surrender of the Scots army Presbyterian power collapsed, and the dream which began with 'God's wonderful Providence in ordering the beginning and foundation of a church here' was once more in ashes. Presbyterianism in Ireland would have to fight its battles by faith alone, unsustained by the 'sword of the Lord'.

Though Cromwell was no lover of Presbyterians – his view was expressed in the Irish context by John Milton where he wrote of 'the blockish Presbyters of Clandeboye ... unhallowed priestlings' – he contented himself with curbing their power, and it was not until the Restoration of Charles II that full-scale persecution began. After an initial period of royal tolerance when a state allowance (the *regium donum*), which worked out at about ten pounds a year, was granted to Nonconformist ministers, the Church of Ireland – now restored to power – began to enforce the full rigour of ecclesiastical law against Presbyterians. Less than a year after the Restoration, the Lord Justices of Ireland forbade meetings of 'Papists, Presbyterians ... and other fanatical persons'. Jeremy Taylor, Bishop of Down, one of the great prose stylists of the English language and an equally distinguished persecutor of dissent, in one day expelled thirty-six Ulster clergymen from their livings. One of the expelled, Patrick Adair, sadly chastened since the heady days of the New Scots Army wrote, 'There came a dark cloud on this poor church.'

There followed a period of which Irish Presbyterians are immensely, and justifiably, proud. The banned ministers preached to their congregation in the fields and woods, and inside the parishes, as Adair recorded, continued quiet pastoral work: 'they did visit the people from home to home and sometimes small meetings in the night time'. In 1698 the Anglican Bishop of Down petitioned the Lord Justices of Ireland to end this 'unreasonable liberty ... they preach in the fields and continue there a great part of the day'.

Field-preaching, however, was not entirely due to persecution and the fear of the sudden arrival of dragoons. There was a great attraction to these 'ancient Christians' in a practice which so strongly recalled the ministry of Christ. As late as the beginning of the nineteenth century, the Seceeders, an evangelical breakaway section of the Presbyterian Church, were still preaching in the open air. John Gamble's *A View of Society and Manners in the North of Ireland*, published in 1813, has a vivid, if romanticized, description of such a meeting: 'the wild glen and the dark woods and foaming torrent – the thin dapper figure – the sharp face and keen visage of the preacher as he projected his head from the little pulpit covered with canvas, placed on the verge of the hill: the immense multitude of all ages and sexes, in scarlet cloaks and grey mantles – in hoods and bonnets and mob caps and old-fashioned hats standing, sitting or lying around.' At about the same time considerably less decorous prayer meetings were taking place among the emigrant Scots-Irish on the banks of a Kentucky river.

The period when it was actually necessary to preach in the open air because of the lack of churches was short. Within a decade of the expulsions from parish churches Presbyterians were putting up simple thatched buildings which they called meeting-houses. The name itself was significant. It indicated that the congregation, not the building, was important and it reaffirmed the Presbyterian principle of the dignity of the individual against the pretensions of ecclesiastical authority and the psuedo-religious magic with which tradition invested churches and shrines.

These first crude buildings were in turn replaced by simple cruciform churches in which the central aisle was specially wide to allow for the celebration of communion. J. C. Breakey, in *Presbyterian Church Architecture in Ireland*, describes the Sunday scene: 'here on Communion Sabbaths were spread the long narrow tables, covered with white linen cloth, to which the people "came forward" from their pews to the singing of the one-hundred and sixteenth Psalm – "I'll of Salvation take the cup".'

The 1680s, the 'Killing Times' in Scotland started a new wave of emigration to the north of Ireland which, like the compulsory emigration from the Borders, was to have an importance out of proportion to its actual size. Soon after Charles II returned to the throne, bishops had been restored in the Scottish Church, with the result that nearly three hundred Dissenting ministers were forced from their livings and became, like Blair and Cunningham in Ulster, martyrs to Episcopal rule. The expelled ministers found support among small tenant farmers, craftsmen and labourers who had little in their lives to replace the 'Godly discipline' and the certainty of election to eternal bliss which the 'auld preachers' of Covenant days had promised them. As in Ulster, an underground Church developed, with secret prayer meetings in houses and open-air services in remote parts of the countryside. These fanatical, devoted people proclaimed themselves the legitimate heirs of the Covenant, 'the true Presbyterian church of Christ in Scotland', and were prepared to challenge those now in authority who in their eyes had broken the solemn treaty which Scotland had made with God. When a few zealots among the new Covenanters brutally murdered the aged Archbishop Sharp of St Andrews – and spent the following night in prayer to celebrate their act – the full force of Government repression was unleashed against them. Covenanting ministers were hunted down, their field services broken up by troops and worshippers killed as they escaped. There were summary executions, men and women were tortured and those who escaped the gallows were transported to virtual slavery in America. Hundreds of active Covenanters and their passive supporters, especially from the counties of the south-west, chose the milder forms of oppression which they might encounter among the valleys of Antrim or the rolling drumlin country of Down.

Years of poverty and oppression had ingrained in these simple, religious peasants an abiding hatred for totalitarian power. This was less a deep desire for democracy than a refusal to recognize any authority which did not meet their own stringent moral and religious standards, an authority which was not 'Covenanted to God'. With their arrival in Ulster a fresh radicalism, a new constancy and courage, was injected into the Scots-Irish bloodstream. In the decade which followed, in places like the lonely valley of Glenwherry in County Antrim, the refugee Covenanters continued to hold services in defiance of the law. There the legendary Scots minister and prophet Alexander Peden preached to them, and from such outlawed gatherings sprang the Reformed Presbyterian Church in Ireland. Unswerving in their faith, whether religious or political, the Scots-Irish Covenanters were to play an important part in the Revolution in America in the 1780s and in Ulster in 1798.

The accession of James II to the English throne turned back the clock in Ireland to pre-Plantation days. As a Roman Catholic monarch, James created a dilemma for many English Anglicans: their religion ordained absolute loyalty to the king and at the same time enjoined utter abhorrence of the religion he professed. In Ireland there was less opportunity for niceties of conscience and in any case such problems were resolved by events. The king appointed as his Lord Deputy a Catholic, Richard Talbot, a survivor from Cromwell's slaughter at Drogheda, who began at once to reverse the anti-Catholic policy of the past century. He replaced Protestants by Catholics in the army, the judiciary and local administration, and he disbanded the militia which Protestants regarded as the guarantee of their safety. The less discreet among the native Irish began to talk of recovering their lost lands and exterminating the planter population. Faced with this very real threat, Anglican and Presbyterian forgot their differences and began to prepare for a common defence.

An even more dangerous situation for the Protestant settlers arose when James, driven from his English kingdom by his Protestant son-in-law William of Orange, turned to Ireland as his power base, a springboard from which he hoped with French help to recover the British Crown. The historian Lord Macaulay, who perceived the settlers as sturdy Protestant Liberals in a nineteenth-century mould, threatened by a Romanist tyrant, let his imagination range freely when he described the situation: 'There was scarcely a Protestant mansion from the Giant's Causeway to Bantry in which armed men were not watching and lights burning from early sunset to late sunrise.'

The panic was increased by a letter found in the streets of the village of Comber in County Down. The Comber Letter was anonymous and written in a semi-literate hand, but the terms in which its message was couched, carefully designed to play on the fears of a new 1641 massacre, could hardly have been bettered by the dirty tricks department of a modern secret service. It was addressed to a local Protestant landowner, Lord Mount-Alexander, and warned 'that all our Irishmen through Ireland is sworn: that on the ninth day of this month they are all to fall on to kill and murder man, wife and child'. It appealed to the landowner to look after himself as he and other Protestant leaders were special targets for the Irish; 'Let no Irishman come near you, whatsoever he be.' Copies of the letter were distributed throughout the planter population, creating the effect which its authors, no doubt, intended. In one place, however, that effect was to have special significance.

Londonderry, with its colonial-style defences built in Plantation days, was a key point in the control of the north. Lord Deputy Talbot ordered the Catholic Earl of Antrim to garrison the city, but when Antrim, with an army of Irish clansmen, arrived the gates were shut against him. The Comber Letter had confirmed the fears of the Protestant inhabitants. Significantly, the shutting of the gates was performed by thirteen apprentices who came almost equally from the English-descended Anglican and the Scottish Presbyterian sections of the community. Behind the walls of Derry, threatened by a besieging force which, if it was not entirely Catholic, was perceived by the defenders to represent Popish aggression, Protestant unity reached its highest point. 'Then', says the Presbyterian historian Thomas Witherow, 'they scrupled not to hear one another's way of worship and sermons.'

Starvation was a far greater threat to the defenders of Derry during the seven-month siege than the army which surrounded them. John Hunter, who kept a diary throughout, wrote, 'Never let poor woman's son meet with such hardships as I met with at that great siege'. In the later months dogs, cats and rats were the luxury items in a pitifully meagre diet. A powerful religious faith, as much as strong political loyalty, sustained the citizens. When relief ships finally broke through in late July 1689, John Hunter was convinced that 'It was never poor starved men in Derry that kept it but the Mighty God of Jacob'.

'The bonfires shone bright along the whole circuit of the ramparts ... and all night

ABOVE *Built by the Norman soldier of fortune, John de Courcy, in the twelfth century, Carrickfergus Castle was the power base for the Scottish Covenanting army which came to reconquer Ulster after the 1641 Rebellion. Here, in 1690, William of Orange landed a month before the Battle of the Boyne* (LEFT).

the bells of the rescued city made answer to the Irish guns with peals of joyous defiance', wrote Macaulay, but he was by no means the first to recognize that the occasion provided good copy. As soon as the guns were silenced George Walker, the Church of Ireland clergyman who had been governor during the siege, rushed straight into print with his *True Account of the Siege of Londonderry*, which inflated the part played by the Episcopalian defenders and denigrated the role of the Presbyterians. Within months an acerbic reply had been written by John Mackenzie on behalf of the Presbyterians. Both Anglican and Nonconformist would in the years to come share the city's slogan of 'No surrender', but more than a century would pass before they united again as they had inside Derry's walls.

Like the 1641 Rebellion, the siege of Derry is now more important as a myth than as an historical fact. The place name was always highly emotive, the city itself a potential flashpoint. The present Ulster troubles began when Catholics attacked a march celebrating the thirteen apprentice boys; one of the most bitter political arguments of the conflict has been about whether the name should be Derry, favoured by Republicans, or Londonderry, favoured by Unionists. In a city much celebrated in song it is ironic that Londonderry suits the slow sentimental ballads which come mainly from Catholic sources while Derry fits best the brisk marching tunes associated with the Protestant cause.

For the thousands of Protestants who emigrated to North America, Londonderry had a more complex significance. It was the symbol of their forefathers' steadfastness and courage, which was why they scattered the place name over New England and the Middle Colonies, but it was also their point of embarkation, their last contact with a familiar world and as such nostalgically remembered. Often descendants two or three generations on, in the heart of a great new continent, had nothing to identify their Irish roots but the word 'Derry' on an old document connected with their grandparents' emigration. To them Derry was a dim place of lost innocence in an island where there were no extremes of heat, no rattlesnakes and no marauding Indians.

A little over a year after the epic siege, the Catholic threat was removed when William defeated James at the Battle of the Boyne. Here that controversial cleric, Walker of Derry, was killed by a cannon-shot and suffered posthumous humiliation at the hands of his recent allies. His body, 'stript immediately for Scotch-Irish that followed our camp ... took off most of the plunder ...'. The Boyne joined Derry as part of Protestant mythology, and emigrant families in the lonely valleys of Appalachia proudly told how an ancestor had defended the Maiden City or stood with William at the Boyne. Two Jackson brothers in the Williamite army were, it was claimed, the grandfather of President Andrew Jackson and the great-grandfather of the Civil War hero 'Stonewall' Jackson.

Even when engaged in an ideological war, the mercantalist instinct of the Scots-Irish was never dormant. When, after the Boyne, the fighting moved to southern Ireland, 'vast numbers of them followed the Army as Victuallers ... and purchased most of the vast preys which were taken by the Army in the Campaign and drove incredible numbers of cattel into Ulster'. This was the beginning of an upward economic thrust which would gather momentum in the eighteenth century and dominate the north of Ireland in the nineteenth. Humble Ulster Scots who 'used to beat upon the Hoof after a Pony laden with Pedlar's goods . . . are now masters of Ships . . . and Warehouses' (Some of the next generation followed the same path to prosperity on the distant banks of the Susquehanna.) For most, however, the Williamite Wars meant loss of property or death by violence or disease. The estates and farms of James's supporters, usually Catholics, were confiscated; other lands were left vacant because the tenants had died or fled. Again, as in the early years of the century, Ulster offered opportunities for immigrants, opportunities which could hardly have come at a better time for the Scots at home.

In the 1690s the Scottish grain harvest failed for four successive years and there was famine in both Highlands and Lowlands. So severe was it that it is estimated between a quarter and a third of the population either died or left the country; 'some die in the wayside some drop down in the street', wrote a contemporary. 'Everyone may see Death in the face of the poor that abound everywhere.' Thousands of the survivors crossed to Ulster, where they were welcomed by landlords anxious for hardworking Protestant tenants. Many better-off farmers, less affected by the famine, also came in search of cheap land. It was this immigration of the 1690s, greater than any of the previous ones, which confirmed the position of the Scots as the dominant element in Ulster.

Almost as soon as victory had removed the native Irish threat, the Protestant authorities in Dublin and the bishops of the Established Church forgot the debt they owed to Presbyterians and renewed their attack on the Dissenting Church. A Parliamentary Act of 1704 made it compulsory for all Government office-holders or members of town corporations to take Communion in the Church of Ireland. This Presbyterians in conscience could not do, so they, like Catholics, were excluded from even the humblest Government jobs and were totally unrepresented on the councils of boroughs, even where they might make up eighty per cent of the population. Already ordinary Presbyterians were liable to fines for failing to attend Episcopal services and their ministers to a crippling penalty of one hundred pounds for performing their pastoral duties. These last two laws were repealed in the Toleration Act of 1719 but the idea of the Presbyterian Church as a non-Church persisted until the middle of the nineteenth century when the Chief Justice of Ireland, pronouncing judgement in a bigamy case involving marriage by a Presbyterian minister, said categorically, 'The law of this country does not recognize the Orders of the Presbyterian Church'.

This non-recognition of their ministers was the greatest religious disability imposed on Presbyterians. The Catholic priest could be outlawed by the Penal Laws brought in by a bigoted Anglican-dominated Parliament, but the State did not deny that he was validly ordained and could administer the Sacraments according to the rites of Rome. On the other hand, because the ordination of a Presbyterian cleric was not recognized, the marriages he performed were invalid, making Presbyterian couples fornicators and their children bastards. Apart from the shame it brought on pious, respectable people, the law led to costly legal complications about inheritances. Church of Ireland bishops were active, using their position as members of the House of Lords and their own ecclesiastical courts to compel Presbyterians to conform. One minister who suffered from their attentions wrote, 'Our prelates are violent where I live. Four of my flock have been lately delivered to Satan for being married by me.' The Dissenters, despite their lack of trust in worldly authority, finally appealed to the Lord Lieutenant of Ireland to restrain the bishops:

> We are surprised to find some officials in this part of the Kingdom indeavouring to deprive us of what we have so long peacably injoy'd as appears by their pursuing both ministry and people in their courts for non-comformity to the Rites & Ceremonys of the Church, the ministry for solemnizing marriage clandestinely, as they pleased to call it, & make void such marriages by obliging people so marry'd to confess publicly themselfs guilty of the damnable sin of fornication to the no small grief of Your Petitioners hereby made infamous, their children uncapable of succeeding to their estates & of diverse other priveledges as being bastards ...

The petition had no effect and the Episcopal attacks continued, 'numerous and violent prosecutions ... of many ... as fornicators merely for co-habiting with their own wives'.

There were also indirect attacks, such as the refusal of landlords, the vast majority of whom belonged to the Established Church, to allow Presbyterian meeting-houses to be built on their land. Thomas Mills, the Bishop of Waterford, was beside himself with rage 'at the boldness of the dissenters for building a meeting-house ... so near the Cathedral'. It would be wrong, however, to imagine Ulster Presbyterians as a mild people, quietly submitting to persecution. They regarded the members of the Episcopal Church as idolaters and heretics and made no secret of the fact that if the Lord saw fit to restore them to power in the land they would enforce conformity to Presbyterianism; 'toleration of all religions is not farre from blasphemy', wrote one Scottish divine. Neither could they refrain from proclaiming their God-given mission, 'the Prospect of Establishing what they called the Kingdom of Christ'. To the Church of Ireland this was plainly 'assuming and insolent behaviour', as in their view God had clearly indicated his preference by providing the Established Church with the full protection of the law and its bishops and rectors with fat and comfortable livings. The Presbyterian Church expressed its position in the blunt prayer of the old County Armagh minister, 'May the Lord protect his ain Kirk from the Whore that sits on the Seven Hills and her bastard daughter, the Church of Ireland'.

Education was highly esteemed among the Scots-Irish, not least because it was the hallmark of the minister or the schoolmaster, the two most important people in the congregation. J. M. Barkley describes how a poor Ulster student might walk hundreds of miles to university in Glasgow or Edinburgh, 'his bag of oatmeal on his shoulder to pay for his lodgings'. As early as 1691 the Presbyterian Synod in Ulster decreed that no one should enter the ministry without a degree.

The minister was at the same time very much a man of the people, working the manse farm which went with his living. John Stevenson, in *Two Centuries of Life in Down*, describes the lifestyle of the Rev. John Kennedy of Benburb as seen through his diary, 'in fair or foul weather travelling far, baptising, marrying, catechising, visiting the sick and dying, attending markets, buying cattle. He quarries, carts manure, plants hedges, sows, reaps – his life is half that of a pastor, half of a farm labourer.' John Kennedy's laconic record illustrates an important facet of early Presbyterian life, the degree to which religion and everyday life were bound together. In the year 1725–6 he records, 'March 4 sowed parsneps. Friday 11 cleaned some seed corn. Saturday 12 laid quicks [whitethorn cuttings] with Tom McCulloch. Sabbath 20 Proverbs 16:20 Romans 9:2 baptised a child to Jos Car.' For him a heavy rainstorm was 'Judgement-like' and, as he noted, at the beginning of each calendar year he would 'renew Covenant with God for me and mine'. The minister had a generous and trusting nature but even in a pious Presbyterian congregation that trust was sometimes misplaced: 'Friday 11 July went to seek Dan McLean, he is gone with my two guineas.'

In the early decades of the eighteenth century Ireland escaped briefly from the grip of its history, and there was a breathing space between endemic sectarian or social conflicts. The Presbyterians lived in quiet, inward-looking rural congregations like that portrayed in the diary of John Scott, a divinity student of Donaghadee. Among a people denied influence in greater matters, the events of parish life were of absorbing importance. On a summer Saturday afternoon in 1707, 'Jamie Allen ... firing a musquet at a bird' on the thatched roof of the meeting-house, set the building on fire, to the intense excitement of the village. The great event of the following year was the November storm in which a ship ran on the rocks 'a little below the meeting-house and was staved to pieces'.

John fell in love with the minister's daughter, whom he prudently disguised in the diary under the name of 'Doa'. She appears to have been a coquette, perversely frustrating his elaborate schemes to see her but at other times encouraging the bucolic romance. 'I was for sometime at the Turf stack cum Doa. Fraiday 21st November after supper I met with Doa at the haystack ... presented her with a broad piece of gold.' This 'broad piece' was one of the gold coins, of French, Spanish or Portuguese origin, circulating in Ireland at the time. Despite his many gifts and his frequent outpourings of love, John lost his Doa. She became the second of three wives of the Rev. Robert 'Greeting' Gordon, a deeply emotional man who fathered twenty-five children, and frequently wept in the pulpit.

The Presbyterian congregations were largely rural, though this was to change in the course of the eighteenth century; they were also poor, almost as poor as their Catholic fellow countrymen. Ministers like John Kennedy lived on an income derived from three sources – the produce of his farm, the *regium donum*, or small Government pension which had been renewed by William III (the efforts of the bishops prevailed on the High

Church Government of Queen Anne to cancel it in 1710) and stipends which each family in the congregation contracted to pay for the upkeep of their pastors. The poverty of the countryside, bad harvests and the conflicting, and legally enforceable, demands of the landlord for rent and the local rector for tithes meant that often these stipends were not paid. In 1717, a year notorious for crop failure, only one minister in the Route Presbytery of north Antrim received a stipend. In these years the minister fell back more and more on the manse farm to support his family. As J. M. Barkley in his study, 'The Presbyterian Minister in Eighteenth Century Ireland', puts it, 'This bound minister and people closely together. If the harvest was good they rejoiced together, if it failed they faced want and starvation together.' This togetherness of pastor and flock was a great unifying force in Presbyterianism and played no small part in the great transatlantic emigrations and the success of the Scots-Irish as pioneers in the New World.

Tithes were not only a burden but also an intense irritant to Presbyterians, and they continued to be so for over a century and a half. It was particularly galling to have to pay for the upkeep of an Episcopalian clergyman you might never have seen because he did not even live in the parish, while your own clergyman, whom you knew as a devoted counsellor and friend, went in want. Archbishop Boulter, worried about his clergy's income, told the Lord Lieutenant with considerable understatement, 'Scotch Presbyterians, as a great part of the Protestants in the North are ... do not pay tythes with any great chearfulness'. It is far from edifying to read the letters of these rich gentlemen, the bishops and the landlords, squabbling over the shillings of the tenant farmers, the prelates arguing that high rents made the lower classes unwilling to pay tithes and the landlords claiming that the tithes prevented them from getting as much rent as they should. It does not seem to have occurred to either that the rents were too high and the tithes morally indefensible.

The kirk was the centre of Presbyterian life, the Kirk Session its court of morals. Church members were called before the Session to answer for sexual offences, for sabbath breaking, for blasphemy and the very frequent offence of scandalmongering. Raymond Gillespie, in his study *Colonial Ulster*, has examined the Antrim session book for four years in the 1650s and concludes that 'by the standards of contemporary England this incidence of adultery (63 cases) and fornication (67) was low ... the East Ulster settler was less likely to commit adultery than murder'. But whatever the statistics, the Dissenting communities seem to have been obsessed with the sins of the flesh. Carnmoney session book entries for May 1686 consist of a long recital of sexual offences: 'Joan Gordon fornicatrix with the said William Martin ... Katherine Cook confest her relapse into fornication ... Thomas Howe fornicator with Barbara Macdonald ... Agnes Macdonald cited for her fornication with George Bodan.' Some are recorded in more detail: 'May 15, 1686, Margaret Dury called apeared and confest that she had brought forth a child in fornication.' Margaret, apart from standing on the stool of repentance and admitting the lurid details before a congregation equally divided between those who were shocked and those who enjoyed every salacious moment, seems to have been treated leniently, merely being exhorted to report frequently to the elder responsible for her area. These elders had the duty of overseeing an area, which could mean spying on church members, 'every elder duily inform himself . . . whether there be . . . any scandalous sin and report the same to the session'.

Unlike Margaret Dury's experience, the story of Isabal Car is a tragic and frightening one. She confessed that 'Alex Wilson sometime agone was in her house and after door shut . . . he sitting on a chest joyning to the bed on which she sat, said to her this a convenient time and to play with thee if thou be willing'. She denied any guilt in the incident, 'but seemed troubled for the dishonour to God'. When the Session decided that she should appear again on the same charges Isabal appears to have been overcome by a morbid terror and literally to have died of fright.

From one session book comes the cruel little story of Mary Wilson. Convinced that Mary was lying when she accused the respectable Adam McCrogh of being the father of the child she was carrying, the elders instructed Agnes Craford, the congregation's midwife, to use the psychological moment when she was in labour to force her to confess.

> Agnes told her there being something extraordinary in her labour which God in his Righteous Judgement might do if she disembel and she did not know but she might be a grave to her child. Wilson cried out what would you have me say crying biterly. Agnes said will you tell ye truth she reply'd if I were to be a grave to my child I have no other thing to say but Adam McCrogh is father to my child after which within a quarter of an hour she was delivered.

The court dealt with many less serious matters, such as petty theft or wife-beating on a Sunday. James Russell was accused in October 1690 of 'being scandalously overtaken with drink on ayne fair day', John Wilson that 'by his playing on the fidle he decoyed young people and servants from their work'. George Sheldon and John Strean were charged with using the Bible for fortune-telling and George Russell of stealing sixpence halfpenny from the collection box.

The elders and ministers themselves were also kept under close scrutiny. From time to time the Kirk Session held Privy Censures, meetings of the elders at which each in turn left the room while his conduct, private and public, was discussed in great detail by his fellow officer-holders, and he was dealt with according to the findings. This game, where judges were judged, with its infinite possibilities for innuendo, for malice, for paying off old scores, where the reputation of the 'unco Godly' could be destroyed in a few minutes, must have been both exciting and hard on the nerves; small wonder 'there were few . . . who were not rebuked'. Ministers too were frequently censured: 'some Ministers, their wives and children are too gaudy and vain in their apparel . . . sumptuous dinners . . . be forborn in Minister's houses'. These plain-living early Presbyterian congregations had something of the atmosphere of Chinese revolutionary communities in the twentieth century.

A feature of Ulster people was their comparatively mild treatment of witches. Scotland, particularly at a time when extreme Calvinism was at the height of its power, had one of the blackest records for witch-hunting in Europe, but that hysteria disappeared from the make-up of the Scots in Ulster. It is true the province had its share of witch scares: ministers' wives seem to have been a particular target for sorcery. The wife of James Shaw, 'a zealous, worthy preacher', died in childbirth 'wronged by the sorcery of some witches in the parish'. Mrs Anne Haltridge, the aged widow of the minister of Islandmagee, was so tormented by a mischievous, and plainly supernatural, boy that she too died. Cows in Ulster fields lost their milk, houses were haunted ('the turf clods flew like swallows about the room'), but the fear of witches never became a mania as it did elsewhere, threatening the vulnerable of society, the eccentrics, the epileptics, the mad and the solitary. The Kirk Session, too, was cautious in investigating the occult and kept a sharp eye out for the practical joker, a spirit that haunted most Scots-Irish communities.

The nineteenth-century historian J. R. Green, writing of the settlers' achievement in the seventeenth century, said: 'In its material result the Plantation of Ulster was undoubtedly a brilliant success. Farms and homesteads, churches and mills, rose fast amid the desolate wilds.' Modern scholars would hardly recognize in this bright, optimistic picture the Ulster of the early eighteenth century. Much of the inefficient agriculture which had come from Scotland or existed in pre-Plantation Ireland still remained. The countryside had little of the hedged, closely cultivated appearance of today. 'Towns', small groups of homes usually occupied by an extended family of fathers, married children, uncles and cousins, dotted the landscape; they survive today in names like Martinstown or Tweedstown. Around them was a strip system of unfenced fields, the arable 'infields' closest to the 'town' while the 'outfields' were devoted to grazing. Evidence of this 'rundale' organization of farming was to be found as late as the 1930s at Evishnablagh in County Antrim. The settlers in general had better houses than the natives, the better-off with stone and timber-framed buildings, but many lived throughout much of the seventeenth century in what were called 'Irish houses', crude dwellings of mud, roofed with branches and rough thatch and having neither chimney nor windows. The manse, the meeting-house and the homes of the bigger farmers were strong structures with small windows; John Kennedy roofed his meeting-house with wooden shingles in December 1726. Wheeled transport was confined to the well-to-do and the tenant farmer used a primitive form of sled. Grain was cut laboriously with a sickle, and ploughing by the tail – tying the plough to the horse or bullock's tail – was still practised despite official prohibition.

It would be misleading to think of Episcopalians and Presbyterians simply in terms of 'haves' and 'have nots'; many of the poor belonged to the Church of Ireland. But there was between the two faiths a social as well as a religious divide, and that class distinction took physical shape in the high stone walls that went up around the estates of the wealthy landowners. Another significant division between the two was their conflicting views of history. The gentry believed in a static concept of society. They saw the social order which had arisen in a century of settlement as an immutable fact sealed by the blood of Derry and the Boyne. The prayers which they prescribed for poor children attending their schools perfectly expressed their outlook: 'Teach us to be Contented with our Lot, submissive to our Superiors and humble and modest to all.' The Dissenters, on the other hand, took a Heraclitean view of history, perceiving all things as flowing on towards an end Heaven had predestined for them.

Many of the richer Ulster Scots deserted the faith of their forefathers for the Anglican Communion and the company of what they considered the better class of people. William Montgomery, scion of the great Planter House of Montgomery, and author of the Montgomery Manuscripts, was one of these. He found comfort in looking back to the early days of the settlement as he imagined them to have been: 'Now everybody minded their trades and the ploughs and the spade – building and setting trees in orchards and gardens. The old women spun and the young girls plyed their nimble fingers at knitting – and everybody was innocently busy. Now the Golden peaceable age was renewed, no strife, contention or Scottish or Irish feuds.'

That was the Ulster Eden that never was, the dream of an old gentleman in a comfortable study. But outside, in the bleak reality of a land where poor Ulster Scots were third-class citizens, the real vision was still there. For the ragged preacher or rent-racked farmer there was no complacent nostalgia but a burning hope for a future where in 'Christ's Kingdom' justice and truth would reign.

4 • A NEW GLIMPSE OF ZION

'This stern and virile people . . . formed the kernel of . . . the pioneers in their march westward.'

Theodore Roosevelt, *The Winning of the West*

'BRETHREN, LET US depart for God has appointed a new country for us to dwell in. It is called New England. Let us be free of these Pharaohs, these rackers of rents and screwers of tithes and let us go unto the land of Canaan. We are the Lord's ain people and he shall divide the ocean before us.' The scene is a bare room with whitewashed walls, the year is 1718, the speaker a tall man in his early fifties with a gaunt face and faded blue eyes. He is dressed in a tattered Geneva gown worn over an old, once respectable, suit of broadcloth. His audience sit on three-legged stools, mesmerized by the angry hypnotic cadences of his sermon. Mr James McGregor, Dissenting minister of the Aghadowey congregation in County Londonderry, is announcing plans for the first mass emigration of Scots-Irish to the New World.

It is the beginning of a great ethnic venture, a venture which will throw up, among other things, a family richer than any the world has ever seen, a ruler with more power than the Caesars of ancient Rome and a gentle alcoholic songwriter whose words will be better known than Shakespeare's. But on that Sabbath morning in June, in the thatched meeting-house of the Aghadowey Presbyterian congregation, such worldly outcomes are not to be thought of. The poor tenant farmers, the housewives and mothers of large families, the weavers and the landless labourers who make up the audience are caught once more in the dream which brought their grandfathers and great-grandfathers to Ulster, the dream of a new Zion, a Garden of Eden, where the land is fertile and free, where, without landlord or bishop, the Ulster Calvinists will establish God's kingdom on earth.

Eighty years before McGregor's successful voyage, there had been an abortive attempt by a much smaller group of Presbyterians, led by Robert Blair and John Livingstone, to reach Massachusetts. After two months of winter storms in the Atlantic their tiny ship, the *Eaglewing*, returned to Carrickfergus. Intensive persecution in the 1630s had been the cause of this hardy venture. Now in the eighteenth century Presbyterians were still second-class citizens in Ulster.

Removed from the intoxicating rhetoric of the meeting-house, economic grievances were more important to the layman. After a hundred years in the Promised Land of Ulster, the great majority of the Scots-Irish were still poor tenant farmers without any hope of owning their farms, or else they were weavers dependent on the vagaries of the linen trade. The early years of the eighteenth century had not been kind to either. A series of calamitous crop failures had brought famine. Deliberate discrimination by the

British Parliament against Irish agriculture and Irish trade had ruined many farmers and craftsmen. Farm leases granted in the 1690s, when there was a large immigration from Scotland, were falling due and landlords were often doubling the rent in the new leases. Catholics, whom landlords found much more docile than Presbyterians and who, because they were glad to get land on any conditions, would pay more rent, were often preferred as tenants. This was particularly galling as, less than thirty years earlier, Presbyterian tenants had stood side by side with Church of Ireland landlords against these Irish Catholics in a common Protestant defence of their Ulster homes. The Anglo-Irish establishment now chose to forget the blood shed in their defence and the Presbyterians were left with a deep sense of betrayal.

James McGregor saw himself as the Scots-Irish Moses but he was not leading his people into the unknown. In the last decades of the seventeenth century there had been a steady trickle of emigrants from Ulster to Maryland and the area close to Philadelphia. More important for encouraging fresh emigration was the presence of Presbyterian ministers from Ulster in the Middle Colonies. The most famous of these was Francis Makemie, who came from County Donegal to Maryland in the 1680s and is now regarded as the Founding Father of American Presbyterianism. About the same time William Homes, from the Derry-Donegal border, worked as a pastor and teacher at Martha's Vineyard. His son Robert, a ship's captain and brother-in-law to Benjamin Franklin, began what was later to be the very dubious business of sea captains touting in Ireland for emigrant business.

Business and political networks, either Masonic or family based, were always a feature of Scots-Irish society, and William Homes seems to have been at the centre of such a network for promoting immigration to New England. Information and on-the-spot help provided by these networks forged a strong link between Ulster and the New World from the closing decade of the seventeenth century.

But it was the vision and drive of James McGregor which gave the impetus necessary for mass emigration. He organized five ships to carry a large part of his congregation, along with people from neighbouring congregations, from Londonderry to Boston. McGregor sailed in the first ship, and on 31 October 1718 he presented a petition to the Massachusetts House of Representatives asking for a grant of land for the Ulster settlers. In general, the New England Puritans did not welcome the immigrants. As people of English descent they despised both Scots and Irish, and the newcomers were obviously uncouth and poor. It is typical of the prejudice which the Scots-Irish have always attracted, from pamphleteers in the seventeenth and eighteenth centuries to the mass media in the late twentieth, that the New Englanders labelled the Ulstermen as 'illiterate'. A petition signed by these immigrants shows that ninety-seven per cent could write – no mean standard at that time for poor people.

The Rev. Cotton Mather, New England's leading Congregationalist divine, saw the usefulness of McGregor's people. They would act, he argued, as a buffer between the white population and the hostile Indians. Accordingly, Governor Samuel Shute of New

Londonderry, symbol of Scots-Irish dominance over the native population, was also the port of embarkation for hundreds of thousands of emigrants to the New World. The first mass exodus to New England in 1718 left from Derry, as did the colonists who filled the Juniata Valley in the Allegheny Mountains, and people from north-west Ulster who went with the land promoter James Patton to the Shenandoah Valley.

England granted them the right to settle on the frontier. McGregor chose an area north of the Merrimac River in modern New Hampshire, and christened it 'Londonderry' in honour of his people's 'finest hour'. Londonderry spawned a group of Ulster settlements in southern New Hampshire with names like Antrim and Hillsborough.

Another party of settlers from the western area of County Derry established a settlement at Casco Bay, and the name Belfast appeared on the map of Maine. In Massachusetts there were settlements at Worcester, Pelham and Colerain. At Worcester the newcomers first felt the dislike of the Congregationalists who controlled New England: their meeting-house was torn down by a Puritan mob. It soon became clear that these descendants of the Pilgrim Fathers were, if anything, less tolerant masters than those the Scots-Irish had fled in Ulster. They demanded a total conformity to their mode of worship which the proud and faithful Presbyterians would not give. This early feud continued into the nineteenth century when the Scots-Irish, now emerged as a powerful political and social group, resented the pre-eminence given to the early Puritans in American mythology as pioneers and founding fathers. Certainly the Ulstermen injected a new dynamism into the society of New England which had grown static and self-regarding. They pushed the frontier north and westwards, moving up the river valleys and into Vermont. Some generations later they crossed the Green Mountains to descend into the valley of the Ohio.

Seven years after the five ships sailed to Boston there was a new upsurge in emigration from Ulster. This lasted until 1729, and for the rest of the century, with the exception of the years of the Revolutionary War, the numbers of emigrants to America rose and fell in a graph which reflected accurately the economic health of Ireland. Now the settlers headed for Philadelphia and the ports on the Delaware. The prospect of complete freedom of worship under the Quaker Government of Pennsylvania and reports of the rich valleys in the hinterland – 'This country abounds in fruit . . . chestnuts, walnuts and hazel nuts, Strawberrys, Bilberrys and Mulberrys, they grow wild in the woods and fields in Vast Quantities' – drew far greater numbers than had sailed to New England. In one week in August 1728 the port of Newcastle recorded the arrival of two thousand people from the north of Ireland. Until the Revolution put a temporary stop to emigration, it was estimated that a quarter of a million Scots-Irish came to the North American colonies. But, in the light of modern scholarship, this figure is probably too low. The estimates were based on Irish shipping figures, many of which were missing, and besides, numbers of Scots-Irish sailed from English and Scottish ports. What is reasonably certain is that by mid-century at least one-sixth of the white population of British North America was Scots-Irish.

'The whole North is in ferment and people every day are engaging . . . to go next year': in 1728 the Protestant Archbishop Hugh Boulter reported to the British Government on the emigration fever which had spread throughout the north of Ireland. Primate Boulter was expressing the alarm felt by the Protestant aristocracy at the prospect of large numbers of Presbyterians moving to America and removing Protestantism's front line of defence. 'Not one in ten' could pay his fare, wrote Boulter, in an effort to belittle the emigrants and the idea of emigration. While the Archbishop exaggerated the figures, it was true that only the better-off tenant farmers or those who could sell the leases of their Ulster farms could afford to pay the passage as well as raise the money to pay for land in the New World, and subsist there for a year until the first crops were harvested. The rest, men and women, sometimes whole families, went as indentured servants or redemptioners.

The indentured servant pledged himself to work for four years for subsistence alone. The pledge was normally given to the ship's captain who, on reaching America, sold the indenture to the highest bidder. The redemptioner gave a similar pledge, but with the proviso that on arrival he could attempt to raise the money to buy his freedom. Notices of the sale of indentured servants, 'Just imported and to be sold, Irish servants, men and women of good trades from the North of Ireland', were as much a feature of the Philadelphia press as slave auctions in Charleston newspapers.

Profit from indenture sales, after paying off the passage money, was high and the American Quakers were quick to seize the opportunity. One Philadelphia Quaker wrote to a co-religionist in Ireland, 'Procure ... four lusty servants and agree to pay their passage. At this side sell two and pay the other passage with the Money.' The American Friends never had it so good. There was no reason why, with a neat combination of philanthropy and sharp practice, the meek should not inherit the earth. They were to discover that this was not necessarily true if one was trying to manipulate the Scots-Irish.

In April 1763 a County Down farmer, Robert Smillie, wrote to the *Belfast Newsletter*, 'As many of my friends and countrymen are about to go to the Provinces of North America I thought it my duty to prevent them being treated in so barbarous and inhumane a Manner as many were last year who went on board the *Sally* from Belfast ...'. When Smillie sent to the newspaper a letter he had received from his emigrant son John about his experiences on the voyage, he was contributing to a discussion which recurred constantly in the *Newsletter* columns. On the one hand there were horror stories from emigrants, and on the other, advertisments placed by shipowners extolling the comfort and safety of their vessels. From time to time satisfied groups of passengers would publish a letter of thanks to the captain, but overall the picture was a grim one.

The ships were designed primarily for cargo, and below decks only children could stand upright. The *William*, which sailed from Newry to Boston in 1766, had a height of four feet nine inches between the decks and was described as 'roomy'. Berths were crowded together, and until late in the century there were no portholes, the only source of fresh air being a few overhead hatches. Here men, women and children ate, slept, performed the functions of nature, were born and often died. The stench was indescribable, and smallpox and cholera frequently broke out. On some voyages half the

The Ulster Scots, contrary to the myth so assiduously propagated by their nineteenth- and twentieth-century apologists, shared much of the primitive living conditions of their Catholic fellow countrymen.

passengers died, and the mortality among children was very high. There were no legal limits on the numbers of passengers, and humanitarian efforts by the Pennsylvanian authorities to impose some were foiled by the British, to whom the profits of shipowners were paramount. Sea captains were autocratic and often brutal, cutting the food rations to increase profits and flogging recalcitrant passengers.

But it was the natural hazards of the crossing which brought the worst hardships. Ships were blown off course by contrary winds or becalmed for weeks. Voyages estimated to last about eight weeks stretched to over three months; the longest was a seventeen-week journey in 1773. Food ran out and there was barely any drinking water. When the *Seaflower* sailed from Belfast to Philadelphia in 1741 six of the dead were eaten by survivors. The *Providence*, sailing from Portrush to New York, foundered and the captain and crew took the only lifeboat, leaving the passengers – including women and children – to drown.

On every voyage there were the small family tragedies, a mother dying in childbirth, an aged relative succumbing to the rigours of the voyage. Robert Witherspoon, who crossed to Charleston as a little boy, remembered with great emotion how his grandmother died on the voyage and was buried at sea amid a raging storm. The letter from his son John in Pennsylvania which Robert Smillie published in the *Belfast Newsletter* gives the most vivid account of a transatlantic voyage. It was written from Fishing Creek on the Susquehanna and reads like a more realistic and horrifying prose version of Coleridge's 'Rime of the Ancient Mariner':

> We had a South-West Wind which drove us so far North that our Weather became extremely cold ... On July 6th we had a Storm which continued nine hours; on the 12th we espied a Mountain of Ice of prodigious Size ... on the 16th we espied a sail ... we gave her chase and fired six guns at her ... In this manner did the Captain behave, giving chase to all ships he saw whither they bore off east or west. [Captain Taylor of the *Sally* was playing at being a privateer] ... August the first our weather became extremely warm and the crew very weak [Smillie uses 'crew' to mean passengers] ... the next 12 days we lived on two biscuits and a half for that time ... we had but half a pint of water per day ... Our Ship was truly a Spectacle of Horror. Never a day passed without one or two of our crew put over Board. Many killed themselves by drinking Salt Water and their own urine was a common drink; yet in the midst of all our Miseries, our Captain showed not the least remorse or pity ... August 29th we had only one Pint of Water for each person [left] and our Bread was done. But on that Day the Lord was pleased to send the greatest Shower of Rain I ever saw which was the Means of preserving our lives. After this we had fair winds ... On the first of September we sounded ... and the next morning we saw land.

Pennsylvania was, like the other North American colonies at the beginning of the eighteenth century, a narrow strip of settled land with a vast, virtually unexplored,

The Scots-Irish wrested control of eighteenth-century Philadelphia (ABOVE) *from the Quakers and kept a radical edge on revolutionary and post-Independence politics in America's first capital. Today there is hardly a trace of their influence in the modern multi-ethnic city* (BELOW).

hinterland of wooded hills, valleys and mountains intersected by a network of rivers and inhabited by a few Indian tribes. In 1681 the Quaker William Penn had been granted by Charles II the lands which became Pennsylvania, and he had established that rare privilege in those days, freedom of worship. To the colony came English, Welsh and some Irish Quakers. These were followed by immigrants from the Rhineland, members of German Protestant sects – Amish, Mennonites, Dunkers – who had suffered religious persecution in their homeland. The Quakers had settled in the coastal fringe around Philadelphia, the Germans a little further westward. The Scots-Irish passed through these settled areas to the frontier, where the land was cheapest, though for many of the Scots-Irish the price was academic. They refused to pay anything, saying that the land belonged to God, not William Penn, and He had intended it for His own people, the Presbyterians from Ulster.

On the Octorara Creek, which flows along the boundary of present-day Chester and Lancaster counties, a series of Scots-Irish settlements grew up. These were continually renewed throughout the eighteenth century by settlers fresh from Ulster, and later they provided springboards for new settlements, particularly in western Pennsylvania around the growing town of Pittsburgh. After Octorara, the Ulster people pushed on into the wilderness in a north-westerly direction, along the east bank of the Susquehanna, founding the townships of Pequea, Donegal, Paxtang and Hanover. The broad Susquehanna, 'the far reaching river', brought their westward advance to a halt until a Yorkshireman called John Harris provided a ferry at the point where modern Harrisburg spans the river. Then the Ulstermen, fired by stories of a beautiful, fertile, empty valley, poured across the river into the Cumberland Valley, 'the seed plot and nursery of their race'. Today their progress can be traced in the line of Presbyterian churches they founded – Upper Octorara, Donegal, New Londonderry and Paxtang.

The Ulster settler usually walked to his land grant, or the land on which he intended to squat, his family beside him, his possessions, tools and clothing strapped on a cow or mule. James Magraw took three days to get from Harris's Ferry to his land in the Cumberland Valley because 'the children could not walk as fast as Jane and me'. Donegal Township in Lancaster County, a rolling plain with deep limestone soil, was the sort of place to convince the weary settlers that they had found their Promised Land. Here they built a meeting-house at Donegal Springs, where on the long hot Sabbath, with its morning and afternoon sermons, the worshippers and their horses could ease their thirst. Today, in this quiet place on the banks of the Susquehanna, it is possible, walking among the gravestones of eighteenth-century Pattersons, Pedens and Moffetts, to imagine the joy of men and women who were for the first time owners of their own land and free to worship God as they chose.

Smaller numbers of Scots-Irish pushed the frontier northwards from Philadelphia into the modern Bucks and Northampton counties. The most important of these settlements was at the fork of the Neshaminy River. Here William Tennent, an Ulster clergyman, set up his famous 'Log College' to educate ministers and teachers for

ABOVE *The Scots-Irish of the Appalachian valleys gather at Sycamore Shoals before their great victory at King's Mountain. Painting by Lloyd Branson.*

RIGHT *After the battle the British commander Patrick Ferguson dies in the arms of his mistress, thinly disguised as a redcoat soldier.*

LEFT *Andrew Jackson, soldier, statesman and Southern gentleman, a towering figure among American Presidents.*

ABOVE *Jacksonian democracy was based on a new style of politics, one of appealing directly to the people.*

Sam Houston, 'Liberator of Texas', came from a Scots-Irish family in the Shenandoah Valley.

the Middle Colonies. From the Log College many American educational institutions, including Princeton, were founded. This early network of schools placed education in the Middle Colonies largely in Scots-Irish hands and enabled them to have a major influence on political thought.

Throughout the eighteenth century Pennsylvania drew the majority of the Scots-Irish immigrants, though some came through Charleston to South Carolina, drawn by a bounty offered to Protestant settlers. The new arrivals at the Delaware ports pushed on to the Cumberland Valley, either immediately or after spending two or three years on the coast to earn money for land and farm tools. By the 1740s the Cumberland Valley and the neighbouring York and Adams counties were overflowing, and the younger sons of the original settlers, who would not inherit the family farm, moved out. Some went westwards up the Juniata Valley, scattering place names like 'Fermanagh', 'Derry', 'Tyrone' and 'Armagh' among the ridges of the Allegheny mountain range. A clergyman travelling through this land of deep, quiet valleys reported: 'the inhabitants of this country, miles around are Scots-Irish ... They are Presbyterians ... happy people to whom the Providence of God has given this pleasant, fertile and retired abode.' The idyllic existence, if indeed it appeared as idyllic to the inhabitants as it did to a passing preacher, was soon to be destroyed. However, in the diaspora which took so many Ulster people on from the Cumberland Valley, the great majority travelled southward through the Great Valley, across the Potomac and into the Valley of Virginia.

Outside Tinkling Springs Church, in the Shenandoah Valley of Virginia, there is a large stone block 'Sacred to the memory of the immigrants who turned this wilderness into habitations'. In the area around Tinkling Springs, in the counties of Augusta and Rockbridge, the Scots-Irish identity is still strong today. This land, between the Blue Ridge and the Appalachian ranges, was divided in the eighteenth century into two massive land grants, the Beverley and the Borden. Families from the Cumberland Valley began to settle these grants in about 1739, and within ten years the valley was filled exclusively with Ulster people – McClures, Houstons, Colters, McKees. Although Virginia was ruled by a Protestant Episcopalian establishment, the new Presbyterians were able to maintain freedom of worship west of the Blue Ridge. They also kept their distinctiveness as a largely peasant farmer community from the slave-owning Tidewater aristocrats.

James Patton, an Ulster sea captain and entrepreneur, owned a large area in the Beverley grant and he added to his considerable fortune by promoting direct emigration. In Ulster the winter of 1739 had been the winter of the Black Frost. Unprecedented cold had blackened the landscape like the aftermath of a great fire. Patton's agents, with stories of the Shenandoah, its warmth, its forests filled with game, its 'old Fields' already cleared by Shawnee Indians and rich in grass, had little trouble persuading a dispirited people to take ship.

In the 1740s the volume of Ulster immigrants steadily increased. The Shenandoah

Donegal Springs Church, which replaced the original log church built by the first settlers, is modelled on the Presbyterian Church in Donegal town in Ireland. In the late twentieth century the nuclear accident at nearby Three Mile Island cast a chilling shadow on this, the first American Eden of the Scots-Irish.

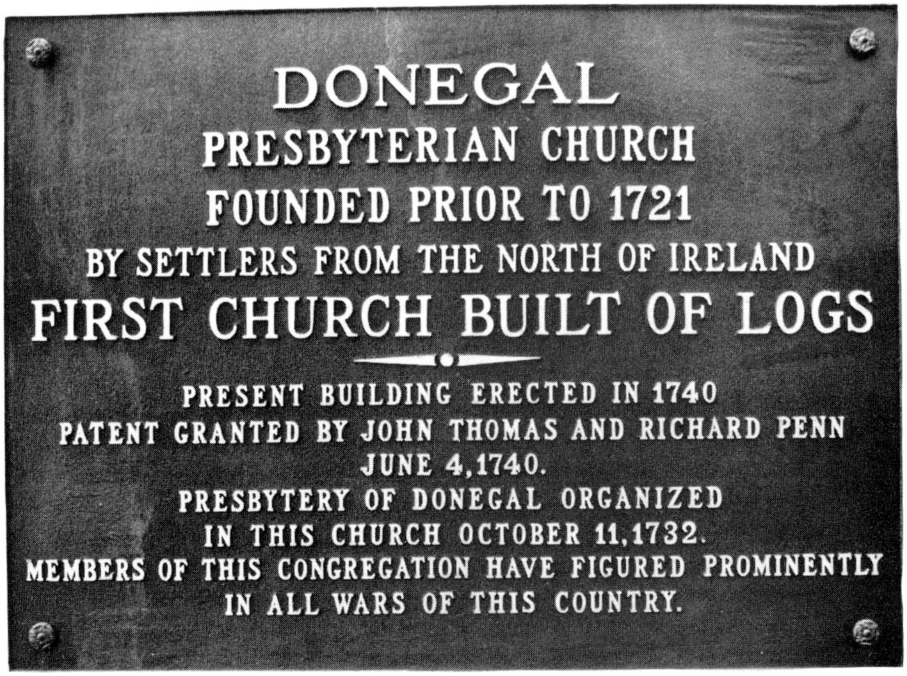

grants soon filled up and the new settlers moved farther down the Valley of Virginia. They crossed the James River where it cuts a gap between the Blue Ridge and an eastward spur of the Appalachian range, and settled from there to the site of the present city of Roanoke. Here the valley ended, and, faced by the Appalachian ridges to the west, the majority took a southerly direction into the Carolina Piedmont. This was to be the third great area of Scots-Irish settlement.

From both the Valley of Virginia and the Piedmont, smaller streams of settlers moved into the mountain valleys of Appalachia; from the Piedmont they filled the counties of western North Carolina, around Asheville. A little later they crossed the Appalachian range through the Cumberland Gap into Kentucky and Tennessee. As the last quarter of the eighteenth century began, the Scots-Irish dominated a one thousand one hundred-mile frontier along the spine of Appalachia from Pennsylvania to South Carolina.

The early Ulster frontiersmen have always been seen from an extreme point of view. To their nineteenth-century apologists they were the epitome of all the virtues, godly, brave and chivalrous, to contemporary English writers like William Strickland, 'savage backwoodsmen . . . possessing all the vices of civilized and savage life, without the virtues of either'. Irish American writers, pursuing some quaint theory of Irish nationhood, chose to deny their existence. Modern scholars, working on documentary fact rather than political, social or religious prejudice, have now provided the material from which a reasonably complete and balanced picture of this 'bold and hardy race' can be created.

Of all the ethnic groups in Pennsylvania they were the most successful settlers. Not as adept traders as the Quakers, nor as successful farmers as the Germans, they could cope better than either with frontier conditions. There is little doubt that their earlier experiences in the Ulster Plantation had moulded them for this second, and in many ways similar, experience. The English settlers who had come earlier had, after their initial thrust, been unenterprising, clinging for over a century to the Atlantic coastlines and river estuaries. The Ulster people, on the other hand, penetrated far and fast into the wilderness, having little fear of the unknown; they learned quickly to use Indian paths and Indian methods of hunting and exploration. They cleared the heavily forested land in a crude but quick and effective manner, and they established permanent settlements more rapidly than any other immigrant group. These Irish settlers were not exclusively Presbyterian; Catholics and Episcopalians were prominent among them if not large in numbers. But the Presbyterian radical ethos, which saw the possession of land in the frontier as the key to personal liberty, dominated this pioneering drive inland and did much to create the American Old West.

The settlement of a newly arrived family was a communal effort. Scots-Irish rode in from miles around to cut down the trees around the cabin site, burn the brushwood and plant the first crop of corn around the tree stumps. The family's first log cabin was built by a similar cooperative effort. A single-room cabin could be built in a day and was followed by a boisterous frontier party with large quantities of home-made whiskey, fiddle music and dancing. Staid Quakers and Germans were shocked by the rowdy merriment of the Irish. It seems as if the broad horizons of America and the unaccustomed sense of freedom released a repressed exuberance in these normally dour Presbyterians. The Calvinist Reformation had bottled up the bacchanalian spirit of the medieval Scots; in the ferment of frontier life, the cork popped.

James Magraw described the first days of a settlement when he wrote in 1733 from the wilderness of the Cumberland Valley to his brother at Paxtang, in the settled lands east of the Susquehanna. For his cabin he selected level ground close both to an Indian path through the woods and a stream of 'sweet water' coming from a spring. He and his friends, the Sloans, Magees and Moores, had collectively built eighteen cabins – the beginnings of present-day Shippensburg – and planted corn and potatoes. Frontier life was uncertain and often tragically short. One of the first jobs was to select ground for a graveyard, and work on the cabins was stopped while they buried 'Hugh Rippay's daughter, Mary . . . a very purty girl who died of faver'. The major threat, however, was not from fevers. Magraw implored his brother, '. . . get some guns for us. There's a good wheen of ingens about here.' Ulster dialect expressions like 'a good wheen', meaning a large number, survived in the Ulster immigrant communities, and many were incorporated into the newly forged dialects of America. In the rural districts of eastern Tennessee people still use Scots-Irish terms like 'forenint' (opposite to) and 'thole' (to endure).

The immigrant soon began to look like a much rougher version of the frontiersman in the Currier and Ives prints. The clothes he brought from Ireland wore out quickly as he moved through heavy undergrowth, cut trees or broke the virgin soil with a hoe. Much of his first year's food supply came from hunting bears, deer, squirrel and raccoon, so animal skins replaced cloth. And, being highly adaptable, he took on an Indian style of dress, hunting shirt, deerskin breeches, coonskin cap and moccasins. He allowed his hair to grow long, plastered it with bear fat and tied it in a pigtail. Within a year at the frontier the transformation would be complete.

Families adjusted to an entirely different diet. The abundance of game roused the Ulsterman's inbred hunting instinct. In Ireland he had been known to desert his plough in mid-field to go chasing hares or rabbits; here he would neglect his maize or potatoes for the exciting job of feeding his family with his long rifle. Meat had never been plentiful in the homeland; now the settlers learned to eat all kinds of game. In the first year of settlement, while waiting for the harvest, the diet was almost exclusively meat and wild fruit and the new immigrants suffered from the lack of grain-based foods and potatoes, which had been their staple diet in Ireland. But with the reaping of their first American crops they found themselves with a diet much richer and more varied than they, or their ancestors, had ever experienced. A new and exotic addition to their table was bear meat, and it was not unknown to see in the corner of a log cabin a bear cub in a cage being fattened up for the next wedding, corn husking or other festive gathering. However, it was the love of hunting rather than the need for food which motivated the frontiersmen.

Their slaughter of wildlife was indiscriminate and enormous. David Noel Doyle, in *Ireland, Irishmen and Revolutionary America*, says '... as they had virtually exterminated deer and wolf in Ulster so now they helped to do the same to bear, wild turkey, passenger pigeon and certain deer populations from Pennsylvania south'. They came at a time when national characteristics were being formed, and it was they, rather than pacific Germans or business-absorbed English, who gave America the tradition of hunting and rifle lore.

The pursuit of game made the settler an expert marksman – he could hit a running squirrel with his long-barrelled rifle – and a very useful Revolutionary soldier. It also made him chillingly casual about taking life, animal or human. David Kilgore was a good example of the settler-hunter-soldier type of frontiersman. His grandfather, John, a Presbyterian elder, had at the age of seventy led his family in Biblical style from their County Down farm to Chester County in Pennsylvania. After the death of the patriarch, the family moved on to the Cumberland Valley, and in 1767 grandson David travelled hundreds of miles into the unexplored valleys of western Pennsylvania. Far from other settlers, he cleared a farm and set up a grist mill. Once, when he returned after nightfall to his cabin, his wife Sarah greeted him with, 'If you had come home earlier we would have had wild turkey for dinner. There was a gobbler calling in the thicket.' David promised to get the turkey cock in the morning, and before dawn he took his rifle and crept out of the house. Moving through the undergrowth as the sun rose, he heard the call again. Then he saw the eagle feather and black head of an Indian looking towards the cabin as he imitated the turkey. At close range Kilgore blew the Indian's head off.

Sarah Kilgore spent much of her time alone with her children in their cabin in the valley of the Loyalhanna, a massive mountain range separating them from any form of civilization. But like other Scots-Irish frontier wives she had little time to worry. Not only did she work beside her husband in the fields, she was also responsible for an elaborate domestic economy. She gathered the wild fruit which supplemented the family diet, made preserves from wild grapes and ground the Indian corn for johnny cake. Most households tanned their own leather and this was the housewife's responsibility. She also scutched the flax which her husband grew, spun the linen thread, wove the cloth and made the family's clothes. All this time she was teaching her growing family to read and write and, almost yearly, undergoing the terrible ordeal of childbirth in a lonely cabin without medical help. Many women did not live beyond their early thirties, to be replaced immediately by a new teenage wife from the local community. Headstones in Scots-Irish graveyards often record a man and the three or four wives he has worn out in a lifetime. In his *The Scotch-Irish of Colonial Pennsylvania*, Wayland Dunaway says, 'On some towering peak of Pennsylvania, the Commonwealth should erect to the Scotch-Irish wife a monument as a worthy memorial of her character and deeds'.

The shock of new surroundings was much more severe on immigrants to the southern colonies. The Witherspoons, pious Covenanters whose forefathers had fled from Scotland to Ulster during the 'Killing Times', arrived in Charleston in 1734. They were put on a boat 'with tools and one year's provisions' and travelled up the Black River to their land grant in the present Williamsburg County. They had been led to expect an already settled area but found 'nothing but a wilderness and instead of a fine timbered house, nothing but a mean dirt house'. They allowed the fire which they had brought with them to go out and, as they had no means of re-lighting it, the father of the family set out along the forest-lined river to get help without any idea where he was going. By chance he found the home of another Ulsterman, Roger Gordon, and brought home the comforting fire. When night came on, 'wolves began to howl on all sides'. Next day they experienced their first tornado, a weather phenomenon of which they had never even heard; 'We all sincerely wished ourselves again at Belfast.' Later, when they had grown accustomed to life in South Carolina, they could laugh at those early experiences; 'One morning when we were at breakfast, there was a "travelling possum" on his way, passing by the door: my mother screamed out saying, "There's a great bear!" Mother and we children hid ourselves behind some barrels and a chest whilst father got his gun.'

Samuel Houston, whose two grandfathers had emigrated with their families, left a detailed description of life among the early immigrants in the Shenandoah Valley. Their cabins

> had but one door and no windows except holes between the logs and the light shone down from the top of a log chimney ... Their bedsteads ... mostly crossticks with thick clapboards on which were laid skins of bears, buffaloes &c ... Their food consisted chiefly of venison, bear meat, Buffaloe, raccoon, turkey, Pheasant, wild geese & pigeons &c., the river fish & Eels, Irish potatoes, Pumpkins, Turnips & cabbages were their principal vegetables ... their bread coarse Indian corn meal made in wooden morters by wooden pestles ... they had pewter Basins, plates and tankards who were able to procure them; but most persons used trenchers and platters made ... out of yellow Poplar wood.

Although most of the people Houston describes were American-born from Pennsylvania, New Jersey or Maryland, their links with Ulster were still strong. These were not the sentimental ties of the nineteenth-century Catholic Irish but purely practical ones. When a wedding dress of fine linen which had been brought out from Ireland fifty years before was taken carefully from its chest to serve another young bride, it was spoken of as 'clothes from home'. Baking was done Ulster-style on a griddle suspended from a 'crook' or crane over an open fire. Transport was primitive and wheel-less, as in Ireland: two poles, one on each side of the horse, like cart shafts, were fastened to the harness and a board was fixed between the poles to support the load, with the pole ends trailing on the ground.

But whatever the hardships, the Scots-Irish lived in the Shenandoah Valley as they had never lived before. 'They have Bread, Meat of many Kinds, Milk, Butter & cheese & all in great plenty & of the best Quality ... they raise a Brood of Youth, young Men

& young Women, for Size, Activity & Complection, such as I have never seen before.' Small wonder that the diarist Philip Fithian found them up to more than clearing land and hunting buffalo: 'An Irishman . . . was taken in an attempt to spend the Night with a Matron of the town – Her Husband found them in Bed . . . the Gallant leapt out the window quite naked . . . His Breeches, Waistcoat etc he left behind. With these the angry husband heated the stove. He ought to have added the sinning Wife.'

The Ulster immigrants became much more Indianized than any other settler group, basing their calendar of farmwork, their natural medicines and their fighting habits on what had been traditional for centuries among the natives of America. Faced for the first time with an abundance of land, many of them were totally wasteful of its resources. Having farmed an area for several years without any attempt to preserve its fertility, they would move on to virgin land to start again the cycle of 'slash, burn and plant', mirroring the nomadic pattern of Indian agriculture. Their use of forest herbs was based on Indian lore; their method of cultivating corn, moulding up the top soil into ridges, was the Indian method. They also learned how to grow tobacco, pumpkins and gourds and to mill their corn in the native fashion. Professor Estyn Evans, in his highly perceptive analysis, 'The Scotch Irish: Their Cultural Adaption in the American Old West', also traces deeper and subtler adaptations, the result of that rarely recognized quality in the Scots-Irish make-up, their chameleon-like ability to absorb and reflect their surroundings, however new or alien: 'The "backwoods" life which the Scotch-Irish adopted was well named, for it took shape in the shadow of the woods and derived much of its colour, sustenance and its superstitions from them.' In fact the Scots-Irishman became in many ways so like his Indian neighbour, and his aims – possession of the hunting grounds and unlimited access to the empty lands west of the white-settled area – were so close to the Indian's aims that a clash was inevitable.

Few of the pioneer artifacts which tourists see in American folk parks today owe their origins to the Scots-Irish. The magnificent Conestoga wagon, with its boat-shaped structure and elaborate braking system was designed by German immigrants. So too was the Kentucky rifle, the 'frontiersman's best friend'. That perennial symbol of pioneer life, the log cabin, is also basically of German design, although the settlers from Ulster incorporated in it some features of the stone-built cabins of their homeland. German-built houses in Pennsylvania had their chimneys – stone structures – in the middle of the house, thus conserving the heat of the fire and warming two rooms. The Ulster people, coming from a milder climate, unwisely put their fireplaces in the gable end. Only a small number of early cabins had windows and most that had used oiled paper instead of glass. Samuel Houston was proud to remember his father's 'squared log house with its glass windows . . . the admiration and wonder of the neighbours'.

Although initially they copied Indian farming practices, the more thrifty and settled Scots-Irish soon recognized the superiority of the German methods. They did take some time, however, to learn advanced cattle-rearing techniques. The Germans harvested hay and other winter cattle foods, something unknown in early eighteenth-century Ulster. They housed their cattle and stored the fodder in basements throughout the winter and were able to keep large herds all year round. A Scots-Irish settler kept only three or four cows in poor condition. 'With a little corn fodder and straw in the hard winter weather, many cattle in the Spring were weakened and needed help to rise before they ventured seeking early grass.' But as the Ulstermen acquired more capital their cattle husbandry improved, and by the second half of the eighteenth century they had become good cattle drovers, the first in the great tradition of the American West, bringing meat to the market on hoof.

The arrogance of the Ulstermen and the exclusiveness of the Germans did not make them easy neighbours and they tended to keep separate. The Germans were hardworking, frugal and generally quiet people. The Scots-Irish were also industrious but hard-drinking, noisy and quarrelsome as well. The Germans were conservative – if any Ulster settler of the 1740s came back to twentieth-century Pennsylvania he would find his Amish neighbours not greatly changed – but conservatism was not a virtue in the New World. The Scots-Irish, lightly burdened with traditional skills but ever ready to adopt the skills of others, prepared to a foolhardy degree to tackle anything, and convinced, often with little justification, that they were right, provided the proper metal from which to forge the cutting edge of a pioneering nation.

5 · BLOOD ON THE BUCKSKIN

'During the late and present Indian War, the frontiers of this Province have been repeatedly attacked . . . by skulking bands of Indians, who have with the most savage cruelty murdered men, women and children. . . .'

Scots-Irish Remonstrance to the
Pennsylvania Assembly, 1764

'Troublesome settlers to the Government and hard neighbours to the Indians.'

James Logan, Colonial Secretary,
on the Scots-Irish, 1730

IN 1720 JAMES LOGAN, the Colonial Secretary of Pennsylvania, was extremely worried by the aggressive movements of Indian tribes on the borders of Quaker and German settlements. He wrote to a friend, 'I thought it might be prudent to plant a Settlement of those who had so bravely defended Derry and Inniskillen as a frontier in case of any Disturbance'. Once again the Scots-Irish were being cast in the role which they had sustained in Ulster, the unpaid protectors of the status quo. Partly as a result of Logan's plan and partly because the frontier drew the Ulster settlers like a magnet, a protective semicircle of Scots-Irish townships formed round the old Quaker farmlands. Once the newcomers were established in force, there was continual friction between them and the Indians. The Ulster people almost totally disregarded the treaties setting limits to white settlement which the Quakers had made with the Indians. They moved into Indian-designated lands and were quick to resort to violence if any attempt was made to stop them. But it was the outbreak of war in Europe, between France and Britain, which finally set the frontier alight.

At that period France controlled the St Lawrence area of Canada and claimed the interior of the present United States, from the Great Lakes to the mouth of the Mississippi. The French recruited Indian tribes in the area as allies and planned a series of attacks from the west on the British seaboard colonies. The Scots-Irish on the frontier from Pennsylvania to the Carolina border took the brunt of the attacks. After the French war ended it was succeeded by a purely Indian attempt, under Chief Pontiac of the Ottawas, to drive the colonists into the sea, so that for ten years there was almost continuous frontier war.

A small leather-bound diary-cum-account book preserved by a Cumberland Valley family gives the flavour of those days better than the massive historical tomes which have been written about them. On the first page are the words 'James McCullough his Book, 1747'. McCullough left Belfast in 1745, and landed at Newcastle on the Delaware. He appears to have stayed there for about four or five years, then moved to the Cumberland Valley and eventually to the Conococheague Creek area near modern Mercersburg. Here he farmed and carried on his other trade of weaver. The diary entries are a mixture of cash accounts – 'ows 7 shillings and one pence to James Friers widow' – family events – 'Jean McCullough did enter to John Robisons Scol upon Tuesday ...' – and farm records – 'I did begin to plow corn June ye 23'. Then the first clouds began to gather: 'July ye 12 was put to flight by a fals Alarm from ye Ingens'. The Indian raiding parties were now coming across the Appalachians into the Cumberland Valley. At first their attacks were by night, then they became bolder and struck even in the middle of the long summer days. A favourite ruse was to hide in the woods until the settlers came to work in a nearby field. Then, after the white men had left their muskets with their food and drink under the shade of a tree at the field's edge, the Indians would attack, '7 killed loading a Wagon in ye field'.

Behind McCullough's terse entries lies a story of official blundering and cowardice and of terrible sufferings endured by the people of the Cumberland Valley. On 13 August 1755 he writes, 'Cornel Dunbar and his Army did camp at Henry Palens'. Dunbar's force was part of the British army retreating after their disastrous defeat in Western Pennsylvania in July 1755. The British commander, General Braddock, had been killed and the headlong flight of his troops left the frontier settlers without protection, and for the next two years McCullough records with monotonous regularity the murder and kidnapping of friends and neighbours: 'Robert Clogston his son and Betty Ramsey her son was killed ... Nov ye 9th John Wood and his wife and mother in law and John Archer's wife was killed and 4 children carried off ... Alexander Miller killed and 2 of his children taken.' The diarist leaves to the imagination the gruesome details of these events.

McCullough's intelligence, humour and stoical acceptance of the situation comes through his laconic prose. He carried on his business even through the worst times: 'May ye 27th David Stoner credit to 6s. 6p for three yeards of Linen.' (Stoner was an ancestor of the present owner of the diary.) One deeply sarcastic entry reflects what must have been the general feeling of the settlers about the British authorities and their monarch safe in his English palace: 'God bless King George – wherever he may be'. On 26 July 1756 came McCullough's personal tragedy: 'John and James McCologh was taken Captive by ye ingins.' These were his two sons, aged eight and five. (McCullough was inconsistent in the spelling of even his own name.) The boys were snatched while playing in a ravine close to their home. Beside the date of the capture McCullough transcribed a quotation from the Book of Jeremiah: 'Weep not for the dead ... but weep sore for him that goeth away; for he shall return no more, nor see his native country.' In the case of the younger boy the words were prophetic; James disappeared completely.

But, after years of agonizing search, the father found John at an Indian camp. The boy could no longer speak English and wept bitterly when he was taken from his Indian family. He had to be tied up for the journey home.

Situations like that in the Cumberland Valley in the 1750s brought out the best – and sometimes the worst – in the Scots-Irish. Inevitably hundreds deserted their homes and fled to defended towns like Carlisle, or to the colony's heartlands around Philadelphia. But where defence was possible they stayed resolutely by the farms they had carved out of the wilderness.

Joseph McClintock lived in Sherman's Valley, in the Blue Mountains to the west of the Cumberland Valley.

> Unwilling to quit his new habitation, and lose the fruits of his hard labours, he surrounded his house with a pallisade, & the families that were in the valley, resorted there, on the first appearence of the savage enemy. Ignorant of the state of the little garrison, the Indians hovered on the sides of the hills, which overlooked it, for several days ... He had only 13 men [his neighbours] with him; and to impress the savages with an idea of their numbers & courage, he caused the women and girls to be dressed in men's clothes, to be paraded with the men, & with a drum which he had made, he made the valley resound with martial music & exercised the little company every day in sight of the enemy. By this strategem he kept them at bay many days.

At last, McClintock, knowing the Indians were getting suspicious, chose a moonless night and led his party of men, women and children out of his home-made fortress. 'With silence and haste they ascended the mountain, undiscovered by the Indians, who lay upon it; by the good providence of God, they arrived with their wives and their little ones at Carlisle, in safety.'

James Logan, himself an Ulster Quaker from Lurgan, County Armagh, added a footnote when he made the proposal to use the Ulster people as a defence: 'Such people, if kindly used, will be orderly and easily dealt with.' Logan's smugness was typical of the Quaker-dominated Pennsylvania Assembly during the Indian Wars. They refused to act against the Indian raiders and, by exempting the pacifist Germans from military service, placed almost the entire burden of frontier defence on the Scots-Irish. The Colonial Governor, Robert Morris, thoroughly irritated by the Quakers, wrote to the military commander, '... they propose to gain the Affections of the Indians now Employed in Slaughtering the People and are entering into an Enquiry what Injustice has been done to them'. A modern Ulster Unionist would, no doubt, be tempted to draw parallels between Pennsylvanian politicians in the eighteenth century and British ones in the twentieth.

Although the Scots-Irish frequently reacted violently in comparatively trivial matters, they could be deceptively inert when under real threat. Their families were being slaughtered, and instead of military help they were being given prim moral lectures. For

ABOVE *Pontiac, chief of the Ottawas, became the symbol of Indian resistance to British settlement in the eighteenth century. It was the Scots-Irish who bore the brunt of his surprise attacks in 1763 and two Scots-Irish leaders, George Croghan and Sir William Johnson, negotiated the peace which brought to an end what became known as Pontiac's War.*

OPPOSITE ABOVE *The murder of the Tully family – a romanticized version of the brutal slaughter of Scots-Irish during the Indian Wars. The historian Francis Parkman wrote of search parties finding 'the half consumed bodies of men and women, still bound fast to trees where they had perished in the fiery torture'.*

OPPOSITE BELOW *The Scots-Irish militia from Paxtang (Harrisburg) – the Paxton Boys – butchered peaceful Indians in revenge for Indian outrages. According to a contemporary the murders took place 'through the connivance, if not the encouragement of the Christian-professing Magistrates . . .'.*

two years the initiative remained with the Indians, their war parties striking at will and retiring to the safety of their lands beyond the mountains. Then the Scots-Irish patience broke. There was, however, a measured and icy coolness about their reaction. They allowed Indian raiders to escape so that they could be followed by scouts and their villages located. They drilled their own undisciplined frontiersmen into small, highly mobile strike forces which could move through the wilderness as quietly as the Indians themselves, and they waited for the opportunity to apply their own radical solution to the problem.

John Armstrong was born in the parish of Brookeborough, in County Fermanagh, an Ulster Plantation enclave with a long history of intermittent guerilla warfare against the native Irish. In his veins ran the blood of the wild Armstrong mosstroopers, seventeenth-century raiders from the Scottish Borders. He was of a comparatively well-to-do family and he arrived in the Cumberland Valley as one of the official surveyors for the Pennsylvanian Government. That job was not in itself a sinecure. The Scots-Irish had no love for surveyors as their arrival generally meant that squatters would have to pay for their land. (In 1733 two surveyors who came to work in Donegal Township found themselves surrounded by 'a very great number ... many having clubs'.) However, Armstrong successfully laid out the town of Carlisle, elegant and symmetrical, around a square dominated by a large Presbyterian church. He became a leading man in the area. In the early years of the Indian Wars he built a chain of forts in the Cumberland Valley which offered refuge to the local families during Indian attacks. Kittanning on the Allegheny River, in what is now western Pennsylvania, was identified as the chief base for Indian terrorist offensives, and Armstrong raised a force of three hundred frontiersmen, almost entirely Scots-Irish, to attack it. From a rendezvous point in the Juniata Valley, north of Carlisle, he advanced with amazing rapidity across unmapped mountains and through thick forest to the raiders' stronghold. The Indians were taken by surprise, their village and much of their fighting strength were wiped out and Armstrong returned to Carlisle victorious, showing true Ulster thrift by bringing back the scalps of his enemies for which there was a considerable Government bounty. By this time his fellow Ulstermen had achieved the unenviable record of being the first white people to scalp *en masse*.

Pontiac's War, launched in 1763 after a brief period of peace by the Ottawa chief at the head of a confederacy of Indian tribes, was even more brutal, and this time the Scots-Irish were taken by surprise. Forts fell to the Indians and whole settlements were wiped out. In Shippensburg alone there were one thousand five hundred refugees and in Carlisle 'every Stable and Hovel was crowded'. The Presbyterian Church in Ireland raised money for their relief.

As the stories of real, or imagined, Indian atrocities became known – men and women roasted over a slow fire, school children killed and scalped, a funeral party ambushed and the corpse taken from the coffin and scalped – Scots-Irish blood rose. Parties of rangers organized from the settlements went in hot pursuit; they seldom brought back live captives. Armstrong struck again deep into Indian territory and destroyed enemy bases. An appeal addressed to the Pennsylvania Assembly on behalf of the inhabitants of the frontier counties struck a very practical note. It asked that the bounty for Indian scalps (which included women over ten and male children of any age, but which had ceased at the end of the previous war) be restored and made 'adequate to the Dangers attending Enterprises of this nature'.

A bounty was welcome to a frugal people but its absence did not mean that they stopped killing Indians. Eventually they went too far, even at a time when public opinion was hardened by bloodshed. At the Conestoga Manor near Paxton (modern Harrisburg) in Pennsylvania a group of unarmed Indians lived under Quaker protection. They were suspected of collecting information on potential targets among the settlers for their countrymen. A band of Scots-Irish from Paxton attacked them, killing six Indians. Two weeks later the 'Paxton Boys' followed the fourteen surviving Indians to the workhouse at Lancaster, where they had been taken for safety, and perpetrated a massacre which outdid the redskins at their worst. A fellow Scots-Irishman, William Henry, saw the aftermath. Across the bodies of an Indian and his squaw, 'lay two children of about the age of three years, whose heads were split with a tomahawk and scalps taken off ... a stout Indian ... his legs chopped with a tomahawk, his hands cut off ... the brains splashed for three or four feet around ... men, women and children spread about ... shot, scalped and cut to pieces'.

Paradoxically, this horrible deed was the beginning of a process which was to democratize Pennsylvania with undreamed-of effects when that colony became the 'keystone' of the Revolution. While the Quaker lands around Philadelphia were shocked by the Lancaster massacre, reaction on the frontier ranged from disapproval of its barbarity to whole-hearted support for the Paxton Boys. There were about one hundred and fifty Indians living in Philadelphia, and both Scots-Irish and Germans now demanded their expulsion. A force of six hundred, mainly Ulstermen, marched on the Pennsylvanian capital to kill the Indians. The Government called in troops, and a major clash with the Ulstermen seemed inevitable. But, as the sides faced one another, the crisis petered out into a petition of grievances presented to the Pennsylvania Assembly in which the Scots-Irish pinpointed the political sharp practice by which the Quakers maintained control of a province in which they were now in a minority. This was the first stage in the process by which the frontier radicals were to destroy the conservative oligarchy which ruled Pennsylvania.

Neither the ruthless efficiency of John Armstrong, nor the brutality of the Paxton Boys, was typical of the Scots-Irish people who defended the frontier in the Old West. Most were ordinary, decent people anxious to improve their land, make money and leave a better way of life for their children. For over one hundred years in Ireland there had been a constantly recurring threat to their possessions and their lives. The fact that the

Ulster dangers were re-emerging in America bred in them a deep-down anxiety and suspicion. As individuals they would react suddenly, without establishing the facts. When Cornstalk, the defeated chief of the Shawnee tribe, was trying to negotiate peace terms at a fort in the Valley of Virginia, he and his son were murdered by the local militia as an instant reprisal for the killing of a settler called Robert Gillmore. 'This rash act was generally condemned', wrote the Rev. Samuel Houston in his account of the event. Houston, recording the Shawnee raids into the Shenandoah – 'they came over the mountains at the head of Kerr's Creek and swept all before them', described Cornstalk's death in sympathetic terms. When the chief's son cried in fear at the sight of the approaching militia, 'his father calmly reproved him and, almost unmoved, saw the guns presented and received their fire'.

Most settlers lived through these times in constant fear, but remained stubbornly determined not to abandon their homes and farms. Joseph Doddridge, in *Notes on the Settlement and Indian Wars*, described his experiences as a child when the express messenger came at dead of night to warn of an Indian attack:

> The express came softly to the back window and by gentle tapping wakened the family. This was easily done as an habitual fear made us ever watchful. The whole family were instantly in motion. My father seized his gun. My stepmother waked up and dressed the children as well as she could, and being myself the oldest of the children, I had to take my share of burdens to be carried to the fort. Besides the little children, we caught up what articles of clothing and provision we could get hold of in the dark for we derst not light a candle or even stir the fire. All this was done with the utmost dispatch, and the silence of death. The greatest care was taken not to awaken the youngest child. To the rest it was enough to say 'Indian' and not a whimper was heard afterwards.

John Craig, first pastor of the churches of Augusta Stone and Tinkling Springs at the 'Triple Forks of the Shenandoah', criticized those who ran away to the coast, and contrasted their behaviour with the ever-growing legend of their forefathers' achievements at the siege of Derry and the Battle of the Boyne – 'a scandal to our nation, falling below our brave ancestors'. Craig was a gentle scholar but that did not prevent him from fighting beside his congregation. His musket lies beside his deerskin-bound Bible in the church museum.

It is now forgotten that this war between Indian and settler, unlike the later Indian Wars, was an evenly matched struggle. The Indian tribes were generally as well armed; they had been accumulating guns for some years and were also being supplied by the French. Initially, they were much better organized for war and they had the advantage of safe bases beyond the great mountain range. It is not an exaggeration to say that at this point two nations were engaged on behalf of their distant masters, the French and British, in a struggle for what was to be the world's richest continent. From this struggle, with its extreme barbarity, its great human tragedy and its very broad spectrum of

ABOVE *Little wooden Baptist churches, many still to be found in Appalachia, illustrate the mass desertion of Presbyterianism for a livelier and more primitive faith.*

BELOW *The Scots-Irish tradition of an open-air faith, which began with 'field preaching' in Ireland and Scotland, takes a picturesque form in this mass baptism in a Tennessee mountain creek.*

Elijah Oliver's dwelling house (ABOVE) *and barn* (RIGHT) *at Cade's Cove in the Great Smoky Mountains in North Carolina. The Oliver house is a double house: the 'dog run' joining both sections provided an open-air bedroom in the hot summer nights.*

human behaviour and moral standards, the Scots-Irish emerged as a steel-hard people.

After Pontiac's War there was a decade of peace before the third great conflict between Indian and settler, the Revolutionary War, broke out. This vital period, when a fresh westward thrust of settlers once again exacerbated Indian-Scots-Irish relationships, is described in the singularly unbiased diary of the Rev. David McClure. McClure was unlike other Scots-Irish clergymen in several respects. He grew up in Massachusetts and became an itinerant Congregationalist clergyman. A much more sophisticated man than the 'fighting parsons' like the Rev. John Elder, who was originally from Randalstown, County Antrim, and became commander of the Paxtang Rangers – 'truly the terror of the Indians' – or the Rev. John Steel who led the militia in the area of the Cumberland Valley where James McCullough lived, McClure learned Indian languages and tried to understand the Indian way of life. He was deeply interested in such things as the 'conjuring places' where the Indian doctors practised their native medicines. He could listen sympathetically to the lament of the chief for the vanished Indian towns, 'on the seashore and on the rivers where ... you will scarcely see an Indian'. And he recognized the damage which his white compatriots, especially the rum sellers, were doing to the American natives.

McClure's diary gives a vivid description of the Pennsylvanian frontier just before the third great Indian War. He travelled on horseback into the wilderness of western Pennsylvania, camping under the stars: 'I spread a bearskin for my bed ... kept awake by the howling of wolves'. There were a few widely scattered settlements east of Fort Pitt (modern Pittsburg) and some pioneers were moving into the upper reaches of the Ohio Valley. McClure saw the new lands with the freshness of the earliest Scots-Irish, half a century before:

> The soil is luxurient ... white and black oak, Chestnutt, Black Walnut, Hickory ... the sweetest red plums grow in great abundance ... grapes wind round the trees ... the pleasantness of this solitary wilderness ... In the middle of the Creek a small flock of wild geese were swimming, on the bank sat a large flock of Turkies and wild pigeons covered one or two trees ... we had our choice for supper.

The Indians, at this time, were prepared to forget the past wars much more readily than the white settlers were, but what they would not tolerate was the continued encroachment on their hunting grounds. Their argument was simple and logical: the white settlers raised cows and sheep, whereas 'The buffaloes are our cows, the deer are our sheep'. As McClure rode on his evangelical mission from camp to camp among the Indians he found behind the elaborate courtesy with which he was received a growing hostility. Already in New England and eastern Pennsylvania there were signs of the coming conflict between the colonies and the home country. McClure learned that British agents were at work among the Indians: 'a War Belt had been sent to the Indians ... informing them, that the Calvinists refused to obey the Great King of England: and if

Life in the mountain valleys of North Carolina, Tennessee and Kentucky altered little in the first hundred years of settlement. The coming of the railroad in the 1880s began the process of change; the mail catalogue system and the Government relief schemes after the Great Depression accelerated it.

he should send an army to chastize them ... his friends, the Indians were invited to join them.' McClure also, by chance, met Simon Girty, the notorious renegade from the Scots-Irish community of Paxtang, but he had, of course, no inkling of the murderous role Girty was destined to play in the coming war. What he did see clearly and with deep indignation was that the British plan to use Indians against the colonists was the blueprint for massacre. McClure returned to Massachusetts in time for the opening shots on 19 April 1775 – 'the Regulars marched into the country and killed several men at Lexington'.

The village of Hanna's Town in Westmoreland County, Pennsylvania, was rebuilt in the 1980s, almost exactly two hundred years after it was destroyed by British-led Seneca Indians. It had been built round the tavern of Ulster-born Robert Hanna, and nearly all the inhabitants of the village and surrounding countryside were Scots-Irish. Today Hanna's Town is a log-built folk village, but in the latter part of the eighteenth century it was the county seat and the centre of justice. McClure called there and instituted unsuccessful proceedings in the presbytery court to 'fix the Guilt of Fornication on Rob Newel and Mary Bay'. He does not, however, mention the trial of the Rev. Robert Huey which absorbed the attention of the inhabitants of Hanna's Town during those dangerous times.

Robert Huey had come to western Pennsylvania from Kilrea in County Londonderry, but he turned out to be not quite the saintly pastor the settlers had been led to expect. He was accused of a variety of crimes, being so drunk he had to hold on to the walls, swearing 'by his Maker', buying a 'black Barcelona handkerchief' on a Sunday, and so on. None of this in itself was very remarkable; other frontier ministers faced trial on similar charges. But it is astounding that at a time when bears were running away with their hogs, wolves snatching their sheep and vast flocks of passenger pigeons ravaging their corn, and when British agents were urging the Indians to cut their throats, these Ulstermen, absorbed with the 'shalt nots' of their Calvinist faith, spent weeks and months digging up evidence against the convivial cleric.

It was also typical of these people that when the Revolution came, tiny Hanna's Town – thirty cabins in the middle of hundreds of miles of empty forest – issued its declaration of independence, its own challenge to the Mother of Parliaments sitting in faraway Westminster. The fruits of that brave, but rash, action came when a British military commander based on the Great Lakes targeted the village for a terrorist raid.

In March 1829 Elizabeth Brownlee petitioned the state legislature of Pennsylvania for a pension. Elizabeth, who was born in Londonderry in 1755 and emigrated with her family at the age of sixteen, told the story of her ordeal following the destruction of Hanna's Town in her pension claim. What happened at the little village in Westmoreland County on 13 July 1782 was typical of what was happening to isolated Scots-Irish settlements from New England to South Carolina.

Elizabeth and her husband Joseph – she carrying their baby, he their little boy – were trying to escape through the woods with a group of their neighbours when an Indian war party caught them. The Indians hacked Joseph Brownlee and his son to pieces. Then they killed everyone else except Elizabeth, the baby and two other women. For thirteen days Elizabeth, carrying her child, was marched across mountainous country from western Pennsylvania to Buffalo in up-state New York, where she was taken ill,

> with the fever and ague, [and] a council was called to determine on the mode of putting her to death! At this council was a white man who had the command of a party of Indians, who was called Capt. Lottridge. He told them that she was so far reduced that she could afford them no amusement in dying by any mode of torture they could inflict; but advised them to take her to Niagara and exchange her for rum.

Elizabeth's life was saved, and she was eventually sold with her child for thirty dollars and two gallons of rum.

The horrors which had marked the earlier frontier wars were repeated: mothers forced to watch while Indians, under British command, swung their infants by the feet and bashed out their brains; settler-soldiers like William Crawford cooked alive over a slow fire. Again the Scots-Irish reeled under the shock, then struck back. Andrew Lewis from the Shenandoah Valley, whose father, it was claimed, had murdered his landlord in Ireland, led a thousand frontiersmen to defeat the Shawnees at the battle of Point Pleasant on the Ohio. The Scots-Irish settled west of the Blue Ridge made up the expeditionary force that destroyed the British bases from which Indian attacks were directed. Riflemen from the same settlements so cowed the Cherokee to the south of them that this potentially powerful British ally was virtually neutralized. Although the Scots-Irish were also to perform bravely against British regular troops in the eastern war zone, the eventual American victory would not have been possible without the protection from Indian attack afforded by the Ulstermen in buckskin.

6 · GOD-PROVOKING DEMOCRATS

'Call it not an American Rebellion, it is nothing more nor less than an Irish-Scotch Presbyterian Rebellion.'

Captain Johann Heinricks, German mercenary
serving with the British *c.* 1780

Hi! Uncle Sam!
Wherever there was fighting,
Or wrong that needed righting,
An Ulsterman was sighting
His Kentucky gun with care:
All the road to Yorktown,
From Lexington to Yorktown,
From Valley Forge to Yorktown,
That Ulsterman was there!

American Revolutionary ballad

THE FIRST CRACK in the British Empire appeared on 4 July 1776, when a group of backwoods Scots-Irish assembled on the banks of Pine Creek, on the west branch of the Susquehanna, and declared themselves independent of Great Britain. These frontiersmen were, in the best traditions of their race, occupying land for which they had not paid, and their creation of a tiny, landlocked republic in the heart of Pennsylvania, based on what they called the 'Play-Fair System' was, cynical observers said, no more than a device to ensure that they would never have to pay. It was a coincidence that on the same July day, two hundred miles away in Philadelphia, other men were approving a document about certain 'unalienable rights . . . life, liberty and the pursuit of happiness'. It was no coincidence, however, that some of the key people voting on the American Declaration of Independence at that Philadelphia meeting were also Scots-Irish.

One of the vitally important men in the American Revolution never crossed the Atlantic and died thirty years before Jefferson drew up the Declaration of Independence. Francis Hutcheson was born at Saintfield in County Down four years after the Battle of the Boyne. The son of a Presbyterian minister, he was educated at Glasgow University, and after a period as a schoolmaster in Dublin, returned to lecture at Glasgow. Here he proved to be the most charismatic of teachers and influenced a wide range of pupils, from the great economist Adam Smith to a dour student for the ministry from County Donegal called Francis Allison.

Hutcheson was one of the greatest thinkers in a golden age of philosophy, a founding spirit of the Scottish Enlightenment whose bright vision illuminated the Calvinist gloom of his fellow Scots-Irish. The implications of his political and social beliefs will be discussed in a later chapter; for the moment only his profound influence on Revolutionary America concerns us. Hutcheson wrote, 'If the plan of the mother-country . . . degenerates by degrees from a safe, mild, and gentle limited power to a severe and absolute one; or if . . . oppressive laws are made with respect to the colonies . . . they are not bound to continue their subjection. There is something unnatural in . . . remaining subject to the direction of and government of a distant body of men.' He might well have been writing after the events which led up to the Declaration of Independence instead of half a century before. It was evident from the Coercive Acts passed at Westminster, and the high-handed, and often illegal, actions of British officials, that the Mother of Parliament had degenerated from a kindly, if ineffectual, parent to a 'severe and absolute one'. Following the classic political prank, the Boston Tea Party, the port had been shut down and democracy suspended in Massachusetts – clearly the 'oppressive laws' of Hutcheson's phraseology. The philosopher's many disciples among Scots-Irish politicians had little difficulty in reaching Hutcheson's conclusion that current British attitudes had released them from their bond of allegiance.

Hutcheson's pupil Allison had emigrated to Pennsylvania and set up a school at New London, an early Scots-Irish settlement in Chester County, where he taught, undiluted, the Hutchesonian doctrine. On a farm about a mile from Allison's academy, Thomas McKean, whose family had come from Ballymoney, County Antrim, was growing up. The future signatory of the Declaration of Independence became one of Allison's students, as did Charles Thomson, from Maghera in County Londonderry, the longtime Secretary of the Continental Congress. Several other students at New London also emerged as Revolutionary leaders. Allison himself lacked the magnetism of his master, but he was totally dedicated to passing on Hutcheson's message, and his influence on the generation growing up in the 1740s was immense. Radical doctrines were spread through the network of Scots-Irish schools; Presbyterian education sowed the seeds of revolution. Hutcheson reached from the grave through the medium of Allison to inspire the youth of a land he had never seen.

The top tier of Revolutionary philosophers and propagandists was made up of the quartet of the three Virginians, Thomas Jefferson, James Madison and Patrick Henry, and the Englishman Thomas Paine, but the second tier consisted of Scots-Irish Revolutionary committee men like Thomas McKean, Charles Thomson and James Smith. The ideas of Hutcheson, formulated in the quiet of Glasgow University, were essentially philosophical exercises, even if they were of the Utilitarian School, but the boys who emerged from the New London school became men of action.

With other Scots-Irish and some German allies they destroyed the grip of the old Quaker oligarchy on the Philadelphia Assembly and took over political control of the colony. This was essentially an internal quarrel, best exemplified in the march of the

ABOVE *The committee appointed to draw up the Declaration of Independence, headed by Thomas Jefferson, report to the Scots-Irish president, John Hancock (seated in the foreground) and the Ulster-born Secretary of Congress, Charles Thomson (standing beside Hancock).*

RIGHT *Though the Declaration was written by the English-descended planter Jefferson, Scots-Irish apologists claim to discover basic Ulster Presbyterian radicalism behind its elegant prose.*

IN CONGRESS, JULY 4, 1776.

The unanimous Declaration of the thirteen united States of America,

When in the Course of human events, it becomes necessary for one people to dissolve the political bands which have connected them with another, and to assume among the powers of the earth, the separate and equal station to which the Laws of Nature and of Nature's God entitle them, a decent respect to the opinions of mankind requires that they should declare the causes which impel them to the separation. —— We hold these truths to be self-evident, that all men are created equal, that they are endowed by their Creator with certain unalienable Rights, that among these are Life, Liberty and the pursuit of Happiness. — That to secure these rights, Governments are instituted among Men, deriving their just powers from the consent of the governed, — That whenever any Form of Government becomes destructive of these ends, it is the Right of the People to alter or to abolish it, and to institute new Government, laying its foundation on such principles and organizing its powers in such form, as to them shall seem most likely to effect their Safety and Happiness. Prudence, indeed, will dictate that Governments long established should not be changed for light and transient causes; and accordingly all experience hath shewn, that mankind are more disposed to suffer, while evils are sufferable, than to right themselves by abolishing the forms to which they are accustomed. But when a long train of abuses and usurpations, pursuing invariably the same Object evinces a design to reduce them under absolute Despotism, it is their right, it is their duty, to throw off such Government, and to provide new Guards for their future security. — Such has been the patient sufferance of these Colonies; and such is now the necessity which constrains them to alter their former Systems of Government. The history of the present King of Great Britain is a history of repeated injuries and usurpations, all having in direct object the establishment of an absolute Tyranny over these States. To prove this, let Facts be submitted to a candid world. —— He has refused his Assent to Laws, the most wholesome and necessary for the public good. —— He has forbidden his Governors to pass Laws of immediate and pressing importance, unless suspended in their operation till his Assent should be obtained; and when so suspended, he has utterly neglected to attend to them. —— He has refused to pass other Laws for the accommodation of large districts of people, unless those people would relinquish the right of Representation in the Legislature, a right inestimable to them and formidable to tyrants only. —— He has called together legislative bodies at places unusual, uncomfortable, and distant from the depository of their public Records, for the sole purpose of fatiguing them into compliance with his measures. —— He has dissolved Representative Houses repeatedly, for opposing with manly firmness his invasions on the rights of the people. —— He has refused for a long time, after such dissolutions, to cause others to be elected; whereby the Legislative powers, incapable of Annihilation, have returned to the People at large for their exercise; the State remaining in the mean time exposed to all the dangers of invasion from without, and convulsions within. —— He has endeavoured to prevent the population of these States; for that purpose obstructing the Laws for Naturalization of Foreigners; refusing to pass others to encourage their migrations hither, and raising the conditions of new Appropriations of Lands. —— He has obstructed the Administration of Justice, by refusing his Assent to Laws for establishing Judiciary powers. —— He has made Judges dependent on his Will alone, for the tenure of their offices, and the amount and payment of their salaries. —— He has erected a multitude of New Offices, and sent hither swarms of Officers to harrass our people, and eat out their substance. —— He has kept among us, in times of peace, Standing Armies without the Consent of our legislatures. —— He has affected to render the Military independent of and superior to the Civil power. —— He has combined with others to subject us to a jurisdiction foreign to our constitution, and unacknowledged by our laws; giving his Assent to their Acts of pretended Legislation: — For Quartering large bodies of armed troops among us: — For protecting them, by a mock Trial, from punishment for any Murders which they should commit on the Inhabitants of these States: — For cutting off our Trade with all parts of the world: — For imposing Taxes on us without our Consent: — For depriving us in many cases, of the benefits of Trial by Jury: — For transporting us beyond Seas to be tried for pretended offences — For abolishing the free System of English Laws in a neighbouring Province, establishing therein an Arbitrary government, and enlarging its Boundaries so as to render it at once an example and fit instrument for introducing the same absolute rule into these Colonies: — For taking away our Charters, abolishing our most valuable Laws, and altering fundamentally the Forms of our Governments: — For suspending our own Legislatures, and declaring themselves invested with power to legislate for us in all cases whatsoever. — He has abdicated Government here, by declaring us out of his Protection and waging War against us. —— He has plundered our seas, ravaged our Coasts, burnt our towns, and destroyed the lives of our people. — He is at this time transporting large Armies of foreign Mercenaries to compleat the works of death, desolation and tyranny, already begun with circumstances of Cruelty & perfidy scarcely paralleled in the most barbarous ages, and totally unworthy the Head of a civilized nation. —— He has constrained our fellow Citizens taken Captive on the high Seas to bear Arms against their Country, to become the executioners of their friends and Brethren, or to fall themselves by their Hands. —— He has excited domestic insurrections amongst us, and has endeavoured to bring on the inhabitants of our frontiers, the merciless Indian Savages, whose known rule of warfare, is an undistinguished destruction of all ages, sexes and conditions. In every stage of these Oppressions We have Petitioned for Redress in the most humble terms: Our repeated Petitions have been answered only by repeated injury. A Prince, whose character is thus marked by every act which may define a Tyrant, is unfit to be the ruler of a free people. Nor have We been wanting in attentions to our Brittish brethren. We have warned them from time to time of attempts by their legislature to extend an unwarrantable jurisdiction over us. We have reminded them of the circumstances of our emigration and settlement here. We have appealed to their native justice and magnanimity, and we have conjured them by the ties of our common kindred to disavow these usurpations, which, would inevitably interrupt our connections and correspondence. They too have been deaf to the voice of justice and of consanguinity. We must, therefore, acquiesce in the necessity, which denounces our Separation, and hold them, as we hold the rest of mankind, Enemies in War, in Peace Friends.

We, therefore, the Representatives of the united States of America, in General Congress, Assembled, appealing to the Supreme Judge of the world for the rectitude of our intentions, do, in the Name, and by Authority of the good People of these Colonies, solemnly publish and declare, That these United Colonies are, and of Right ought to be Free and Independent States; that they are Absolved from all Allegiance to the British Crown, and that all political connection between them and the State of Great Britain, is and ought to be totally dissolved; and that as Free and Independent States, they have full Power to levy War, conclude Peace, contract Alliances, establish Commerce, and to do all other Acts and Things which Independent States may of right do. —— And for the support of this Declaration, with a firm reliance on the protection of divine Providence, we mutually pledge to each other our Lives, our Fortunes and our sacred Honor.

John Hancock

Button Gwinnett
Lyman Hall
Geo Walton.

Wm Hooper
Joseph Hewes,
John Penn

Edward Rutledge

Thos Heyward Junr.
Thomas Lynch Junr.
Arthur Middleton

Samuel Chase
Wm Paca
Thos Stone
Charles Carroll of Carrollton

George Wythe
Richard Henry Lee
Th Jefferson
Benja Harrison
Thos Nelson jr.
Francis Lightfoot Lee
Carter Braxton

Robt Morris
Benjamin Rush
Benja Franklin
John Morton
Geo Clymer
Jas Smith
Geo Taylor
James Wilson
Geo Ross

Caesar Rodney
Geo Read
Tho M:Kean

Wm Floyd
Phil Livingston
Frans Lewis
Lewis Morris

Richd Stockton
Jno Witherspoon
Fras Hopkinson
John Hart
Abra Clark

Josiah Bartlett
Wm Whipple
Saml Adams
John Adams
Robt Treat Paine
Elbridge Gerry

Step Hopkins
William Ellery

Roger Sherman
Samel Huntington
Wm Williams
Oliver Wolcott
Matthew Thornton

frontiersmen on Philadelphia in 1763, but it resulted in the colony being given an advanced radical constitution which would serve as an inspiration when delegates from the other colonies assembled in the Pennsylvanian capital to debate whether 'to continue their subjection' to Britain. The immense energy of people like Thomson, McKean, George Bryan (Bryan came from Dublin, but if Presbyterianism was the distinguishing badge of the Scots-Irish he must be included) and Joseph Reed, in organizing and manipulating the political committees provided a solid basis for revolution in the Middle States. The journalism of Paine and the fiery rhetoric of Patrick Henry sent waves across the political waters, but it was the lesser-known Scots-Irish who maintained the steady flow towards independence.

Pennsylvania was truly the 'keystone' of the Revolution. It dominated the Middle States which linked the focal points of revolt, Massachusetts in the north and Virginia in the south, but it was also the most vulnerable to British persuasion or British military might. The interests of the middle classes living on the coast in Pennsylvania, New York or New Jersey were vested in trade with Britain. Their cultural links with the mother country were close; they drew their liberalism from British Whiggery and they could not help being involved in British national pride, which had ballooned with Britain's rise to world power in the previous decade. The Scots-Irish politicians had no such conflict to resolve. They owed little loyalty to the London Parliament and they drew their hunger for liberty from a different source.

It would be wrong, however, to visualize the run-up to the Revolution in a Hutchesonian world where men behaved rationally. The ordinary Scots-Irish were motivated less by political theories than by the divide between the frontier, which had austere religious principles – if it seldom lived up to them – and the coastal towns and settlements, which were perceived as hedonistic, godless and corrupt. The Ulster frontiersmen, heirs of the early Calvinists, with their vision of an imminent millennium, saw that the City of Brotherly Love was clearly not the City of God. They had always withheld a degree of consent from such governments, just as in the twentieth century many Ulster Protestants withhold total consent from a British Government, of whatever political shade, which inevitably has materialist aims and *laissez-faire* morals.

In more mundane matters these sons of pioneers were reacting to much of what Britain or the Atlantic establishment in America did. The London decrees restricting further westward encroachment into Indian territory they regarded as intolerable interference. When the Ulster-American settlers, who had migrated from their first New Hampshire homes to the Green Mountains of Vermont, resisted the encroachment of New York land speculators, they were making a statement about liberty as well as defending their farms. The men of Paxtang signalled the beginning of the end for old colonial rule as they marched on Philadelphia in 1763. What followed a decade later, when the protégés of Allison harnessed Scots-Irish and German resentment and took over the colony, was the rehearsal for revolution.

In the years of political wrangling which preceeded the final breach between Britain and the North American colonies, it is significant that the Scots-Irish were the first to mention guns. Hanover, just north of Route 78 which links Philadelphia and the Pennsylvanian state capital of Harrisburg, was one of the most prickly and self-opinionated of the Ulster settlements. In 1774, reacting to a British Coercive Act aimed at punishing Boston for the Tea Party, Hanover passed a resolution opposing the 'iniquitous and oppressive' action of the London Parliament and adding in sinister undertones, 'our cause we leave to heaven and our rifles'. In the early 1770s, committees and associations appeared with the limited aim of boycotting British goods; it is worth noting that the Scots-Irish associators of Lancaster (an organization dedicated to resisting tax impositions), were instructed to keep their rifles in 'good order and repair', with powder and shot handy. While the politicians were spreading the gospel of revolution, the Ulster backwoodsmen were spoiling for a fight.

In the late nineteenth century, when the remote descendants of the eighteenth-century Ulster immigrants gathered at one of the congresses of the American Scotch-Irish Society, no claim was too extravagant, no epithet too hyperbolic to be applied to the Scots-Irish role in the Revolutionary War: 'the Gulf Stream among the most stupendous of the works of creation; ... the Scotch-Irish race just as remarkable.' The Rev. Dr Thomas Murphy, addressing the third Scotch-Irish Congress in 1891, saw the War of Independence and the formation of the American Constitution as the 'consummation of that sublime movement of humanity' for which the Scots-Irish had been training for 1,800 years. Every likely American Revolutionary name, including those of Admiral John Barry, the 'father of the American Navy', who was a native Irishman from Wexford, 'Mad' Anthony Wayne, one of the most successful of Revolutionary generals but whose family, originally of English descent, came to America from County Wicklow, and General John Sullivan, who as his name implies was an Irish Catholic, was claimed as Scots-Irish.

Equally absurd was the view promulgated by Michael O'Brien in his book *A Hidden Phase of American History*. O'Brien, a late nineteenth-century emigrant from County Cork closely connected with extreme Irish Nationalists, worked his way through the muster rolls of the Revolutionary armies, searching for Catholic Irish names in an effort to establish that it was the native Irish, not the Scots-Irish, who had fought the good fight for American nationhood. The truth was that the Catholic Irish were too few in number to be of great significance while their Presbyterian fellow countrymen, first, second and third generation, supplied about forty per cent of the American fighting men. The roster of Washington's army shows a Scots-Irish element much larger than that of any other group. David Doyle makes the shrewd point that, while the native Irish joined not for motives of 'self-sacrificing patriotism' but because they needed to improve their lowly status in a new and Protestant-dominated land, the Scots-Irish, however they might be stirred by memories of landlord oppression and agrarian troubles, fought for American reasons in an American context.

The degree and nature of Scots-Irish involvement varied from colony to colony and between backwoodsman and town dweller. Pennsylvania, where they were strongest, was to be the pivot of revolution, the link between the rebels of New England and the rebels of Virginia. At the same time it was also one of the most vulnerable colonies. The support for independence, particularly around the Atlantic ports, was far from unanimous. There was a strong sense of 'Britishness' among the better off; many people depended for their livelihood on the rich trade with the motherland, and an even wider group of farmers in the old counties around Philadelphia – professional men, tradesmen and merchants – did not wish to disturb a comfortable status quo. Against this background the patriots, committee men, associators and radical journalists had to create the right political climate for armed rebellion.

In Virginia the Scots-Irish of the Valley area had always been on much better terms with the people of the Tidewater and the Virginia Assembly than their Pennsylvania counterparts with the authorities in Philadelphia. So when an impassioned Patrick Henry cried to the House of Burgesses, 'Give me liberty or give me death', the Colters, Patricks and McAfees on the other side of the Blue Ridge thought his phraseology a bit extravagant but largely agreed with his sentiments. They quietly cleaned their long rifles as they waited for 'the next gale that sweeps from the North' which would bring to their ears 'the clash of resounding arms'.

In the Carolinas the separation between the coastal population and the back country people, largely of Scots-Irish origin, was not only social, racial and political but also physical; there was a large tract of virtually empty land between the plantations around Charleston and the Piedmont settlements. The frontiersmen, cut off and alienated, had little inclination to support the Tidewater gentry in a fight for independence, which they saw would only strengthen the power of the Charleston government.

Scots-Irish individuals, too, had widely differing attitudes and motives. Clerics, like David Caldwell, who operated in the south, were inspired by a burning patriotism when they preached their anti-British sermons. The wealthy businessman John Hancock, whose people came from County Down, was the first to sign the Declaration but he was involved less because of his declared 'eternal enmity to tyranny' than because British taxation and British interference with trade curbed his God-given right to make money. British ministers, he said, will 'thrust their dirty hands into the pockets of every American'. Marksman Timothy Murphy had different reasons from either Caldwell or Hancock for his patriotism. He shot dead a brigadier-general because the redcoat officer represented to him the high-living corruption and oppression of the just which a Puritanical frontiersman might expect of the British ruling classes.

Many Scots-Irish, both as individuals and as groups, set definite limits to their patriotism. Farmers west of the Susquehanna protested loudly when their indentured servants left the cornfields to fight for their country. Others, especially in the Carolina backwoods, were loyalists and fought alongside the British troops. The case of Alexander Chesney illustrates some of the contradictions always inherent in the relationship between

Ulster Protestants and the British authorities. Chesney was born on a tiny farm at Dunclug near Ballymena, now overbuilt by housing estates but in the 1750s a country area seething with discontent. He went to South Carolina with his parents and seven brothers and sisters in 'the Snow [a merchant ship] called James and Mary'. During the Revolutionary War he served as an officer in the loyalist militia, although his younger brother was fighting with the rebels. With the British defeat, Chesney returned to Ireland, and in 1798 he again served as a British officer when the men who were boys with him twenty years before at Dunclug were in armed rebellion against the British Crown.

Personal circumstances decided for some their political stance. Scots-Irish historians usually fail to mention Simon Girty, who has passed into American mythology as the epitome of treachery and cruelty. Girty was not only Scots-Irish but very much a product of the society he grew up in. His family lived at Sherman's Creek in the Pennsylvania mountains, in that band of frontier society where the men of the family took refuge from a poverty-stricken existence in heavy drinking. Simon saw his father killed by an Indian in a drunken quarrel and he, with the rest of his family, was later carried off by an Indian war party. As a young man he came back to white society, only to be despised as an illiterate 'half-Indian'. Highly intelligent but deeply frustrated by his treatment, Girty returned with two of his brothers to the Shawnee tribe, where they became totally Indianized. During the Revolutionary War Girty was a remarkably effective leader of raiding parties, taking particular delight in torturing the better-off Scots-Irish who fell into his hands.

A few Ulster Scots managed successfully to keep a foot in both camps. The journalist Hugh Gaine from Belfast, who arrived in New York in 1745 without even the customary bundle containing a spare shirt and hose over his shoulder, had everything to lose if he made the wrong political decision. As the British pulled out of New York after their first defeat, Gaine prudently painted out the crown from the 'Bible and Crown' sign over his printing shop. When the royal armies returned he moved to the patriot-controlled Newark, New Jersey, where he ran a newspaper backing the American cause, while his original journal continued to print in New York and support the British interest. Gaine survived to become a rich and respected American citizen.

Nothing illustrates the difference between eighteenth- and twentieth-century society better than the fact that a one-man school, attached to a church in the heart of the country, could generate political power to influence the destiny of a nation. A study of a few of the lawyers and businessmen who emerged from Francis Allison's academy also shows that eighteenth-century politics could tolerate, and even encourage, a degree of individualism (that ineradicable virtue or vice of the Ulsterman) which would be totally unacceptable within a modern British – or even American – party machine. Charles Thomson from County Derry was orphaned on the voyage to America by the death of his father, just within sight of the Delaware shore. Sold at ten as an indentured servant but within the protected Scots-Irish circle, he was soon displaying his intellectual talents at the New London school. He moved through teaching and business to politics and, as a quiet but extremely effective committee man, spread the Hutchesonian doctrine to those not privileged to have sat at Allison's feet. He is credited with bringing Benjamin Franklin round to supporting independence. For fifteen years he served as Secretary of Congress, and the first draft of the Declaration of Independence, before Jefferson turned it into elegant prose, is in his handwriting. Thomson was that perfect civil servant, sadly missed by twentieth-century Presidents and Prime Ministers: he burnt incriminating papers before he left office.

James Smith, another Ulster-born signatory of the Declaration, was one of Allison's earliest pupils. Trained as a lawyer, he soon discovered that he was unable to break into the moneyed circles of Philadelphia, still dominated by Quaker and English merchants. Grievance sharpened his wit and he turned to politics, using Hutcheson's ideas to urge a re-shaping of American society and a re-thinking of the relationship between Britain and her colonies. When that relationship deteriorated too far for moderately radical solutions, he helped draft the resolutions for independence.

Another hungry lawyer was Thomas McKean who belonged to one of the earliest Scots-Irish families to settle in Pennsylvania. He was a stern Presbyterian jurist, a type as common in Ulster as in the New World, who saw no contradiction between his stance as a godly, upright man and an insatiable appetite for money and social position. McKean, like Thomson, was a great committee man and it was largely through his drive and determination that the Continental Congress – the assembly of representatives from each North American colony which met in Philadelphia during the Revolution – finally voted to break the British link in 1776. George Read, another pupil of Allison, who was also a signatory of the Declaration, came from a very different background. His family, English squires who had settled in Ireland, were now big landowners in Maryland, and Read reflected his social position in his cautious approach to independence. Despite his lineage, he is usually listed as Scots-Irish, and there is some argument for this as he certainly belonged to the Scots-Irish political network and he reflected, if in a more modified form, the Hutchesonian philosophy.

Hugh Williamson, on the other hand, was of traditional Presbyterian stock. He left the New London school to become a mathematician and doctor and a publicist for the American cause. Like his friend Franklin, he operated on the international scene, arguing the American case in Britain. His cosmopolitan radicalism was interrelated to the advancement of science and education just as McKean's was to his family's social progress. In this way Williamson resembled the Presbyterian radicals beginning to emerge at that time in Ulster.

On a Sunday morning in September 1777, under the Witness Oak which still grows beside the eighteenth-century church at Donegal Springs in Lancaster County, sons and grandsons of the Ulster frontiersmen who had created the township half a century earlier

ABOVE *Charles Thomson designed the original Great Seal of the United States in 1782 and as Secretary of Congress was the first to use it to authenticate Congressional Bills. The simplicity and power of his concept expresses vividly the single-minded and often aggressive radicalism of the man.*

BELOW *The bland modern version, in contrast, expresses the modern conservatism of his country.*

now took an oath to defend their new fatherland. Community after community of Scots-Irish were doing the same. In what is now the chocolate city of Hershey, the Associators of Londonderry's Liberty declared their allegiance to the concept of an independent America. One hot May afternoon in 1775 Sergeant James McMichael joined the local company of volunteers at the crossroads in Drumore Township, and in high spirits began the march eastwards through the older Scots-Irish settlements towards the coastal war zone and a series of resounding defeats. The impassioned speeches and the high-sounding oaths taken at recruiting meetings a few months before were to seem unreal to McMichael when he saw his comrades killed around him by the trained musketry of the British regulars. In the midst of military disasters the untrained militia turned to that old Scots-Irish remedy, whiskey, and took out their disappointment, fear and frustration in fights among themselves. Only Washington's timely victory that Christmas at Trenton, New Jersey, restored morale.

Veteran leaders from the Indian Wars twenty years before, like John Armstrong of Carlisle, were given commands in the Revolutionary Army, but often they were more effective as rallying points for backwoods patriotism and as organizers of the war effort than as field officers. The rich Scots-Irish lawyer Joseph Reed, after a successful term as Washington's close military associate in the Jersey campaign, gave up his command and turned to politics.

But the American, like other revolutions, soon threw up talented generals. A pre-emptive strike into Canada in the year before independence was declared produced the most effective of the Ulster-born military men. Daniel Morgan, who came from Draperstown in County Londonderry, led a company of riflemen from the Valley of Virginia in the abortive American attack on Quebec, and distinguished himself after his commanding general, also Scots-Irish, had been killed. In 1777, when the British counter-thrust into up-state New York under General Burgoyne came to grief at Saratoga, Morgan played an important part in this, the first major American victory. Four years later he had switched to the southern war sector, and his own victory at Cowpens in North Carolina was an important step on the road to the final British surrender at Yorktown. Morgan was one of the first American commanders to recognize that marksmanship with the long frontier rifles was a cheaper way to win the war than relying on the mass fire power of short-range military muskets. He was also the type of leader, unorthodox, inventive and daring, to whom the backwoods fighters instinctively rallied.

In the middle war period of 1777–8, despite the elimination of the British army at Saratoga, Washington was hard pressed to keep his forces intact. While the American troops wintered at Valley Forge (their nearby capital of Philadelphia and most of their means of supply were in British hands), endurance of cold and hunger rather than fighting skills were needed, and it was in this that the famous Pennyslvania Line, chiefly made up of Scots-Irish, proved its dour Presbyterian worth. The man who, against great odds, kept the supply lines going, was Ephraim Blaine. Born in the Irish county of Donegal and educated in Pennsylvania by Francis Allison, Blaine had none of the dash of a Daniel Morgan but he did possess a sharp business sense and great organizing skill. He had already learnt the connection between trade and war when he turned from fighting Indians, as a young lieutenant in the French War, to selling them knives, jewellery and rum. Now he had to persuade the farmers of the Ulster communities to part with their grain and hog meat on credit, a job which made Indian trading seem like a sinecure. In those dark days Washington is credited with the remark, 'If defeated everywhere else, I shall make my last stand for liberty among the Scotch-Irish of my native Virginia'. Perhaps this was less of a general compliment to the race than a pointer to the Ulster Pennsylvanian farmers, whose loaded wagons were going to the British in Philadelphia because the British could pay in gold and the hungry patriots at Valley Forge could not.

'We travelled this day about twenty-five miles over pleasant savanna ground, high and dry, having very few trees upon it ... we passed through delicious country ... saw fine bladed grass along the banks of these pleasant rivulets': so that area of the North Carolina Piedmont which lies between the Yadkin and Catawba rivers was described in the early eighteenth century. To this empty, virtually treeless area thousands of Scots-Irish came in the period between 1740 and the outbreak of the Revolution. The Catheys, who originally emigrated from County Monaghan to Pennsylvania, were typical of this southward migration. A generation after their arrival they moved from their home in Lancaster County to the Shenandoah, and from there to what is now Rowan County, North Carolina. Here they were among the inhabitants of the 'Irish settlement' which grew up around the Presbyterian church of Thyatira. In the succeeding decades Scots-Irish, along with Germans, poured down the Great Valley from Pennsylvania, New Jersey and Delaware, and the Carolina Piedmont rapidly filled up. In Rowan County alone the population quadrupled in fifteen years.

But what was important to the American Revolution was not the number of migrants but the change which came over them when they entered North Carolina. It was as if they had broken free from the Atlantic-centred society of the coast, from that frame of mind which accepted that the colonies, however recalcitrant, were extensions of Britain. The umbilical cord was cut, and these were Americans no matter how much they recreated little Ulsters at Thyatira or the Waxhaws.

The Regulator rebellions (1767–71) of North and South Carolina were the first outward signs of this division, which looked forward to the great divide between west and east in the United States of the late nineteenth and early twentieth centuries, the divide between a patrician and Europeanized view of society and the free-wheeling life of the continental interior. The Regulators, of course, had no such historic view. In South Carolina, the rule of law had ceased to operate. 'Married Women have been Ravished – Virgins deflowered ... unheard of Cruelties committed by barbarous Ruffians', Charles Woodmason, a local clergyman, reported. The Regulators, largely Scots-Irish vigilantes, merely wanted to see wrongdoers punished and order restored and, if they

LEFT ABOVE *General Washington visits his army at Valley Forge near Philadelphia. It is doubtful if the Scots-Irish of the Pennsylvania Line, starving and half-naked in the grim winter of 1777 to 78, were quite as enthusiastic about their commanding general.*

LEFT BELOW *Derry-born Charles Thomson, long-time Secretary of Congress, hands to George Washington his commission as first United States President.*

ABOVE *America's greatest humiliation came in June 1814 when a British expeditionary force captured Washington and burned all the public buildings in the national capital.*

sometimes behaved a little like the Klansmen of a century later, many of them had been personally injured, 'Some in their Wives – others in their Sisters or Daughters or by the loss of Horses, cattle and Effects'.

In North Carolina the Regulation movement was a protest at the corrupt rule imposed on the back country people by the gentry of the coastal plantations who controlled the Provincial Assembly. Both rebellions were suppressed by the colonial authorities of the coast, and the five Regulator leaders hanged after the Battle of Alamance in North Carolina became frontier martyrs. All this happened just five years before the first shots at Lexington, so it was small wonder that the people of the Piedmont, already defeated in one rebellion, should hesitate to embark on another, and that they should be unwilling to come to the help of their recent oppressors, now themselves in rebellion against Britain.

The Scots-Irish revolutionaries of the Middle States were well aware of the general indifference of their countrymen in the Carolinas. So the élite of the Republican propagandists, Ulster Presbyterian clergymen, were sent south. Charles Woodmason had less sympathy for these political missionaries than he had for the Regulators: 'Itinerant Presbyterian preachers traverse this country Poisoning the minds of the People – Instilling Democratical and Commonwealth Principles into their minds . . . and laying deep their fatal Republican Notions – Especially that they owe no Subjection to Great Britain – that they are a free People.'

At the solidly Scots-Irish Waxhaws, on the border between North and South Carolina, the Rev. Alexander Craighead converted the entire settlement to revolution. His clerical son-in-law, David Caldwell, preached a highly influential sermon against apathy towards the holy cause of American liberty, 'The Character and Doom of the Sluggard'. There were of course many, particularly in North Carolina, who did not need patriotic sermons to make up their minds. As early as 1775, frontiersmen of Mecklenburg County, reacting to the news from Boston, had declared themselves independent of British rule. Equally some Scots-Irish, like those of the Ninety-Six district of South Carolina, had no hesitation in supporting the British or Loyalist cause. But even when allegiances were clearly defined the quarrel had a local character, and there was an element of moral censure in the attitude of the American Party, with the authority of the Presbyterian Church behind them, towards their Loyalist opponents. Patriot leader Andrew Pickens, who had been born of Ulster parents in Pennsylvania, and came down the Great Wagon Trail through Virginia to Lone Cane Creek in the Ninety-Six district, was a solid farmer and Presbyterian elder. He hardly needed a political reason for disliking his Loyalist counterpart, Irish-born Richard Pearis, who was an itinerant trader and kept an Indian wife as well as a white one. There was also a great mass of uncommitted settlers who watched with interest while the patriots tarred and feathered Scotsman Thomas Brown for laughing at one of the more pretentious speeches on behalf of liberty, or looked the other way when Loyalists raided rebel houses in search of arms.

The decade preceding the Revolution was a time of bitter land troubles in Ulster, and

ABOVE AND RIGHT *The pious and patriotic inscription on Waxhaw Church belies the nature of the boisterous, undisciplined and frequently violent Scots-Irish who inhabited this South Carolina settlement. In contrast, the Irish Covenanters who rest under these headstones lived quiet, godly lives nearby and turned to arms only in resistance to British atrocities during the War of Independence.*

as a result of rising rents, constant evictions, terrorism by agrarian secret societies and a slump in the linen trade, emigration to America reached record levels between 1770 and 1775. Many of these new immigrants found their way to the Carolinas, either overland from New York and Pennsylvania or directly through Charleston. The newcomers had little appreciation of the political situation in America, and no wish to challenge the status quo in a country which had given them cheap land and a chance to be their own masters. In 1771 the Rev. William Martin, a Covenanting clergyman from County Antrim, led five shiploads of his co-religionists to South Carolina (the story of their voyage illustrates how the good organization imposed by a strict religious sect could minimize the sufferings caused by a prolonged voyage and the outbreak of disease). When the brethren arrived at their settlement on Rocky Creek in Chester County they were full of gratitude for the expeditious way the Charleston authorities had processed their land warrants and assisted them with money on their journey inland. It was largely due to British stupidity that nine years later these quiet Covenanters, along with thousands of their less devout fellow Scots-Irish, turned from ploughing, sowing and raising families to fighting a guerilla war.

After the losses in the North the British switched their war effort to the Southern colonies. Military intelligence told them that the majority of the back country settlers were Loyalist, and that a firm display of force would cow the rest. But London's information on the Carolinas in the 1780s proved to be no more reliable than its information on Ulster in the 1980s. The offensive opened well for the British. Charleston, with a large American force, was captured and the British commander, Lord Cornwallis, trounced the American Southern army at Camden. Cornwallis then sent Colonel Banastre Tarleton to win over the back country by burning some 'sedition shops', British jargon for Presbyterian churches. Tarleton, girlish-faced, elegant and sadistic, was exactly the sort of emissary to rouse the hatred of the Piedmont people, and he did so very effectively. On 29 May 1780 he pursued two beaten companies of Americans into the Waxhaws settlement and butchered them, despite white flags and appeals for mercy. One witness to the slaughter was the twelve-year-old son of a Carrickfergus weaver, who was to be one of America's greatest Presidents and who was to harbour a hatred of Britain for the rest of his life. Of more immediate importance than the boy, Andrew Jackson, was the Rev. William Martin. The following Sunday he preached a violent sermon calling on his fellow Covenanters to take up arms. Martin's anger was echoed from other pulpits and the freedom-fighter bands, like that of Andrew Pickens or Francis Marion, 'the Swamp Fox', were swelled with new recruits.

Cornwallis now invaded North Carolina as the beginning of a mopping-up operation by which he would move north, restoring British rule in colony after colony. To protect his left flank he sent Major Patrick Ferguson with an army deep into the outback, towards the Blue Ridge Mountains. This move was intended to frighten the Scots-Irish of the Watauga River west of the Blue Ridge. Instead it incensed them. Over a thousand armed men in buckskin gathered on the banks of the Watauga to hear the Rev. Samuel Doak call on them to take up 'the sword of the Lord and of Gideon'. This scene and what followed were reminiscent of the seventeenth-century Scottish Covenanters going into battle. These long-bearded hymn-singing Calvinists marched over the Blue Ridge and, joined by men from Virginia, caught up with Ferguson at King's Mountain, an isolated, forest-clad hill near the modern town of Gaffney.

The British commander lined up his troops on the level summit of the hill and waited for the frontiersmen to attack, knowing that they could not withstand a bayonet charge from his trained men. Unfortunately for him, these 'over-mountain men' had not learned the rules of eighteenth-century warfare. They fought the battle in native American style, keeping under the cover of the trees, each sharpshooter killing a redcoat with a single shot and then moving back to reload while another settler took his place. Ferguson was killed and his men, after heavy losses, surrendered.

After the battle the summary trial and execution of prisoners began. Presbyterian elders, who officered the settler army, presided as judges and invoked the Old Testament as they paid off old scores against Loyalist fellow settlers. Their commanding officer, William Campbell, was a particularly zealous hangman. He reversed the reprieve granted to fellow Scots-Irishman John McFall and had him executed immediately. Alexander Chesney from Ballymena was lucky enough to escape the gallows, though not considerable ill-treatment: 'Even my shoes and silver buckles were taken off my feet. I was marched in inclement weather without covering or provision.' Reaching the Yadkin River as night fell, Chesney made a classic escape by diving in and swimming to safety.

The destruction of his protective left flank forced Cornwallis back to Charleston and gave the Americans a chance to assemble another Southern army. The fact that the Watauga settlers had beaten a British army in battle gave great impetus to recruiting. In 1781 Cornwallis again began the move northwards, with Banastre Tarleton leading the élite Tory Legion and a regiment of Scottish Highlanders in another mopping-up operation into the back country.

At Cowpens, where the Carolina drovers assembled their cattle for the drive to the Philadelphia market, Tarleton met an American force composed largely of Scots-Irish militia, under General Daniel Morgan. Morgan's military skill held the untrained frontiersmen together under Tarleton's attacks until their superior marksmanship inflicted such losses that the crack British regiments disintegrated. Only one thing marred the great Scots-Irish victory: 'Bloody' Tarleton's speed of flight put him beyond their vengeance.

The two battles, King's Mountain and Cowpens, fought within a distance of a few miles, destroyed the British supply lines. Despite some local successes, Cornwallis's campaign never recovered its momentum and eight months later, hemmed in at Yorktown on the Virginia coast, he surrendered the last British army on United States' soil.

With the exception of Morgan, the Scots-Irish produced no outstanding generals but, as many British field officers testified, it was their colonels, captains, non-commissioned officers and ordinary soldiers who were the backbone of the army. 'Hopping' John Miller set a record by serving in twenty-six battles. From the Waxhaws whole family networks fought for their new country, among them four McCammon brothers and nine Gastons, of whom three died in the battle of Hanging Rock. Nearly all were amateur soldiers, bravely improvising as they went to war. With them began that cherished American myth, 'A well regulated Militia, being necessary to the security of a free State, the right of the people to keep and bear arms shall not be infringed'. Many tributes were paid to them but the finest came not from one of their apologists but from a frustrated opponent: he called them, 'the most God-provoking democrats this side of hell'.

7 • IN SEARCH OF AMERICA

'The gifts of fortune are promised in the West and to the West they bend their course.'

Alexis de Tocqueville

'Isolationism . . . a commonwealth of large or small communities, self-sufficient, self-regarding and suspicious of the outside world.'

Woodrow Wilson

'STAND AT THE Cumberland Gap and watch the procession of civilization, marching single file – the buffalo following the trail to the salt springs, the Indian, the fur-trader and the hunter, the cattle-raiser, the pioneer farmer – and the frontier has passed by.' A young Wisconsin university teacher, by freezing the frame of the moving frontier at this precise geographical point, created the most graphic image in American history and one that quickly caught the popular imagination. The Cumberland Gap, which leads from the toe of the Valley of Virginia through the Appalachian range to the headwaters of the Kentucky River, and from there to the great interior basin of the United States, was known to most Americans, if only from George Caleb Bingham's picture of a fatherly Daniel Boone leading settlers through its romantic defile to the fresh bluegrass prairies. The members of the American Historical Association, to whom Frederick Jackson Turner delivered his famous paper 'The Significance of the Frontier in American History' in 1893, were equally familiar with the Gap as the key point at which the white settlers breached the Appalachian barrier in their surge westward. Turner told his audience, 'the Western wilds, from the Alleghenies to the Pacific, constituted the richest free gift ever spread out before civilized man'. He might have added that the Scots-Irish were poised at three points to the east of the great mountains to take advantage of this unrepeatable offer.

In western Pennsylvania, in the Valley of Virginia and in the Carolinas Scots-Irish settlements were in ferment. Religion, radical politics, resentment of the better-off citizens of the Atlantic seaboard, the need for new land to replace farms worn out by prodigal agriculture, all had contributed, by the early days of the young republic, to a fluid situation which could lead to a fresh revolution or a fresh emigration or both. North and South Carolina had tried rebellion with their Regulator movements and lost.

In 1785 the 'over-mountain men' of the Watauga and Holston river valleys, the men who fled from Carolina after the collapse of the Regulator Rebellion and returned to win the victory of King's Mountain, set up the independent commonwealth of Franklin, called after the great Philadelphian, an honour which he diplomatically ignored. Franklin was founded on the principles which might be expected from a radical frontier society – universal male suffrage, secret ballot, only devout Christians to be office-holders, lawyers and such dubious middle-class characters being barred. With the old Scots-Irish suspicion of official currency, otter skins were designated as legal tender, but this did not prevent widespread forgery, the less upright of Franklin's citizens sewing otters' tails on to worthless raccoon skins. Appropriately, after three tumultuous years of existence, the state of Franklin collapsed in fisticuffs and farce.

Western Pennsylvania would also try rebellion as a result of this disenchantment with the Atlantic seaboard and with seaboard rule. But eventually the Pennsylvanian frontiersmen, like their compatriots in the Carolinas and Virginia, would accept the peculiarly American solution of migration westwards, 'this perennial rebirth ... this expansion westwards with its new opportunities, its continuous touch with the simplicity of primitive society'. Ahead of the pioneers was the true America, unstained by the Atlantic coast with its still colonial culture. 'The true point of view in the history of this nation is not the Atlantic coast, it is the Great West ...' When the Scots-Irish wagon trains began to move, from Rowan County in North Carolina, from Draper's Meadow in Virginia or from the Juniata Valley in Pennsylvania, they carried not only farm tools and furniture but the human characteristics, the political and religious beliefs and many of the social structures which were to go into the making of 'real America'.

Of the three Scots-Irish regions which were primary reservoirs for the great spill-over into the Mississippi basin, the Carolina Piedmont was the most populous and the most isolated from European influences, and it is, through the Journal and other writings of the Reverend Charles Woodmason, the best documented. After allowing for Woodmason's prejudices and his persecution mania, we have the most exact picture which exists anywhere of American frontier life, that 'coarseness and strength' which Frederick Jackson Turner admired.

Woodmason rode through the countryside stopping at settlements to baptize twenty or thirty children or marry a dozen couples. He observed that, despite the dearth of clergy to perform the wedding ceremony, life went on: 'Out of 100 young Women that I marry in a year, I have seen but Six who are not with Child.' Wherever the parson went among the Scots-Irish he saw sexual temptation: 'The Women bareheaded, barelegged and barefooted with only a thin Shift ... The Young Women have a most uncommon Practise which I cannot break them off. They draw their Shift as tight as possible to the Body and pin it close to shew the roundness of their Breasts and slender waists ... and they expose themselves often quite naked.' The fact that a kick from a horse 'received in the scrotum' had left him 'unfit for Nuptial Rites' does not seem to have lessened Woodmason's horrified fascination with the buxom young Ulster women.

Woodmason was a traditionalist, a believer in an immutable social order, but even if he had been the most advanced thinker of his age he could hardly have been expected to recognize in the 'Thieves, Jockeys, Gamblers ... Prostitutes, Felchers, Racers, Fidlers and all the refuse of Mankind' he preached among, a society in embryo, the prototype of America's Wild West. The ingredients were there: an economy based largely on cattle-raising; rustling and horse-stealing accepted as a way of life (Woodmason was picked up by a gang of horse-thieves and taken to their hideout to preach to them); a great deal of heavy drinking and gambling and a readiness to reach for guns to settle a dispute. A somewhat earlier society existed side by side with the Scots-Irish cowboys, 'many live by killing of Deer ... There is not a Cabbin but has 10 or 12 Young children in it – when the Boys are 18 and the Girls 14 they marry ... These people are all from Ireland and live wholly on butterMilk, Clabber and what in England is given to "the Hogs and Dogs".' But at Rocky Mount, also among the Scots-Irish, Woodmason found efficient husbandry, 'the land is good and plowed to the Summit, Spring Wheat, rye, Indian Corn and all kind of Grain and Fruit Trees'.

The Anglican preacher had little sense of humour; when he told his congregation about his unfortunate encounter with the horse he was surprised that 'They laughed as at a joke'. He would have needed, however, more than the average man's ability to laugh things off to cope successfully with the Ulster settlers' idea of fun. When Woodmason invited the Irish Presbyterians to his Episcopal service they 'brought with them 57 dogs (for I counted them) which in the time of the Service they set fighting'. At the same place some Ulster Baptists stole Woodmason's clerical gown and one of them, putting it on, crept into a respectable woman's house and into her bed, 'making her give out next day that the Parson had come to bed of her'. At another township the Dissenters registered their protest by evacuating their bowels on the Anglican Communion table. Small wonder he found it difficult to be civil about the Scots-Irish, 'certainly the worst Vermin on Earth'.

Even when there was no English clergyman to torment, life in the Carolina settlements was lively and often bizarre. The Scots-Irish quarrelled among themselves, fighting, slandering and sueing each other with untiring energy. John Baker had his ear bitten off but accepted this as a natural hazard of an argument; he worried only lest anyone think the ear had been legally cropped for some criminal offence. John McElrath, an early livestock baron, 'with a great amount of land ... and large droves of horses', sought an injunction to stop fellow Presbyterians from crossing his ranch to church. To ensure the legal proceedings went his way he stood outside the courthouse with a horsewhip. Months after the Rev. William Richardson of Waxhaw had committed suicide, rumours went round that his wife had murdered him. The corpse was exhumed and the widow was forced to touch the body in the belief that if she was guilty it would gush blood. When no blood appeared one zealous accuser forced Mrs Richardson's hand so violently down on the forehead of the corpse that the skull was crushed.

We know much more about the faults of the Ulster frontiersmen than about their virtues because the former are amply recorded on court files or in the letters of the many highly placed officials whom they irritated. But if they were quarrelsome and litigious, the Scots-Irish were also warm-hearted and caring. The Presbyterian Church was the

Scots-Irish Settlements in the USA

A
D
A
L. Superior
L. Huron
L. Michigan
MICHIGAN
L. Ontario
L. Erie
NEW YORK
MAINE
VERMONT
NEW HAMPSHIRE
Monmouth
Londonderry
Boston
MASS.
Worcester
CONN
Hudson R.
Susquehanna R.
New York
Princeton
N.J.
Philadelphia
Cleveland
PENNSYLVANIA
Harrisburg
Donegal Springs
Pittsburgh
Hanna's Town
MD
Potomac R.
Washington
DEL.
Shenandoah R.
VIRGINIA
OHIO
INDIANA
ILLINOIS
Bloomington
Mississippi R.
St Louis
MISSOURI
Ohio R.
Charleston
W. VIRGINIA
Lexington
Staunton
KENTUCKY
Cumberland R.
Cumberland Gap
Nashville
TENNESSEE
Tennessee R.
ARKANSAS
APPALACHIAN MOUNTAINS
BLUE RIDGE MOUNTAINS
NORTH CAROLINA
King's Mt.
Waxhaw
SOUTH CAROLINA
Charleston
GEORGIA
MISSISSIPPI
ALABAMA
LOUISIANA
New Orleans
GULF OF MEXICO
N
Key:
Areas of concentrated Scots-Irish settlement 1720-1800
Areas with significant Scots-Irish population 1800-1860
0 250 500 km
0 100 200 300 miles

channel for social welfare. The many orphans and illegitimate children were looked after; money was raised for the sick and needy. In the extended pioneer family the very old and the very young were cared for as a matter of course. One grim frontier fighter, cut off and facing a terrible death, wept because he would leave his little blind son to the mercy of a harsh world. Children were important to these settlers at a period when they did not rate highly in the outside world. Among the most touching relics of frontier life are the home-made dolls or little wooden horses that fathers carved, probably by firelight on winter evenings watched by children, wide-eyed that such wonders as toys could exist in their harsh world.

The little frontier community, created around a Presbyterian log church and often consisting of a few extended families, no matter how uncouth and hostile it might appear to an outsider, was a protective social unit and offered to immigrants a security and standard of living they had not known in Ulster. The Timber Ridge settlement in Rockbridge County, Virginia, was a good example. Here in the 1740s came the Houstons, Todds and Montgomerys, 'following Buffaloe races and Indian paths through the wilderness. These adventurers had chiefly in view the formation of compact settlements for schools and religious societies believing that the interests of themselves and their children depended much on Knowledge, morals and true christian religion.'

The northerly reservoir of Scots-Irish pioneer strength was quite unlike the Carolinas. Western Pennsylvania was legendary country – vast forests filled with wolves and panthers, hundreds of streams where bears fished, open spaces with herds of big black buffalo led by bulls weighing up to a ton. The rivers teemed with fish and, like everything else, they were of epic proportion: 'a fish caught here weighted one hundred and twenty pounds, and the story goes he drowned the man who caught him'. Rattlesnakes were particularly plentiful. The Rev. David McClure was obsessed with killing them; perhaps he equated the rattler with the Serpent in this, his own special Eden. Even the Indian population was sparser than elsewhere and the only white men, apart from military expeditions, were occasional hunters and Indian traders.

Fear of the Indian tribes, and a dispute between Pennsylvania and Virginia about ownership of the territory, delayed large-scale settlement until after the Revolution. Then the Scots-Irish from the Cumberland Valley passed over the Allegheny Mountains into south-western Pennsylvania. 'To the region they gave tone and direction, politically, economically and socially', says Wayland Dunaway. 'It was a characteristically Scotch-Irish community, forming a second and larger reservoir of their race.' In 1784 Arthur Lee noted, 'Pittsburgh is inhabited almost entirely by Scots and Irish'.

Migrants moved their entire belongings in a journey that often took weeks, first crossing the mountains and then using Indian paths through unmapped, heavily forested country. One settler remembered his journey as a small child from the Cumberland Valley just after the Revolution:

We were provided with three horses, on one of which my mother rode carrying her infant, with all the table furniture and cooking utensils. On another were packed the stores of provisions the plough irons and other agricultural tools. The third horse was rigged out with a pack saddle, and two large creels one over each side, in which were stowed the beds and bedding, and the wearing apparel of the family. In the centre of these creels, there was an aperture prepared for myself and sister, and the top was well secured by lacing, to keep us in our places, so that only our heads appeared above. Each family was supplied with one or more cows, which was an indispensable provision for the journey.

These settlements, in Fayette, Allegheny and Westmoreland counties, renewed the old frontier life which had faded from the original Pennsylvania homelands east of the mountain range, but with some significant differences. Silence was the predominant feature of the great forests of western Pennsylvania, and this aroused the dormant superstitions which the settlers had carried all the way from Scotland. On winter nights in lonely cabins families hearing the single isolated cry of an owl accepted that someone in the household would die that year. Sometimes the sounds were not the familiar ones of owls, wolves or panthers, and then the listeners knew that the Devil himself was abroad. In medicine, Indian and Ulster beliefs merged: snakebite was treated by killing the snake and burning it, for erysipelas the blood of a black cat was applied to the infected skin, a child with whooping cough was thought to be cured by the breath of a stallion. Other remedies, if equally impractical, were more enjoyable. André Michaux, coming on a household of adults smitten with measles, 'found them all drinking whiskey'.

As in Plantation Ulster, a network of taverns developed early, and like Ulster the landlords were usually farmers as well. One exasperated traveller, Mrs Sally Hastings, reported, 'Last night was a jovial one. The Landlady had collected a number of persons to husk corn and when their business was finished, they devoted the night to Dancing, Singing and other Exercises.' Being a religious lady she refrained from specifying what the 'other Exercises' were. The custom of waking the dead was also transplanted from Ireland and took on a boisterous nature in the backwoods. Settlers, gathered to pay a last tribute to a friend, sometimes let go in an orgy of dancing, drinking and fist-fights which was as much a relief from loneliness as from sorrow.

The early settler, wrote Dr Benjamin Rush, 'delights chiefly in company – sometimes drinks spirituous liquors to excess – will spend a day or two every week in attending political meetings'. The convivial Scots-Irish radical portrayed here was to give 'tone and direction' to life west of the Alleghenies. Although western Pennsylvania is part of the broad river basin which occupies the interior of the American continent, it was much less cut off from the Atlantic community than the Carolina Piedmont. The Ulster-born Revolutionary William Findley, who had moved from the Cumberland Valley to Westmoreland County, wrote, 'Every year after seeding time a great proportion go over the mountains to bring back their salt – when they visit friends and are informed of the news of the country'.

The political news they heard in the east was little to their liking. Post-Revolutionary America had grown conservative. The eastern politicians, even men like Thomas McKean, were interested in a seaboard republic which would grow wealthy on trade with Europe rather than in pushing on westwards towards that land of plenty which must exist somewhere in the empty heart of the continent. Spain, with jurisdiction in the Mississippi basin, had barred the river to settler traffic, and the American Federal Government showed no inclination to do anything about it. When the new republic set about creating complex financial structures, such as the Bank of North America, the western settlers felt this was not only a betrayal of the Revolutionary ideal of a republic of farmers, craftsmen and merchants but could also mean they would have to pay more tax. Above all they feared the strengthening of central government, and they resented gentlemen politicians like President Washington's authoritarian Treasury Secretary Alexander Hamilton.

The Scots-Irish of the west were ably represented by two spokesmen, William Findley and John Smillie who had survived the dreadful voyage from Belfast aboard the *Sally* in 1762. Smillie came from Greyabbey in County Down, where before the end of the century a Presbyterian clergyman would be hanged for his liberal principles, and he was typical of the best among Ulster-American politicians – radical, determined and deriving his power base directly from the pioneer people he represented. His lucid mind, which had recorded the most graphic account of an emigrant crossing, carried him from the job of carpenter to a seat in the United States Senate. William Findley challenged Hamilton's contemptuous phrase, 'lower orders of people' with 'We had not thought of a Distinction of Orders in Society ... We have few Slaves.'

The declaration of a republic in France excited many Americans who felt that their revolution had stopped half way. Revolutionary clubs were revived in Philadelphia and in western Pennsylvania; Jacobinism was in the air. But what finally brought the frontiersmen to rebellion was something more mundane and far closer to their hearts. Secretary Hamilton, in an effort to raise money to run the new federal structures, imposed a tax on whiskey. As practically every settler west of the mountains had his own private still, it was obvious that such an outrageous proposal had to be resisted. From run-of-the-mill attacks on tax collectors, the Whiskey Rebellion gathered momentum until, in 1794, it became a full-scale challenge to the authority of the Federal Government. Quiet farmers who depended on exporting their grain in the form of whiskey to the eastern towns joined the rebels, 'Tom the Tinker's firebrands'. Their argument seemed unanswerable: 'Why should we be made subject to tax for drinking our grain instead of eating it?' Five thousand angry moonshiners, nearly all Scots-Irish, took over Pittsburgh and the Government was forced to act. An army, in which many former Scots-Irish Revolutionaries served, was sent to western Pennsylvania and the Rebellion collapsed. Most rebels surrendered and were pardoned but some stubborn Ulstermen trekked over the mountains to Kentucky, where beyond reach of the tax men they could distill in peace. Twelve years before the Whiskey migration, two Scots-Irish Baptist ministers, Lewis and Elijah Craig led their congregation from northern Virginia, across the mountains and through the Kentucky hill country to the Bluegrass lands. Here while Lewis preached strong fundamentalist doctrines, his brother devoted his time to inventing equally strong and uplifting bourbon whiskey.

By the time the western rebels were crushed, the idea of a restricted seaboard America was already doomed. In 1794 the British surrendered the string of forts which they had held since the Revolutionary War, and which barred Pennsylvanian expansion to the north-west. The following year Spain opened the Mississippi to navigation and the Scots-Irish were again on the move. Now they travelled by water, as they had travelled along the River Bann in their first incursions into Ulster. Down the Ohio they went, families with all their possessions – clothes, cooking utensils, farm implements, even two or three hogs and a milking cow – aboard a leaky flat-bottomed boat at the mercy of the river currents. Another great diaspora had begun, and the Ulster Americans, careless and intrepid, were in the vanguard.

The most volatile element in the crucible of frontier society was religion. As early as 1738 an immense religious revival, the Great Awakening, began to sweep through colonial America. The moving spirit was the English evangelist George Whitefield, but as the whole structure of Scots-Irish life was built around their Church they soon became involved and deeply divided. Some Presbyterian ministers, like Gilbert Tennent of the Neshaminy Log College, approved of Whitefield's highly charged preaching. Other conservative ministers thought the evangelical movement 'the ruin of Christ's Government'. The Presbyterian Church divided in a bitter controversy between New Side evangelicals and Old Side conservatives.

The Old Side argued that the Church's role was to provide a house of worship and a worthy pastor; it was man's duty to seek his salvation. The New Side said the Church must search even the depth of the frontier wilderness and seek out sinners. John Craig, pioneer minister in the Shenandoah Valley, who came from Donegore in County Antrim, belonged to the Old Side. He was an intellectual and something of a visionary. When he first arrived in the Shenandoah he recognized the landscape: 'From the Dream I had before I left Ireland, I knew it to be the Plot in Christ's Vineyard where I was to labour.' This hardworking, devoted pastor was submitted to constant persecution by New Siders trying to take his congregation away. 'When I administered the Lord's Supper to my people, they mockingly said to their neighbours going to it, "What, are you going to Craig's frolic?"' Evangelical zeal left little room for Christian charity or even good manners.

In the Carolinas the Presbyterian Church faced a deeper crisis. Quite apart from the split between Old Side and New, it was almost impossible to provide the 'learned ministry' of university graduates which Presbyterianism demanded, and because of the

ABOVE *The home of the McAfees, one of the first settler families in Kentucky. The McAfees came originally from County Armagh.* BELOW *The Shawnee Indians tried to forestall the White invasion of the buffalo-rich Kentucky grasslands by attacking pioneer wagon trains.*

lack of ministers many Scots-Irish went over to the Baptists and Methodists who asked for no such credentials from their preachers. This process was accelerated as the settlers moved westward across the Blue Ridge and into the Great Smokies, until the Baptist faith took over from the Presbyterian as the religion of the Ulster Americans in the South.

Woodmason, the Anglican, ever ready for a controversy, was in the heart of the religious turmoil. He blamed the number of bastards among the Scots-Irish on the extravagances of the Methodists: 'Nothing more leads to this Than what they call their Love Feasts and Kiss of Charity. To which Feasts celebrated at Night much liquor is privately carried ... and it is no wonder Things are as they are, when many Young Persons have Miles to walk home in the Dark Night with convoy thro' the Woods. Or staying all Night at some Cabbin and sleeping together, either doubly or promiscuously?' To the New Light Baptists he put a straight question: 'Does bathing together promiscuously stark naked in the Streams and Rivers, as I myself have seen many of You, tend to Edification?' So disturbed was he with the public hallelujahs and the sexual frolics which he was convinced went on in private that he offered to make common cause with the 'beggarly Irish Presbyterians'.

The further the settlers went south or west the more evangelical and non-institutional became their religion. The Revival which began in Kentucky in 1799 made the earlier Revival of Whitefield and Tennent seem like a well-conducted Sunday school. One of the leading evangelists was a Scots-Irish farmer-turned-preacher called James McGready. Immensely tall and thin, with a cadaverous face and fiery eyes, he could wring the heart of the most obdurate sinner. The cynical who came to scoff at his outlandish pulpit mannerisms stayed to cry out their own most secret sins to the multitude. Religious hysteria swept the Scots-Irish townships along the frontier. The great rally at Cane Ridge, Kentucky, in August 1801 drew 25,000 howling penitents. At the preacher's words some fell down and twitched like epileptics, others writhed on their bellies like snakes, while the militants among the converted went down on all fours and barked like dogs to chase the Devil up the nearest tree. With many the reformation was short-lived; they went back within weeks to their more normal occupations of drinking and fornicating. But the Revival destroyed the predominance of the Presbyterian Church in the South. In thousands the Ulster settlers deserted their traditional beliefs for the Baptist faith. The Revival also weakened the structure of all Protestant institutional churches and laid the foundation for the incredible diversification of religious beliefs and practices in the modern United States.

Long before the post-Revolutionary migrations Scots-Irish traders and scouts had gone over the Alleghenies deep into Indian territory. A group of pedlars who rose in status to become merchants operated from the settlements along the Susquehanna from the early years of the century, among them Thomas McKee, James Patterson, the Lowery family of Donegal Springs led by Esquire Lowery, and John Finley who penetrated to

Neighbours gathered together to help each other at corn husking: these occasions usually turned into convivial parties when a great deal of home-made whiskey was consumed.

the Indians' magical land of Kaintuck, 'the dark and bloody land', in 1752, fifteen years before his friend Daniel Boone led the famous expedition there. Best known of these traders was George Croghan, 'a fat, cheerful and cunning rogue', who came from Dublin and, despite his Celtic surname, was a Protestant. The legend of Croghan's dubious land speculations, his sharp trading practices and his lecherous ways spread from Virginia to the Ohio Valley. At the settler soirées, mothers and grandmothers kept a watchful eye on the chastity of their nubile daughters if he was about. But the crafty Irishman was equal to the occasion. 'Croghan generally pushes Aboute the Glass so Copiously and briskly amongst the Old Women that before half the night is over they forget their Errand as well as their Charge and then what follows is easily guest at.'

Croghan was the most highly organized of the frontier merchants, controlling a network of agents and trading posts but he also operated in the field himself, often under trying circumstances: 'I have at this minnit 20 drunken Indians about me.' Traders were frequently murdered or robbed and because of this the single packman was rare. Independent traders usually moved in twos or threes, accompanied by a string of packhorses laden with goods. They brought back to the seaboard towns fine furs and supplies of medicinal herbs. Ginseng was exported in large quantities from Virginia to the Far East, where it went to stimulate the sexual appetites of jaded Chinese mandarins. These glib, humorous pedlars were a vital link between the isolated communities in the Alleghenies or the Ohio or Wabash valleys and civilization. They were the news carriers, maintaining an Irish tradition which went on well into the twentieth century in Ulster, where the herring vendors bowling along the country roads in fast spring carts would bawl out, between cries of 'herrin' alive', titbits of often fictitious local news – 'Poor Charlie's goin' to jail' – or anticipated their less talented brothers of the tabloid press by simply shouting, 'Shocking! shocking! shocking!' More importantly, these frontier traders brought back to civilization reports of empty fertile lands in the interior, thus stimulating new thoughts of migration among the Scots-Irish already restless after a generation of settled farming.

The credit for opening the floodgates of trans-Appalachian migration is generally given to Daniel Boone. Boone, of Quaker stock, lived among the Scots-Irish of the Yadkin River in the Carolina Piedmont, and when he made his first journey through the Cumberland Gap in search of the fabulous prairies of Kentucky he was guided by that far-ranging Scots-Irish trader John Finley. In 1775 Boone was in charge of a team of axe-men who cut the Wilderness Trail, which in the years following provided a road for thousands of migrants to the bluegrass country.

The McAfee brothers, who had come with their parents from County Armagh by way of Pennsylvania to the Valley of Virginia, led a group of Scots-Irish families, McCunes, Magees and Allens, through the Gap and penetrated a hundred miles into Kentucky. They settled at Salt River, where there is a monument to their mother, the indomitable Jane McAfee who walked beside her sons on that two hundred and fifty-mile journey.

Overland migration assumed a patriarchal character. A grandfather – often no older than his early forties because of the custom of teenage marriage – would lead his own family, along with brothers and cousins, in the kind of mass migration which had been impossible when the Atlantic, not the Appalachians, separated the settler from his goal. So the Scots-Irish communities with their complex, and sometimes genetically disastrous, patterns of intermarriage remained comparatively undiluted for another generation.

With the end of the Revolutionary War, emigration from Ulster, suspended during hostilities, began again and increased in volume until well into the nineteenth century. While the traditional entry points of Boston, Philadelphia and New York continued to receive Scots-Irish, there was also a great influx through New Orleans. The frontier, having broken the physical and psychological barrier of the eastern mountain range, moved on with ever-increasing momentum. Kentucky and Tennessee were rapidly swallowed and the settlement line moved down on to the deep black soils of Mississippi. The flamboyant Irishman General Anthony Wayne defeated the hostile Indians of the north-west and opened the settlers' route to what are the modern states of Indiana and Wisconsin. With the purchase by the United States of the western half of the Mississippi basin from France, the great river was crossed and the frontier surged on. Here in the rugged country of the Ozarks, on the Missouri–Arkansas border, the pace for some Scots-Irish inexplicably slowed down, just as a generation earlier in the Great Smokies they had suddenly lost their drive and ambition and settled on poor soils to a frugal existence, lightened only by their own remarkable music-making. But then, perhaps, this quiet, deeply religious, inward-looking life was the Eden they had been seeking.

In May 1975 a twenty-page essay entitled 'The Ante-Bellum Southern Herdsman; a Re-interpretation', appeared in the *Journal of Southern History*. This was a landmark in Scots-Irish studies. Written by Forrest McDonald and Grady McWhiney of Wayne State University in Detroit, it argued that the tradition of cattle-raising and cattle-droving on which the great myth of the American West is based was derived from Irish and Scots practices imported with the settlers from Ulster. The cattle culture of the Scottish Highlands and Borders, the breeding and stealing of cattle which had been the major occupation of those upland peoples, had been transplanted by way of Ulster to Virginia and the Carolinas. The authors could have added that the seventeenth-century Scots arriving in Ireland came into a native pastoral culture which could only reinforce their tribal predilections.

In early pioneer days in the New World, lack of capital had restricted the number of cattle kept by the Ulstermen. Instead they reared hogs, which thrived with little labour or cost by foraging in the Pennsylvania woods. A little later the cleared 'Indian fields' of the Shenandoah and the sparsely forested Piedmont gave better opportunities for cow herds and, as McDonald and McWhiney point out, the local laws were particularly favourable to herdsmen. In North Carolina it was a criminal offence to interfere with livestock grazing on land not under cultivation, irrespective of who owned the land or the cattle.

Despite an unpromising start, cattle numbers in the Scots-Irish settlements increased

ABOVE *The covered wagon or 'prairie schooner' was the vehicle of the great secondary migration into the continental interior.*

BELOW *'Poteen' makers tar and feather an exciseman during the Whiskey Rebellion in western Pennsylvania. The settlers justifiably regarded President Washington's new tax on whiskey a poor way to repay their patriotic service during the Revolutionary War.*

rapidly. In the mid-eighteenth century a frontier traveller wrote, 'From the heart of these Settlements we now got into the Cowpens, the Keepers of these are very extraordinary Kind of Fellows, they drive their Herds on Horseback and they need to do so for their Cattle are as wild as Deer.' The twentieth century would not find it difficult to identify these 'very extraordinary Kind of Fellows' with screen heroes from Tom Mix to Clint Eastwood. The Old West differed little from the Big Country of Kansas or Wyoming.

By the last quarter of the eighteenth century Scots-Irish Matthew Patton was the leading beef breeder in the Valley of Virginia. In 1790 he moved his herd to Kentucky. Twelve years later André Michaux noted, 'the number of horned cattle is very considerable in Kentucky; those who deal in them purchase them lean and drive them ... to Virginia where they sell them to graziers who fatten them in order to supply the markets of Baltimore and Philadelphia.'

One of the drovers who operated on the Great Wagon Trail to Philadelphia was James Patton from Tamlaght O'Crilly in County Londonderry. Through his autobiography, which was privately published by his family, Patton stands out as one of the most appealing and sharply drawn characters in Scots-Irish history. Son of a tenant farmer, he set out for Pennsylvania with a plan to earn enough money in two years to bring his widowed mother and family 'to this land of liberty ... where virtue and good conduct give a passport to the highest stations in Society'. This gullible idealist was duped and exploited at every turn. When his family's passage money seemed within his grasp, he was lured into a crooked dice game and lost everything. At the end of three years he was almost as poor as when he landed. 'I ... sat down by an oak tree and gave vent to a torrent of tears.' He then turned to trading and put all the money he had into dry goods. He set off, his pedlar's pack strapped on a pony, 'whistling and singing in the highest spirits'. After three miles pony and pack fell into a millpond. Trading in North Carolina, he was given a forged banknote and nearly lynched when he innocently tried to use it. Moving up and down the Great Valley buying fur pelts and selling trinkets and handkerchiefs 'at thirteen or fourteen cents advance', he encountered hundreds of cattle moving north, perhaps from the herds of his namesake Matthew, and his Irish peasant instinct was aroused. Maybe he recalled those Irish cattle dealers who bought steers from his father to drive south to the newly booming city of Dublin. A successful deal in furs gave him the capital to buy cattle, and from then on he prospered. His dream of bringing his mother and family from Ireland was realized and he died one of the earliest and richest citizens of Asheville, North Carolina.

Like cattle, hogs were taken to market in herds of from 300 to 2,000. They were driven eight to ten miles a day and stopped at night at 'hog hotels', stockyards with accommodation for the drovers. Pigs are perverse and clever animals which delight in making fools of men, so hog-driving could never become a dignified or heroic occupation. If the hog instead of the cattle culture of the Scots-Irish had gone to the Great West, John Ford would have made slapstick comedies against a sage bush and canyon backdrop.

Hog drovers, hog drovers, hog drovers we air,
A-courtin your darter so sweet and so fair
Can we git lodgin' here, O here,
Can we git lodgin' here.

In their essay McDonald and McWhiney use the term 'Celtic' in its older sense of pastoralist, meaning the peoples who once inhabited the whole of the British Isles, and still in the seventeenth and eighteenth centuries left strong traces of their culture in upland and western areas of both islands. They document the influence of 'Celtic' pastoralism brought in by settlers from the Scottish Highlands, but overwhelmingly by the Scots-Irish. They prove that the cowboy traditions of the Great Plains existed in the Old South before the explosion of 'buoyancy and exuberance' that took the migrant caravans into the Mississippi basin. They rightly challenge Frederick Jackson Turner's view of the cattleman as an environmental phenomenon occuring at a fixed point in frontier evolution, and convincingly argue that the open range tradition of cattle-rearing has its roots in the primitive peoples of the British Isles.

Turner's model of the frontier has its faults, but it offers a clear overview of a confused situation, a chance to identify major issues. 'To the frontier', said Turner, 'the American intellect owes its striking characteristics. That coarseness and strength combined with acuteness and inquisitiveness; that practical inventive turn of mind, quick to find expedients; that masterful grasp of material things, lacking in the artistic; that restless nervous energy; that dominant individualism, working for good or evil ...'. He might well have been ticking off the racial traits of the settlers from Ulster just as he ticked off the pioneer types passing through the Cumberland Gap. At the time when the young Republic was filling its lungs with the first breath of freedom the Scots-Irish were at the peak of their 'restless, nervous energy'. The Scots-Irish politician John C. Calhoun wrote, 'We are great and rapidly – I was about to say fearfully – growing'. The masterful and restless were disappearing westwards or into the political and business world of the east. 'Stand at South Pass in the Rockies a century later', said Turner, completing his famous frontier image, 'and see the same procession with wider intervals between'. But this time the viewer would not have picked out in the procession Scots-Irish communities or family groups but lonely, rugged individuals.

8 • WHISKEY IN THE WHITE HOUSE

'The most roaring, rollicking, game-cocking, horse-racing, card-playing, mischievous fellow that ever lived....'

Contemporary view of Andrew Jackson

'The stage is set, the destiny is disclosed. It has come about by no plan of our conceiving but by the hand of God who led us this way.'

Woodrow Wilson

THERE NEVER WAS a day like it, before or since, in the history of the White House. Scots-Irish frontiersmen, and a good many who were not, crowded the new presidential mansion. They drank all the liquor, ate all the food, scratched the elegant furniture with their spurs, quarrelled, were sick on the lawn and stole the silver. On 4 March 1829 Andrew Jackson, the Carrickfergus weaver's son, was inaugurated as seventh President of the United States, and the grip of the old colonial oligarchies on the chief office of the Republic was broken for ever. There was every reason why the ordinary Americans – farmers, cattle drovers, tradesmen and tavern lawyers – who in the first wave of American populist politics had elected Jackson, should rejoice. For them this was a victory of the South and West over the aristocratic East, of democracy over wealth and privilege. The rich and the privileged saw the event rather differently; this was the beginning of 'the reign of King Mob'. The inauguration celebration only confirmed that view.

The origins of Jacksonian democracy lay in the power struggle between the first political factions of the Republic in the immediate post-Revolutionary period. The difference between the Federalist and Democratic-Republican parties was in simple terms the difference between a readiness to settle for a conservative, élitist republic which would fit easily into the international pattern of the eighteenth century – a 'New Britain' independent of the old but resembling the mother country – and a desire to follow the Revolution to its logical conclusion and bring some, at least, of the principles of the French Revolution to America. The Scots-Irish patriots divided into conservative and radical, according to where their personal interests lay. Successful people like Thomas McKean, George Read and the Ballymena-born James McHenry, who was War Secretary in Washington's cabinet, were Federalists, but the majority of Scots-Irish, led by James Smith and John Armstrong, supported the Democratic-Republican Party.

Many of them, like the west Pennsylvanian radicals William Findley and John Smillie, were deeply suspicious of the Federalist Constitution of 1787, with its tendency to concentrate power at the centre. This sort of suspicion lies deep in the Scots-Irish nature, from recalcitrant clerics like Robert Blair in the seventeenth century, defying episcopal power vested in Armagh or Canterbury, to independent-minded twentieth-century Unionists resenting dictation from Downing Street. Anti-British feeling played no small part in this Scots-Irish support for the Democratic-Republicans. When the treaty with Britain negotiated by the conservative John Jay in 1794 was labelled 'pro-British' there were violent demonstrations in Philadelphia: 'Kick this damned treaty to hell', said the militant Ulster emigré Blair McClenachan.

In the periods of repression before and after the 1798 Rebellion in Ulster, Presbyterian liberals took refuge in America, and because their politics were cosmopolitan, the politics of international revolution, they found no difficulty in transplanting them to America. Dr James Reynolds from Cookstown, County Tyrone, the Rev. John Glendy from Maghera in County Derry, Rowan Hamilton from County Down, Thomas Addis Emmett, William Duane and others provided a middle-class leadership for the thousands of uneducated emigrants (in the period between 1783 and 1815 it is estimated that at least a hundred thousand came in from Ireland). These exiled leaders of the revolutionary United Irishmen found a new mission in America: they organized their compatriots in a political crusade to halt discrimination against Catholics and Presbyterians, against the working class and against immigrants in general. They found their outlets in radical journals, and their campaigns were strident and bitter. They frightened the new American establishment much as the rumbling of the Paris tumbrils had frightened the English one. Harrison Gray Otis, Mayor of Boston and Federal extremist, wrote, 'If some measures are not adopted to prevent the indiscriminate admission of wild Irishmen and others to the sight of suffrage, there will soon be an end to liberty and property'. But although the first year of the nineteenth century saw the election, with enthusiastic Scots-Irish support, of a Republican President, Thomas Jefferson, and the newly built White House was open to all with invitations to dine with 'Mr Jefferson', twenty-eight more years would elapse before the arrival in Washington of the age of the common man

Giant figures dominated the American scene in those early decades of the century: the great jurists Daniel Webster of Massachusetts who, according to Stephen Vincent Benet, bested the Devil in legal argument, and John Caldwell Calhoun of South Carolina, whom many Northerners believed was the Devil himself; John Quincy Adams, scion of a family whose name was virtually synonymous with American politics; Martin Van Buren, consummate political manoeuvrer. But high above them all in executive ability, political skill and appreciation of public wants rose the tall, lanky shape of Andrew Jackson. Though he was not a great political theorist, like his one-time friend and later opponent John C. Calhoun, Jackson brought about a bigger change in American politics than any other individual. He was the most positive personality ever to hold presidential office. Rugged and self-opinionated, no one made executive decisions but 'Old Hickory'. It was inevitable that he should become a folk hero, but the romantic framework that legend

A profile of power in this statue of the young Andrew Jackson at Waxhaw in South Carolina; at this age, however, the future President was more interested in horse racing than politics.

built round him obscures the sharp outline of the hard achiever. If Americans in the doldrums of late twentieth-century presidencies should wish to recall, like King Arthur to a modern Camelot, some past 'Chief', it is not Kennedy or Lincoln or even Washington but Andrew Jackson to whom they should look.

Unlike most great political figures, his private life was genuinely colourful. He was brought up in the Waxhaws when life there was at its most rumbustious. His father's funeral took place during a heavy snowstorm and the drunken mourners lost the body on the way to the churchyard. Two events in his schooldays pointed to the two extremes of his future career. His earliest surviving manuscript is an essay on the feeding of game cocks; when the newly printed Declaration of Independence arrived in the backcountry settlement, nine-year-old Andy Jackson was chosen to read it to the assembled settlers. Four years later the massacre of American prisoners by Tarleton set Jackson off on his career as a boy soldier in the Revolutionary War. Cornered by dragoons in the house of a relative, the thirteen-year-old rebel was ordered by their officer to polish his boots. Jackson's reply was one he was to give time and again in dangerous circumstances, a proud, foolhardy refusal. The officer's sabre cut marked the boy's cheek for life, a symbolic scar made much of in later patriotic portraits.

Jackson studied law at Salisbury, South Carolina, where he paid less attention to his legal studies than to the pretty, and available, mulatto girls of the town. From the chrysalis of the uncouth Waxhaw boy emerged a tall young dandy, horseman and gambler who quickly realized that the future for a Scots-Irish lawyer without rich connections must lie in the West. From the Carolina Piedmont Jackson moved to the Cumberland River Valley of eastern Tennessee, settling at a bunch of cabins with two taverns and a courthouse which was to become Nashville. Here began a lifelong attachment which was to reveal an unexpected side to his character.

When Rachel Robards, after a quarrel with her jealous husband over a young lawyer who lodged with them, returned to the home of her mother Widow Donelson on the Cumberland River, she found a lodger called Jackson in residence. Given Rachel's penchant for young lawyers a friendship rapidly developed, only to be interrupted by the arrival of her husband, Captain Lewis Robards. After a tense scene Jackson wisely left the widow's house and Rachel returned home to Kentucky with Captain Robards. Shortly afterwards occurred an incident which has been described on the one hand as a chivalrous young man honourably escorting an unhappy wife back to her own family and on the other as the romantic elopement of two passionate lovers. The undisputed fact was that Jackson took Rachel from her husband. Although the couple were subsequently married, charges of adultery followed Rachel for the rest of her life and resulted in Jackson fighting several duels, in one of which he killed a man. His single-minded devotion to Rachel was one of the finest elements in Andrew Jackson's many-sided character.

In the roughhouse of frontier justice Jackson quickly made his mark, as ready with a pistol as a legal plea. The courthouse was also the political centre and he helped to draft the constitution of Tennessee. Elected to Congress to represent the new state in 1796, he arrived in Philadelphia just as President Washington was retiring from public life, and with incredible affrontery he attacked the great American hero at the time when the public felt most sentiment towards him. He described Washington as 'over-rated' and accused him of being pro-British. The brash young frontiersman was throwing out his first challenge to the aristocratic clique who ruled the Republic.

There was always the smell of the tavern mixed with the whiff of gunpowder about Andrew Jackson's career. In 1814 when he was already a distinguished lawyer, a mature politician and commander of the Tennessee militia, he was almost killed in a confused hotel brawl with a fellow politician and his camp followers. Jackson was obsessed with personal honour. He would fight a duel or horsewhip a man at the drop of an incautious word. Then, overnight, the hot-headed cavalier would vanish, leaving Jackson the clear-sighted pragmatic politician or Jackson the brave and skilful soldier. Even as he recovered from the wounds of the Nashville brawl, he led his Tennessee militia against Creek Indians who, as allies of the British, had massacred settlers in the frontier territory that is now Alabama. His victory at the battle of Horseshoe Bend was his first major military achievement. Taking part in that battle were a young ensign called Sam Houston, from the Scots-Irish community of the Shenandoah Valley, and a frontier scout named Crockett, whose father had emigrated from County Londonderry. Both were to play significant roles in the history of Andrew Jackson and of America.

When, a year later, an army of British veterans who had just defeated Napoleon landed at New Orleans, Jackson commanded the American forces opposing them. The odds were on the British but Jackson's energy and will to win brought off a victory incredible in its totality. Against British casualties of two thousand, his army suffered thirteen dead and wounded and he became an American hero of the proportions of Washington. But another thirteen years of soldiering and hard politics passed before Old Hickory entered the White House.

John Caldwell Calhoun, whose career ran parallel to Jackson's, was in some ways a more likely candidate for the Presidency but, despite a brilliant political career and two terms as Vice-President, the supreme office eluded him. Calhoun's family had come the traditional Scots-Irish route down the Great Valley to South Carolina. Their experience too was not untypical, a grandmother scalped during the Indian War and an uncle killed by the British Tories during the Revolution, so John Calhoun grew up like Jackson with a strong anti-British prejudice. Calhoun served as Vice-President during Jackson's first term but afterwards the two quarrelled bitterly. Calhoun was by far the most original of the Scots-Irish political thinkers, but he lacked Jackson's pragmatism and his iron will. He was an advocate of states' rights to a degree that could have destroyed federal unity, and in this he bears comparison with modern Ulster Unionists. Jackson, on the other hand, believed passionately in a unified American nation.

Andrew Jackson was effective because he was direct: 'Every friend was an equal and every foe was a hound.' But it would be a mistake to over-simplify or over-sanctify him.

Davy Crockett, the archetypal frontiersman, was the son of a County Londonderry immigrant. His exploits, related in the Crockett Almanac, *began the tradition of American super-heroes which flourishes in modern television cartoons.*

He posed as the enemy of big business yet he himself was a very wealthy man, and much of his money had been made as a lawyer representing large land companies against their tenants. To his voters he was the new style American President – tough, two-fisted and forthright – yet no one was more naturally or more consciously a Southern gentleman. For someone elected on a platform of the equality and rights of man, his policy on Negroes and Indians left a lot to be desired. He worried about slavery only because he knew its extension to new western territories would divide the nation and threaten the union, and it was in his Presidency and with his approval that the process began which removed the highly civilized Cherokee nation under military escort from their lands in Georgia – coveted by some ignorant rednecks, largely Scots-Irish – to the distant lands of Oklahoma.

Yet Jackson was a very great President because he was strong and true to himself. His political style, says David Doyle, 'was carefully crafted by Andrew himself from elements in his own career. He appealed to the dignity of plain people on the farms, in the new factories, on the canals and on the city wharves. This appeal reached out not only to the old Scots-Irish but also to the incoming Catholic Irish who linked Andrew Jackson's achievement of the Presidency in 1828 with Daniel O'Connell's achievement of Catholic Emancipation the same year.'

In the 1820s American settlers were moving in ever-increasing numbers across the Sabine River in the east and the Red River in the north, into the Spanish-owned territory of Texas. After Mexico became independent of Spain, Texas was incorporated into the Mexican republic and was officially opened up to American colonists. However, by 1830, tension between the settlers and the Mexican authorities was growing, and when the megalomaniac General Santa Anna ('If I were God, I'd want more') became dictator of Mexico, the new Texans rose in rebellion. Volunteers from the United States, including Davy Crockett, came south to help the settlers as a large Mexican army under Santa Anna invaded Texas.

Crockett, whose father had fought at King's Mountain, was already an American folk hero. What skeleton of truth there was in his bear-hunting exploits is irrelevant: everything was inflated to the grotesque by his immense inventive powers. He had been promoted by the conservative Whig Party as an answer to the frontier image of Andrew Jackson; he was elected to Congress and there was even talk of him as a presidential candidate. But, despite a vocabulary poetic in its range and a ready rustic wit, he offered no serious challenge to Jackson, and in 1835 a determined effort by his Jacksonian opponents put him out of Congress. Aged forty-nine and deeply disappointed, he told his political supporters, as his plaque in Madison County courthouse, Tennessee, records, 'You can go to hell. I am going to Texas.'

Davy Crockett's observations as a naturalist ('a bear is jest nothin' but a big tail-less dog') should hardly have inspired confidence in his judgement, but he found a group of Tennessee volunteers prepared to follow him south to the former Franciscan monastery

At New Orleans Andrew Jackson defeated the British troops who had beaten Napoleon. His crushing victory on 8 January 1815 ended the last invasion of American soil.

ABOVE *'Remember the Alamo' echoed across the battlefield of San Jacinto in Texas as Sam Houston's men destroyed the Mexican invaders in April 1836.* BELOW *The wounded Sam Houston lays down terms to the Mexican dictator General Antonio López de Santa Anna.*

of the Alamo, the strong-point chosen to halt the advance of Santa Anna. Here one hundred and fifty men, including Crockett and his Tennessee company, faced thousands of Mexican soldiers. The outcome was never in doubt. After a two-week siege the Alamo fell and Crockett and the other defenders were massacred. The man who had created epics of the mind finally died in a real one.

A few months before the Alamo Sam Houston, who had begun his career as a junior officer under Jackson in the war against the Creek Indians, and who had been successively a frontier lawyer, a Congressman, an Indian trader and Governor of Tennessee, was appointed commander of the Texan settlers' army. He opposed the romantic lunacy of defending the Alamo, favouring the guerilla tactics which his Scots-Irish kin practised so successfully against the British in the Revolutionary War, but after the tragic event he took swift and devastating revenge. At the battle of San Jacinto he destroyed a Mexican army which outnumbered the settlers two to one and captured Santa Anna himself. Houston immediately sent news of the victory to his friend and mentor President Jackson, and six months later he became President of an independent Texas. In 1845, the year Andrew Jackson died, Samuel Houston achieved his ultimate aim when Texas joined the United States.

While many American Presidents faded from office tarnished and weary men, Andrew Jackson left the White House with his power hardly diminished. He virtually appointed his successor, Martin Van Buren, and he created a dynasty of Scots-Irish Presidents of whom the next two at least were fashioned in his own image. James Knox Polk belonged to an old Scots-Irish family who had been political kingfish in Mecklenberg County, North Carolina for many generations. Jackson nominated him to succeed Van Buren. James Buchanan, who occupied the chief office on the eve of the Civil War, was a 'log cabin' President and the son of an emigrant from County Donegal. Both men were professionals in the Jackson tradition, skilled in the new populist politics. Buchanan, a Pennsylvanian, faced the dilemma of disapproving of slavery in principle while being forced to uphold it under the Constitution and denounce the abolitionists. Before he handed over to Abraham Lincoln, Buchanan knew that American unity so dear to the Old Chief was crumbling.

The slavery question, which divided the United States to the point of civil war, also divided the Scots-Irish; for many of them the institution of slavery was an offence to their Christian principles, while for others slaves were property and property was something which in the New World they were able for the first time to appreciate. Presbyterian congregations argued the case for and against slavery. In the Northern and Middle States the decision was usually heavily in favour of abolition, obdurate pro-slavery members even being expelled from their churches. The leader of the first anti-slavery party and its presidential candidate, James Gillespie Burney, was the son of Ulster immigrants. In the South, in a dangerous and volatile situation, Presbyterians in the Ulster communities spoke out as their principles dictated. Despite the fact that South

Carolina, with its large Scots-Irish population, was at the centre of the storm, and that John Calhoun – with his belief that a state had the right to 'nullify' a federal decision, whether it be about human rights or taxation – was the ablest and most aggressive exponent of the slavery argument, a large section of the Southern Scots-Irish, particularly the Covenanters, proclaimed their belief that the 'using of human beings as property is a heinous sin against God'. Samuel MacCalla, writing from Chester County, South Carolina, in the early 1830s, when the controversy over the nullification rights claimed by South Carolina was growing bitter, spoke of vigilante companies being formed to prevent the state falling out of line with the Christian and liberal policies which should guide the American people. 'If the Nullies don't go back we will fight ... it will be short and bloody.... We have not only the best rifles but the best marksmen in the State ... they can blow the ball of an otter's eye out at his other end.'

The pro-slavers among the Scots-Irish were even more convinced and militant. The high priest and moral philosopher of that viewpoint was a Mississippi cleric, the Rev. James Smylie, and, incredibly from the standpoint of today, the highly educated and eloquent Calhoun linked the continuance of slavery, and its extension to the west coast of the continent, with a Utopian vision of the American future: 'Our fate as a people is bound up with the question. If we yield we will be exterminated; but if we successfully resist, we will be the greatest and most successful people of modern times.'

In the event, most of the anti-slavery settlers in the Carolinas prudently packed their belongings, sold their farms and moved to the developing lands of Indiana, Illinois and Ohio. The movement came at a time when cotton prices were depressed, and so, as in their departure from Ireland, economic as well as religious factors played a part in the 'Cotton and Conscience' migration of the Scots-Irish from the Old South to the new North-West.

These migrants settled at Bloomington, Princeton and Madison in Indiana, Xenia in Ohio and Sparta, Monmouth and Paxton in Illinois, where they were joined by thousands of others who had migrated from the Middle States. They not only formed a powerful pressure group towards the achievement of Emancipation in 1863, but also provided a conscience for the new Republican Party and fighting power for the Union armies.

'Southerners lost the Civil War because they were too Celtic and their opponents too English', is the conclusion of the controversial book on civil war tactics *Attack and Die*, published in 1984 by Grady McWhiney and Perry D. Jamieson. The authors assume for their argument that the Scots-Irish are a largely Celtic people which, considering their name structures and the successive waves of Celtic tribesmen who populated their Scottish homeland, is not an unreasonable viewpoint. The American South, say McWhiney and Jamieson, has always been dominated by Celtic traditions brought in by the Scots-Irish, the Scots, the Welsh and the native Irish, traditions which placed pleasure above work, and set a high value on time spent hunting, drinking and making music. These 'Celtic' immigrants were mainly country dwellers; they lived in extended families or clans, and they had a highly developed sense of personal honour which often led to violence. An English traveller, looking at the South with all the moral arrogance of a Victorian, observed that, 'the slave-holding states appear to stand in about the same relation to the free, as Ireland does to England'. In the South, 'everything appears slovenly, ill-arranged, incomplete; windows do not shut, doors do not fasten; there is a superabundance of hands to do everything and little is thoroughly done.'

In contrast, McWhiney and Jamieson see Northern society as the product of New England puritan values, motivated by a powerful work ethic, its shrewd, careful and disciplined people dedicated to sober living and material success. 'Yankees were cleaner, neater, more orderly and progressive, worked harder and kept the Sabbath better than Southerners.' So the two regions were not only culturally different, they were culturally antagonistic, and the Civil War was, in a sense, the inevitable culmination of such a clash.

The Celts, McWhiney and Jamieson argue, knew only one method of fighting: to stake everything on one reckless charge which, if successful, would sweep the enemy from the field. They quote examples ranging from Celtic battles with the Romans in the third century BC, through the national wars of the Irish, Scots and Welsh to the final desperate assault of Pickett's Confederate brigade at Gettysburg. Even the famous rebel yells which accompanied these headlong attacks are traceable, say the authors, to the traditional war cries of the Celtic tribes. But the losses which accompanied such tactics were colossal, and the South literally bled to death. At Gettysburg, where charge succeeded charge, the Confederates lost 23,000 men in three days. The Yankees, well equipped and organized, and with a temperament suited to defensive fighting, were bound to outlast their brave but mercurial opponents.

A score or so generals and senior officers on either side were of Scots-Irish stock, among them the overrated Union commander-in-chief George B. McClellan, General Irwin McDowell who suffered the first Northern defeat and Ulysses Simpson Grant who brought about the final Confederate surrender; among the Confederates were General Joseph E. Johnston, the great cavalry commander J. E. B. Stuart and the most famous soldier on either side, Thomas Jonathan ('Stonewall') Jackson. Some of these commanders fit well into the cultural moulds of the McWhiney-Jamieson thesis. George B. McClellan was a superb organizer but lacked fire and dash, as 'cautious as a bank clerk', said one critic. 'Jeb' Stuart, on the other hand, was the archetypal romantic leader, smitten with that Southern disease of chivalry which Mark Twain attributed to reading too much Walter Scott. Riding a splendid horse, his grey cloak lined with red, a red flower in his buttonhole and a peacock's feather in his hat, Stuart led magnificent cavalry raids which terrorized the Union armies in the early days of the war. But at Gettysburg he faced, less successfully, his fellow Scots-Irishman David McMurtrie Gregg, a Northern cavalryman experienced in dealing with Indian charges in the Far West.

In the case of 'Stonewall' Jackson there was a great deal of the Northern Puritan in his make-up. Despite his mastery of the surprise attack and the brilliant encircling movement, he lacked the Cavalier touch and was much more a throwback to the Scottish Covenanting armies of the seventeenth century. The men of his Scots-Irish brigade whom he led in the classic Shenandoah Valley campaign were pure Southern stereotypes, reckless, convivial, hard-drinking farm boys. Fittingly, perhaps, the two traditions appear to blend in Ulysses Grant; he combined a remarkable organizational ability, resilience and energy with an almost unlimited capacity for consuming whiskey and believing in luck. When the 'emotional and inveterate gamblers' of the South staked their last throw with the army of north Virginia, he was an understanding and generous victor.

When Abraham Lincoln was assassinated in 1865, a week after the Confederate surrender, his Scots-Irish Vice-President, Andrew Johnson, succeeded him. The grandson of a County Antrim farm labourer, Johnson was the only President who really belonged to the great anonymous bulk of poor Ulster immigrants. He had no schooling and was taught to read by his wife while he worked as a tailor in a Tennessee mountain town. Despite his Southern background, he opposed the Confederacy and for that reason was chosen as running mate to Lincoln. Johnson's term of office ended sadly; he was impeached by a hostile Congress and acquitted by only one vote.

General Grant, who came from County Tyrone and New England Puritan stock, succeeded Johnson in 1869, but as President he displayed little of the energy which had made him the most successful Union commander. An honest, if lazy, man he was unfortunately to be saddled with one of the most corrupt administrations ever to hold power in Washington. After his Presidency Grant toured Ireland where, with a candour refreshing in a politician, he insulted Protestant and Catholic alike.

The Scots-Irish Presidents and politicians after the Civil War came largely from the North, the offspring of the migration from Pennsylvania westward and northward of the Ohio River to the states of Ohio and Indiana. Many of them were veterans of the Union armies, and most joined the Republican Party from a typical Scots-Irish mixture of moral principles and sharp business acumen. The Republican Party was by now the party of respectability, of the evangelical and upwardly mobile classes; the Democrats drawing much of their support from the underprivileged, and particularly from the newly arrived Catholic Irish immigrants.

Chester Arthur, son of a County Antrim man, was the next Scots-Irish President after Grant, succeeding the assassinated President Garfield in 1881. He came to the White House with an unsavoury reputation, but despite his 'champagne and whiskey' regime, which shocked his pious Baptist supporters, Arthur was a surprisingly honest chief executive. His successor, Grover Cleveland, was also of Scots-Irish stock and while nominally a Democrat he was committed to big business and to maintaining the Gold Standard, something which was to become a presidential issue ten years on. Sandwiched in between Cleveland's two terms of office was another Scots-Irishman, Benjamin Harrison, great-grandson of a signatory of the Declaration of Independence and the shyest man ever to occupy the White House.

Many of the Civil War generals and officers on both sides came from Scots-Irish stock. 'Stonewall' Jackson (ABOVE), *outstanding Confederate general and Presbyterian deacon, was austere and godly. Calvinist plainness was also a marked characteristic of Ulysses S. Grant* (RIGHT), *the most successful of the Union commanders.*

PREVIOUS PAGE *Charleston, South Carolina, in the Civil War: thousands of Scots-Irish fought in both Union and Confederate armies.*

The twenty-fifth President, William McKinley, whose great-grandfather emigrated from County Antrim in 1743, provides a good illustration of how the radical pioneering families of the eighteenth century had changed by the latter part of the nineteenth. McKinley has always been portrayed as the puppet of the businessmen, particularly of the Ohio tycoon Mark Hanna: 'No more backbone', said Theodore Roosevelt, 'than a chocolate eclair.' He was certainly one of the first exponents of baby-kissing politics and 'heart and home' sentimentality as a substitute for policy but there was more to McKinley, the man, than a 'bronze statue looking for its pedestal'. It is to him that the United States owed its first major overseas possessions, Puerto Rico and the Phillipines, what he described as 'an empire of God's righteousness'.

In the terms of his Scots-Irish heritage, the campaign of 1896 which brought McKinley to the White House was a reversal of roles. This Methodist from Ohio represented the power and privilege which his Presbyterian ancestors abhorred, while his populist opponent, William Jennings Bryan, descendant of native Irish kings, spoke for the small farmers, the drovers and independent-minded pioneers of the West. Bryan barnstormed his way across the States, using such slogans as, 'You shall not crucify mankind upon a cross of gold', which sounded uncommonly like Scots-Irish shibboleths from raging radical days. Only the mass machinery of the Republican Party deprived Bryan of victory.

From the mid-nineteenth century many Scots-Irish were motivated in their political choices by the fear of being identified with the poor, ill-educated Catholic Irish who poured into the eastern seaboard cities in their millions after the Irish Famine. For the same reason the name 'Scots-Irish' was revived and promoted to a degree of absurdity, matched only by the cult of native Irishism which began some decades later. Celtic characteristics in the group were played down and Anglo-Saxon traits were stressed. Forgotten were the days when revolutionary Presbyterians in Philadelphia were proud to be called Sons of St Patrick and Andrew Jackson offered the hand of friendship to all Irishmen and women of whatever faith or cultural allegiance.

What was responsible for the change of heart? Victorian values imported from England, with their emphasis on cleanliness and godliness, on education and self-improvement played an important part. The historian Denis Clark sees the Scots-Irish of this period as the intermediaries between the rich industrial bosses and the turbulent working classes. Respectability was the distinguishing badge of these clerks and managers, and that respectability often came from attending the right church, Presbyterian rather than Pentecostal and certainly not Roman Catholic, and from being schooled, even self-schooled, to the right standard. William Holmes McGuffey, the grandson of an Ulster immigrant who grew up in a log cabin in Ohio and who, as a boy, demonstrated both his piety and the sponge-like quality of his intellect by learning the Bible by heart, was 'the schoolmaster to Victorian America'. His *Eclectic Readers*, which he wrote for elementary school children, sold 122,000,000 copies and had an incalculable effect on the hearts and minds of the white Anglo-Saxon Protestant population.

It would be tempting to ascribe the 'Know Nothing' movement of the 1850s to the

WASP aspect of Scots-Irish culture, but the underlying causes were less transient and more sinister. The movement took its name from the password, 'I know nothing', used by members of a secret society, the Order of the Star-Spangled Banner, around which the movement grew. It was anti-immigrant and anti-Catholic, attacking Irish in the Atlantic seaboard cities and Germans in the Middle West. The obvious causes were the sectarian tensions created by Protestant evangelical preachers who used the violent anti-Papal imagery of the seventeenth-century reformers; the confrontational bog Catholicism of the Irish hierarchy (who disliked the liberal intellectualism of their German co-religionists even more than the emotionalism of Protestants); the threat of jobs going to cheap immigrant labour and the very appearance of the ragged disease-ridden immigrants themselves.

In the summer of 1844 sectarian violence, which had grumbled for decades in the growing cities, flared up in Philadelphia into large-scale anti-Catholic riots leaving thirty dead, several Catholic churches burned and thousands of Catholics homeless. By 1855 the 'Know Nothings' had taken control of Massachusetts and most of New England. Polling heavily in the Southern states, in Pennsylvania and New York, they became for a brief time a major force in United States politics. Their official name, 'The American Party', gives a strong clue to the real nature of the movement and the violence which attended it. This was a sudden assertion of tribal panic, that protective mechanism which emerges from time to time from the collective subconscious of a race, like the instinct of sheep to bolt, and which is usually called 'nationalism'. The anguish of its victims, Irish or German, was not lessened by the fact that the same disease was taking root in their own homelands.

The old Scots-Irish tradition was briefly revived in the person of Thomas Woodrow Wilson, twenty-eighth President. His lineage was impeccable. His grandfather, James Wilson, a printer, had emigrated in 1807 from Londonderry to Philadelphia, where he worked on the Jeffersonian newspaper *Amora*; his father, Joseph Ruggles Wilson, was a Presbyterian minister, and Woodrow himself was born in the Presbyterian manse at Staunton in the Valley of Virginia, surrounded by the farms and homes created by eighteenth-century settlers from Ulster. His mother, Janet Woodrow, came from a line of Scottish Presbyterian ministers; an ancestor, Patrick Woodrow, was a Catholic priest who accepted the new disciplines at the time of the Scottish Reformation. Wilson, himself, was conscious of a duality in his genetic make-up. Arthur S. Link, in his article 'Woodrow Wilson and His Presbyterian Inheritance', says, 'To his Scottish ancestors he attributed his introspection, seriousness and tendency towards melancholy. To his Irish forebears he attributed his occasional gaiety and love of life.'

The loving and nurturing nature of the Wilson family home gave the young Woodrow an optimistic view of life which he never lost, even in the dark disappointments of 1919. He was taught at home until he was eleven and developed a close relationship with his father, from whom he derived a powerful Calvinistic sense of mission. The Rev. Joseph

ABOVE *President Woodrow Wilson rides triumphantly through Paris with the French President during the Paris Peace Conference following the First World War.*

LEFT *James Buchanan, Scots-Irish on both sides of his family, was the fifteenth President of the USA.*

Ruggles Wilson was imbued with that Old Testament view of Christianity which distinguished the early Presbyterian divines, but his sternness was tempered with great humanity. Woodrow's high moral tone, which was combined with care and affection for the losers in life, for the oppressed and the victims of injustice, reflected his father's interpretation of Calvinist morality. In later life the scholar-politician recognized the sources deep in history from which his spiritual strength came: 'The stern Covenanter tradition that is behind me sends many an echo down the years.'

Woodrow Wilson was a brilliant political theorist and teacher. In 1902 he became president of Princeton College, where he set in motion a programme of radical reform which, despite heated opposition, broke the snobbery and club-domination which had dragged Princeton down as a centre of learning. In politics he was a Democrat and his success at Princeton led to him being offered the Democratic nomination as Governor of New Jersey. The party bosses recognized they had an awkward customer on their hands when he began, after election, to fulfil his campaign promises. In 1912 Wilson, as presidential candidate, was given the job of unifying the Democratic Party, which, despite the idealism of Bryan's campaign against McKinley, was really controlled by such unsavoury elements as the Irish Catholic ward bosses in the eastern cities, corrupt beyond belief, and the muck-raking press baron William Randolph Hearst. Wilson, incapable of compromising his integrity to the slightest degree, refused the help of Hearst's yellow press and denounced Tammany Hall, that symbol of Democratic corruption in New York. Despite this, his victory at the poll was, in the terms of the electoral college, the greatest until then.

As President, Woodrow Wilson applied moral principles to the business of governing the country. It was the duty of Christians not only to look after their own souls but to obtain social justice for their fellow men. 'Christianity', he said, 'came into the world to save the world as well as to save individual men.' In a land of hard-nosed capitalism he brought in a series of measures to benefit workers, he legalized strikes, sponsored a child labour law and one on workmen's compensation. Although the question of America's participation in the Great War was the major issue of the 1916 presidential election, Wilson's platform was one of social reform, a vision of a new and more equitable society.

When the World War broke out in 1914 it was Wilson's policy to keep America out of the European quarrel, but as German submarines sank American merchant ships carrying food to Britain he began to see United States participation as inevitable; German militarism threatened the principles set forth on another battlefield fifty-four years earlier, 'government of the people, by the people, for the people'. He prepared American public opinion for war using his favourite speech writer, the prophet Isaiah – 'If the watchman see the sword come and blow not the trumpet ...' – and in April 1917, with great personal sadness, he declared war on Germany. America's role, as he saw it, was 'to make the world safe for democracy'.

The decisive role which American troops played in ending the conflict made the President the most powerful man in history, greater than Alexander or Augustus Caesar.

But in Wilson emerged a new, generous type of conqueror, more interested in the problems of the conquered than in the booty of war. His Fourteen Points for peace, including arms reduction, open diplomacy and liberalization of trade, offered the chance of a brave new world, a brotherhood of nations, and when he came to the Paris Peace Conference he seemed like a saviour, inspiring hope and trust in the obscure peoples of Central Europe and the Balkans who had suffered so terribly, not only in the war but in the centuries of tyranny which had preceded it.

For all that he was steeped in their tradition, Wilson forgot what his Scots-Irish forefathers knew only too well, that the men who ruled Britain and Europe were locked into an ancient system of oppression, were hidebound by the tradition of power politics, and were greedy and chauvinistic. To Lloyd George of Britain, Clemenceau of France and Orlando of Italy, Wilson was that inexplicable phenomenon, an honest politician. Clemenceau complained, 'Fourteen Points! God Almighty had only ten commandments'; the cynical old French blasphemer was quite unable to recognize goodness in a fellow statesman.

The American leader was forced to compromise. He found himself at a conference dominated by shabby secret deals, by nationalistic avarice cloaked in fine phrases, and his high-minded idealism was an anachronism. When he returned home his plan for a League of Nations was rejected in his own land. The Ulster immigrant's grandson had returned to the Old World to remake it according to Christian principles, which his people had believed in but seldom lived up to. His failure was the ultimate failure of the Scots-Irish vision.

9 • MOUNTAIN MEN AND MILLIONAIRES

'The half-civilized, half savage pioneers who roamed the West in search of beaver ... were the supreme examples of the destructive impact of the wilderness on inherited traits and institutions.'

R. A. Billington

'Without prudent children or others to guard it, it is a natural consequence that a man's wealth will begin to waste away with his mental and physical energies.'

Thomas Mellon

IN 1825 THOMAS HART BENSON of Missouri (who once exchanged shots with Andrew Jackson in Nashville), worried about the perennial debate on American expansionism, spoke of 'the Rocky Mountains ... a convenient, natural and everlasting boundary'. While the vertebral mountain range was not destined to be the national boundary, it did provide for the Scots-Irish their final frontier. Reports of vast beaver populations in the streams of the Rockies, combined with a rapidly expanding market for furs in the cities of the East, drew, from the 1820s to the 1840s, an assortment of trappers and traders, impecunious gentlemen and social misfits to the area which was to become the states of Colorado, Utah, Idaho and Montana. Among this new breed of Mountain Men were French Canadians, Mexicans, Germans and English, but once again, as in Appalachia but to a much lesser extent, the Scots-Irish, along with Scots and native Irish, dominated.

Kit Carson, the most famous of them, was the grandson of William Carson, an Ulsterman who had moved south from Pennsylvania along the Great Valley route to North Carolina. Kit was born in Missouri, and at the age of sixteen he ran away from an apprenticeship in the saddlery trade to join an early expedition along the Santa Fé trail. He became in turn a trapper, a scout, an Indian agent and the commander of a brigade in the Civil War. Soft-spoken, abstemious and gentlemanly, he was in total contrast to his fellow Mountain Men. Less well known was Kit's elder brother Moses, a formidable, six-foot hunter, 'with one good eye and a few fingers', who survived the terrible mountain life to a retirement in California, where one of his favourite anecdotes was how he won a lawsuit by temporarily turning Catholic. Another descendant of Ulster migrants who came down the Great Valley wagon trail was Hugh Glenn: he was to be remembered for his epic fight with a wounded white grizzly. Some, too, were fugitives

The Rockies offered a new life style to the pioneers, abundant game for food and a chance to make a fortune in the fur trade.

from justice, like Bill Craig who fled his native Greenbriar County, now in West Virginia, after killing a man. Among the Catholic Irish pioneers in the Rockies, Tom Fitzpatrick from County Cavan stood out as a fearless explorer and a great leader of men.

John Colter, one of the earliest of the Mountain Men, came from the tight-knit Scots-Irish community of the Shenandoah Valley; the location of the Colter family farm is still identifiable in Augusta County. Colter joined the expedition of Captain Meriwether Lewis and the Scots-Irishman William Clark, which President Jefferson sent in 1803 to explore the upper reaches of the Missouri River and, at the end of his tour of duty two years later, he decided to remain in the mountains to trap beaver. In 1807 Colter began his great journey, which took him – alone and on foot – across the then unexplored Grand Teton and Yellowstone regions. He was the first white man to see the famous natural wonders of the hydrothermal region which are major tourist attractions today: the great geyser Old Faithful, with its regular patterns of short and long eruptions; the magnificent Yellowstone Falls; the deep lion-coloured canyon; the boiling springs on the edge of the Yellowstone Lake; the Two-Ocean Pass, where a stream from the snow peaks divides in two – one branch going east to the Atlantic, the other west to the Pacific – and where trout can swim across the mountain range.

Colter's trek in the autumn and winter of 1808–9 across heavily wooded, broken country, often at heights above nine thousand feet, without maps and carrying a pack of thirty pounds weight as well as a gun and ammunition, was an incredible feat of endurance. There was the constant danger of encountering grizzlies capable of tearing a man open with a single blow of their claws. In the intense cold of the mountain nights Colter often slept in the open, while the branches of the trees cracked like pistols in the frost and the Northern Lights moved in crimson curtains overhead. After sundown wolves replaced grizzlies as the prime danger; a later Mountain Man, Osborne Russell, awoke to find his fire had gone out and he and his horse surrounded by a circle of glaring wolves' eyes. Game was plentiful but spasmodic in its occurrence. Colter, like later travellers, must at times have been reduced to eating thistle roots and berries. Probably, he too was prodigal of the endless meat supply, killing an elk or bison and taking only a few of the choicest cuts. Local Indians were unpredictable, varying between extreme and often embarrassing hospitality and a hostility from which the best a captive could hope for was a quick and merciful death.

As he moved across the Yellowstone Colter, with the strong visual memory of the solitary man, absorbed the wonders around him, the tar springs, the mud geysers, the warm waters where breeding algae and bacteria create prismatic patterns, what he called the 'Hot Springs Brimstone' but is now the world-renowned Mammoth Hot Springs, and the sulphurous North Fork of the Shoshone River to which, with Scots-Irish bluntness, he gave the name of 'Stinking River'. But when he returned to St Louis, Missouri, the headquarters for trapping expeditions, he was written off as a liar and a fantasist, another of the Irish breed of tall tale tellers. His former leader, William Clark, took Colter's story more seriously and incorporated his information in the Lewis and

ABOVE *Fort Laramie, built by Ulsterman Robert Campbell on the Oregon Trail, was a rendezvous point and refuge for trappers.*

LEFT BELOW *The Lewis and Clark expedition to the headwaters of the Missouri in 1803 brought the explorer John Colter to the West.*

LEFT ABOVE *Colter kills the leading Indian in his epic race for life.*

Clark map of 1814. The region of the tar springs on the Shoshone River was given the name of 'Colter's Hell'.

To the trappers who followed him into the area, Colter's famous 'race for life' was much more impressive than his exploration of Teton and Yellowstone. During his epic walk Colter had become friendly with the Crow tribe of Indians, and he helped them in a battle with their traditional enemies, the Blackfeet; the prestige and firepower of even a single white man was prized in these tribal conflicts. In the spring of 1808 he and another trapper called Potts were canoeing along the Jefferson River in search of early beaver when, coming round a bend, they found themselves at the edge of a large camp of Blackfeet. The Indians ordered them ashore and for the white men there was no choice but to obey. At that point Potts lost his nerve and fired on the Indians, killing one. He was immediately cut to pieces and his entrails were thrown in Colter's face. Colter now expected a slow and terrible death. Instead he was told to strip naked and run. He obeyed, and when he saw a group of young braves set out in pursuit he knew that his scalp was the prize.

Against all odds, running across a plain covered with sage and cactus, the explorer out-distanced all but one of his pursuers. Halfway to the comparative safety of a cottonwood forest on a loop of the Jefferson, Colter, virtually worn out, saw an Indian with an upraised spear closing in on him. The brave, equally exhausted, charged, but Colter caught the spear, threw the Indian to the ground and killed him with his own weapon. Reaching the Jefferson, Colter hid in the stream under some driftwood until nightfall, with only his mouth and nose above water.

Hiram Chittenden, nineteenth-century historian of Yellowstone, described the end of Colter's race for life: 'For seven days he wandered naked and unarmed; over stones, cacti and the prickly pear, scorched by the heat of noon and chilled by the frost of night, finding his sole subsistence in such roots as he might dig, until at last he reached Lisa's trading post on the Bighorn River.'

Professor Ray Billington, doyen of historians of the American West, speaks of 'a reversion to the primitive' among the trappers who flocked into the mountains in the post-Colter period. These 'half-civilized, half savage pioneers ... were the supreme examples of the destructive impact of the wilderness on inherited traits and institutions'. Similar reversions, though to a lesser degree, had taken place among the Scots-Irish at Paxtang in Pennsylvania and Waxhaw in South Carolina. Billington quotes the example of 'Big Phil' Gardner, so called because he came from Philadelphia, who not only killed and ate an Indian fellow trapper during a hunting trip but, having been cut off in the high mountains by early snowstorms, lived comfortably through the winter by consuming his Indian wife.

Only a few of the Mountain Men were cannibals and for the majority there were less *outré* culinary delights. After weeks of beaver hunting on lean rations, trappers like Bill Craig and Moses Carson would let themselves go in a gargantuan feast. Osborne Russell describes an occasion when the assembled hunters sat around the camp fire as a butchered elk impaled on wedges of timber cooked over the flames. Buffalo ranked higher than deer meat in the trappers' preferences and was second only to the 'honey-fed' flesh of the black bear. Dinner at sundown usually began with drinking warm buffalo blood, followed by the roasted intestines of the animal which were sucked sizzling down the throat like spaghetti. The main course was the prime rib and rump steaks. 'A son of Erin . . . sat opposite with an Elk rib in one hand and a butcher knife in the other . . . sweat rolling from his face mingled with the channels of grease which ran from the corners of his mouth.'

Many of the Mountain Men were deeply religious; a high valley among the snow-capped Tetons would sometimes ring with two or three hunters singing rhymed psalms remembered from a church-going youth in Kentucky or Ohio. The literate sought comfort from loneliness and the constant presence of death in these dangerous lands by reading aloud to themselves from their Bibles. To men brought up on hell-fire preaching this area of awe-inspiring scenery, where the earth was almost as active as the wildlife, was a place where the natural and supernatural met; the geysers emerging from underground at temperatures of several hundred degrees were 'the breathing places of his Satanic Majesty'.

Their inbred Calvinism did not, however, deter the mountain pioneers from heavy drinking and indiscriminate, bizarre sexual encounters with Indian women. Nor did it make them any less ferocious in battle. They were always heavily armed with rifle, revolver and tomahawk, and they killed Indian braves with as little compunction as had earlier generations of Scots-Irish on the Appalachian frontier. The Indians, said one trapper, 'gotta larn t'respect decent Christians'.

Not all the Scots-Irish in the Rockies were primeval men living in the nineteenth century. Robert Campbell, born in 1804, who belonged to respectable farming stock, claimed descent from Scottish noblemen and he never forgot that fact. He went to America in 1824, like many young men of his class, hoping to make a fortune. He had contracted tuberculosis, the great killer disease of damp Ulster, and he was advised to look for a cure in the high altitudes of the Teton mountains. There he joined Tom Fitzpatrick and Jim Bridger in a trapping expedition and took part in the battle of Pierre's Hole, when the trappers defeated raiding Blackfeet. He stayed in the trapping business until 1835, organizing and leading groups of hired trappers, and formed a company to trade in furs with W. L. Sublette, the great trapper-cum-entrepreneur.

In the late 1830s Campbell, now settled in St Louis, went into real estate and then into banking. He became an important figure in the West, served as an Indian commissioner and built Fort Laramie. When he died in 1879 he was a millionaire, a fact which, when the last of his sons died without an heir in the 1930s, set afoot the greatest genealogical search Ulster has ever seen. In an effort to establish kinship with the Campbell fortune hardly a tombstone in west Ulster was left unturned.

With the ruthless exploitation of the beaver, the supply of furs began to dry up in the 1840s. At the same time a change in fashions brought a fall in the demand for skins. The

THE TESTING OF THE FIRST REAPING MACHINE NEAR STEELE'S TAVERN, VA. A.D. 1831.

The first mechanical reaper invented by Cyrus McCormick was tried out near Steele's Tavern in the Shenandoah Valley.

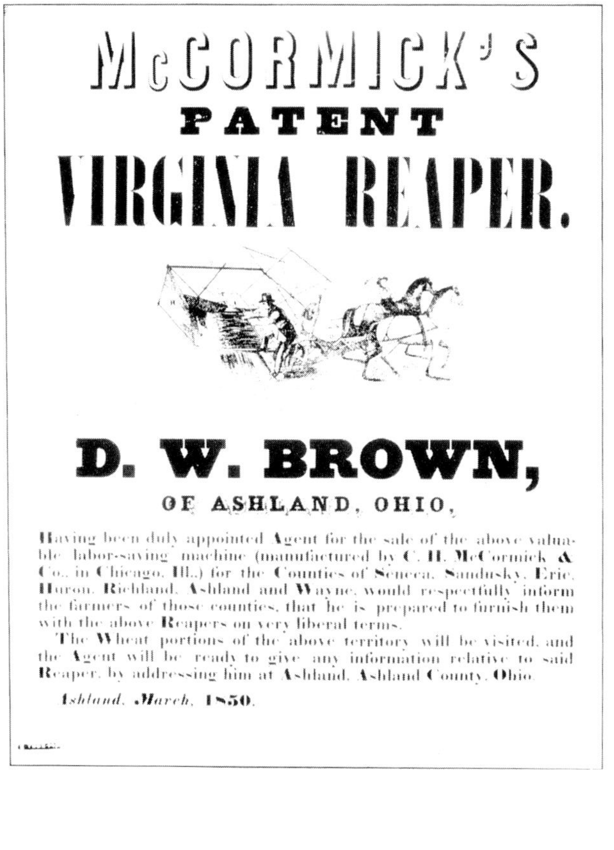

era of the Mountain Men and the Fur Frontier came to an end. A few, like Campbell, had made a fortune but the majority of the trappers died in poverty in St Louis or other growing towns of the West. The more fortunate stayed in the mountains and became indistinguishable from the Indians among whom they lived.

The age of the Scots-Irish millionaire arrived with Cyrus McCormick of Steele's Tavern in the Shenandoah. The first McCormick immigrants were Thomas McCormick and his wife Elizabeth who settled in Pennsylvania. The family later moved to Virginia where Robert McCormick, a grandson of Thomas, worked up an idea for a mechanical harvester. The prototype was improved by his son Cyrus, who began to manufacture the reaper at a small settlement on Lake Michigan, later to be the city of Chicago. Cyrus was a superb businessman, using newspaper advertising and manipulating newspaper editorials to promote sales. The glossy McCormick posters, showing the machine driven by a smiling boy and easily pulled by two horses, were years ahead of their time in sales psychology. The very idea of such a labour-saving device appealed to the Calvinist consciences of Northern businessmen and politicians at a time when they were trying to prove that the Great Plains to the west could be successfully exploited without the un-Christian system of slavery. Another McCormick poster, which shows pioneers on a rock looking out over a seemingly endless prairie of grain, was prophetical as well as promotional. The McCormick reaper unlocked the Midwest as the granary of the world.

A more colourful but far less effective inventor than McCormick was Robert Fulton, a man of Renaissance versatility from the Scots-Irish colony of Little Britain in south-eastern Pennsylvania. Fulton went to post-Revolutionary France and built a submarine for Napoleon, but when it failed to sink ships, he switched sides and launched torpedo attacks on the French Fleet for the British. However, the Admiralty in London preferred the Nelson touch and turned a blind eye on the genius from Pennsylvania. Fulton returned to America and employed himself more usefully building steamboats for the Hudson River.

Alexander Brown could well be chosen as the unknown soldier of that great army of Scots-Irish merchants, manufacturers and bankers who dominated much of America's commercial life in the nineteenth century. He arrived in the first year of the century from Ballymena in County Antrim, reputed to be the sharpest business town in Ireland, and apart from his talent for making money he was entirely undistinguished. Brown set up a fiscal business which spanned the Atlantic, and his firm, Alexander Brown & Sons of Baltimore, is the oldest banking house in the country.

A. T. Stewart, from the Lisburn district south-west of Belfast, was also typical but in a different way. He was the pioneer of the department store, and his famous Marble Store near City Hall in New York was renowned for its harsh working conditions, low wages and rigid Sabbatarian attitudes. The Chicago department store of Carson, Pirie was founded by William Carson from Newry, County Down, who later brought two fellow shopkeepers from Newry, George and Robert Scott into partnership. From

County Armagh came Andrew McNally, founder of the Rand-McNally publishing company.

Two names, Getty and Mellon, dominate by sheer weight of dollars the Scots-Irish business world. The first of the Getty family, James, emigrated from County Londonderry in 1780 and bought the land which was to be the site of the great Civil War battle of Gettysburg. Unlike the Mellons, the Gettys started on a downward path: habitually drunken, John Getty fell off his horse and froze to death. Then the family got on to the evangelical spiral which took them 'out of this mire of ignorance and shame in which my Grand-Father and Father left me on account of the Demon Drink'. In the twentieth century the oil king Paul Getty not only looked like an old Ulster farmer but behaved like one, keeping his women in order with promises about his will. Thomas Mellon, the founding father of America's richest business dynasty, wrote an autobiography, *Thomas Mellon and His Times*, which revealed not only the inner thoughts of a rising tycoon but, in its way, much of the Scots-Irish business soul. Thomas was born on a small farm in the west of County Tyrone in 1813. The name Mellon or Mallon is a common Catholic Irish one and, while Thomas investigated the kingly antecedents of the Irish Mellons, he dissociated his family from them, claiming instead a Scottish Presbyterian ancestry. The Catholic Irish, he wrote, were 'a class largely trained to a vicious disregard of law and order'.

When Thomas was five his family emigrated to western Pennsylvania, where his uncles and grandparents were already settled. There the Mellons farmed in Westmoreland County. It is illustrative of the new attitude among some Scots-Irish that they now, in contrast to a century earlier, looked down on the Pennsylvania Germans, 'who did not come up to the Scots-Irish standard of morality – sexual intercourse and religious observances'. Thomas decided, as did many other Scots-Irish in nineteenth-century America, that the key to riches no longer lay in the possession of land. He became a lawyer in the growing town of Pittsburgh and at the age of forty-six was elected to a judgeship. On the bench he was clearly on the side of the moral majority. Having pronounced the death sentence on 'both males and females', the judge believed there was 'too much time wasted and expense incurred by the public on their behalf'. The growing tendency for criminals to commit suicide should 'not be discouraged'. Judge Mellon had as little taste for Jews as for Irish Catholics. When a lawyer came before him with an application for a charter for a Jewish burial ground, he smiled, 'A place to bury Jews? – with pleasure, with pleasure'. Mellon's position on the bench, hearing suits involving the business secrets of hundreds of litigants, put him in a unique position as an investor. He bought up real estate at the most advantageous prices and soon his investment income far exceeded his judge's salary. For him the fire which destroyed Pittsburgh in 1845 was a blessing: it created a booming real estate market where the pickings were rich for someone who already held mortgages on much of the building land.

Thomas Mellon was a tight-fisted man, his main interest business success, his only

ABOVE *The Mellon building, Pittsburgh. Mellon dominance is still in evidence everywhere in modern Pittsburgh, the city on which the Mellon fortune was founded.*

LEFT *Thomas Mellon from County Tyrone, founding father of America's richest business dynasty.*

pleasure watching his wealth grow. He tried to make his elder sons, T.A. (Thomas Alexander) and J.R. (James Ross) models of his cautious money-grubbing self. He advised them to 'make no friends' and warned them against 'theatre-going, party going and writing letters to girls'. American patriotism, usually high in the Scots-Irish scale of values, meant little to him. When the Civil War came he told them to 'avoid the folly of soldiering'. What worried him most about that terrible conflict was the additional tax he had to pay. J.R. and T.A. took his advice, and grasping the opportunities offered by war became, by their early twenties, two of the richest men in America.

Thomas Mellon made a trip to Ireland in 1882, and when he landed at Cork all his prejudices were confirmed. A cripple 'born footless' arrived to push his luggage on a handcart. 'The cripple was doubtless kept for the purpose', to appeal to his charitable feelings. Among the Catholic Irish he realized there were 'many good, industrious and humane people . . . but these were exceptions to the rule'. Irish nationalism was anathema to him; 'the Irish political agitator and the American labor agitator' were his twin devils. His solution to the Irish problem was appealing in its simplicity – disperse the native Irish as widely as possible over the world, where they would disappear like a bad smell in the fresh air of other cultures. 'Cromwell', he wrote, 'was the only ruler who understood them and governed them accordingly.'

The second generation of Mellons were all wealthy men; the fourth son, Andrew William (A.W.) became, as Secretary of the Treasury, one of the big political figures of the 1920s, the age of President Calvin Coolidge and the high noon of hedonistic materialism in America. Andrew looked like a remote intellectual but he was, in fact, a hard pragmatic monetarist. The only things which disturbed his calm were Congress attempts to tax the rich, the promoters of such measures being little better than the 'bloody bolsheviks' lately come to power in Russia. He favoured easy credit and low interest rates as a means of maintaining a boom economy, and when the Wall Street crash came in 1929 his policies were blamed for the collapse of the market. By this time the Mellon financial empire contained such giants as Gulf Oil and Alcoa (the Aluminium Company of America), and these companies were among the first to cut wages and shut down enterprises, thus deepening the financial slough into which the country had sunk.

Much of the success of the Mellons in their many enterprises, from the Mellon National Bank of Pittsburgh onwards, was due to the way they cooperated as a family, a cooperation which was maintained even after each of the judge's sons had become independent operators with widely differing business interests. However, when the remaining sons, J.R., R.B. (Richard Blair) and A.W., all died during the 1930s the 'Mellon machine' ceased to function as such. Today the family are better known for the foundations and trusts, which give money to a wide variety of causes, artistic, environmental and political. A.W. not only gave the country its National Gallery of Art, with typical modesty refusing to have his name in the gallery's title, but also donated a priceless collection of Old Masters which he had acquired in secret negotiations with the hated Bolshevik Government from the Hermitage Museum in Moscow.

Mellon generosity, like other large-scale benefactions in the USA, was tax deductible and usually cost the family relatively little. The story is told of A.W. that he asked for Raphael's portrait of Giuliano de'Medici to be removed from his drawing room because he did not like the face of the sitter. Perhaps his sensitive soul felt that the Italian merchant prince, munificent in his patronage, was looking down on the Scots-Irish one.

Scots-Irish preachers down the centuries had exhorted their people to seek a city on a hill; instead they founded two cities in valleys. Pittsburgh was the western capital of the Scots-Irish 'empire', just as Belfast was the eastern one. In the mid-nineteenth century there were many similarities between the two, and only a few which reflected much credit on the entrepreneurs responsible for their development.

The natural setting of Pittsburgh, where the Allegheny and Monongahela rivers joined to form the Ohio, and forest-covered hills rose on three sides, was perhaps the most beautiful site for a city anywhere in the world. André Michaux, coming there in 1803, found 'the air very salubrious ... intermittent fevers are unknown'. Fort Pitt, around which the town grew up, had been the key point in the defence of the Middle Colonies from French and later British attacks. The situation also had great commercial advantages.

Trade came in on the Allegheny from northern Pennsylvania and on the Monongahela from northern Virginia and south-western Pennsylvania; the broad Ohio was the waterway to the Mississippi Valley and New Orleans. A seemingly inexhaustible stratum of coal, up to twelve feet thick in the surrounding hills, was the basis for large-scale heavy industry. In 1815 *Niles Weekly Register* believed that Pittsburgh was going to be the 'greatest manufacturing town in the world'. A year later the former frontier post became a city. Pittsburgh coal, the inhabitants boasted, was only handled twice. It was shovelled into a railcar at the coalface, run out of the mine and down the hill to the foundry, where it was dumped at the door of the furnace. The Scots-Irish firm of Jones and Laughlin, with their vast American Iron Works, dominated the city industry, and by the late 1860s were producing nearly half of America's iron.

'The masters of Pittsburgh are mostly of the Scotch-Irish race ...', wrote James Parton in 1866, 'and the great firms are usually composed of near relatives ... the visitor generally finds the old man bustling about the works ... his eldest son is keeping the books, a son-in-law or nephew is making up the wages accounts, and a younger son is in the warehouse'. Everybody worked hard in Pittsburgh, the employers and their sons impelled by a relentless Presbyterian work ethic, the employees because that was the only way to survive in the harsh working conditions of the time. The French traveller Michel Chevalier observed: 'There is no interruption of business for six days a week except for three meals, the longest of which hardly occupies ten minutes.' On Sundays, however, everything that could possibly stop came to a standstill.

Living conditions in the city by the mid century were appalling. Bituminous smoke from hundreds of factory chimneys was trapped in the triangle between the rivers. A point was reached when it was necessary to keep the street lighting on all day. James

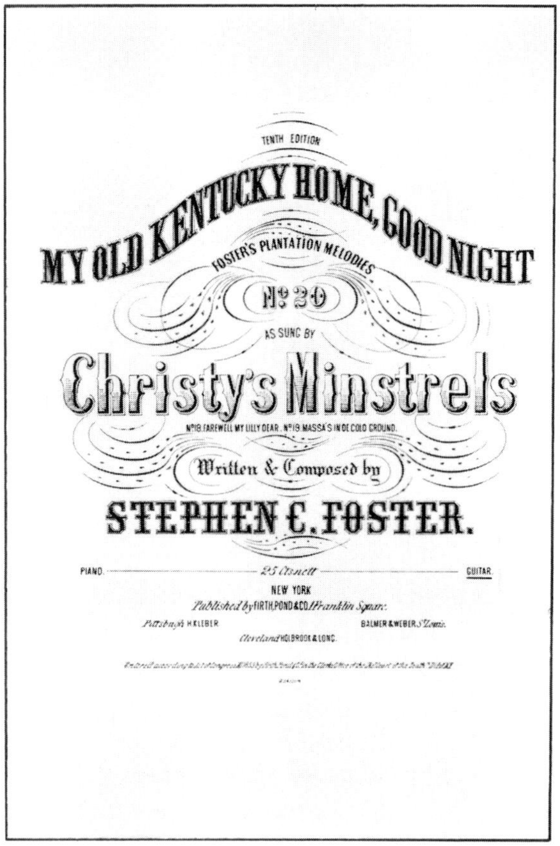

Stephen Foster, descendant of a County Londonderry immigrant, was America's best loved lyric writer.

Parton describes looking down on the city from Washington Heights: 'the entire space lying between the hills was filled with the blackest smoke, from out of which the hidden chimneys sent forth tongues of flame, while from the depth of the abyss came up the noise of hundreds of steam hammers . . . hell with the lid taken off.'

If the early Mellons owed much to Pittsburgh, the city in the twentieth century owes much to the Mellons. Richard King Mellon, son of R.B., was the driving force behind the great effort to clean up and rejuvenate the city after the Second World War. Working largely behind the scenes, R.K. used his influence to push through anti-pollution legislation and induce Mellon-controlled companies to take part in the redevelopment programme which had produced the Golden Triangle of business skyscrapers at the junction of the rivers. Mellon money helped to build and maintain the University of Pittsburgh, the remarkable Cathedral of Learning, and what was the Mellon Research Institute has now become the city's second university, the Carnegie-Mellon. The Richard King Mellon Foundation, one of the largest in the United States, directs much of its funds towards Pittsburgh projects.

The second generation of Mellons sought relief from the smoke and grime of Pittsburgh in the healthy air of the Westmoreland County hills. J.R. built an Alpine-style castle with an extensive pleasure ground around it and R.B. bought up 1,800 acres of beautiful countryside at Ligonier from which he created the Rolling Rock Country Club, one of the most exclusive in America. Behind the high walls are golf courses, swimming pools, ski slopes, trout streams, a route for an English-style fox hunt and some of the finest stables in the country. As one cynic put it, 'The Mellons fixed up Rolling Rock the way God would have if He'd had the money'.

Emigration from Ulster resumed immediately after the American Revolution and it quickly reached record levels, 10,000 coming in 1783 alone. The Napoleonic Wars again slowed down the transatlantic traffic, but the agricultural slump which followed the Battle of Waterloo sent numbers up again, until by 1832 65,000 people a year were leaving Ireland for America. The Ulster immigrants in the post-Revolutionary period were mainly small farmers and skilled artisans, while labourers made up the bulk of those from the rest of Ireland. In 1832 *The Londonderry Journal* reported: 'Most of those who have sailed from this port are, as usual, small farmers . . . in decent circumstances and of the Protestant religion.' The Ordnance Survey two years later examined the religious make-up of two thousand emigrants from Londonderry County and found that 60 per cent were Presbyterian, 30 per cent Catholic and 10 per cent Church of Ireland.

But even the indentured servants from the North of Ireland were no longer humble chattels. The *Belfast Newsletter* of 28 October 1783 has a report of male servants who, 'not contented with . . . plenty of good provisions and a daily portion of grog, insisted on having access to the women, which being refused them, they broke in the bulk head that separated the females from them. A mutinous riot ensued. . . .' It was these emigrants, somewhat better off than their predecessors, and even more adventurous and independent-minded, who swelled the great internal migrations sweeping across the Mississippi basin in the South and into the North-West territories beyond Ohio, and twenty years later crossing what was then mapped as the 'Great American Desert', but was soon to become the cattle range country of Kansas, Nebraska and the Dakotas.

These great 'prairie schooner movements' created isolated settlements of Ulster Scots from Texas to Oregon, but in the mainstream the Ulster people were fused with an ever-increasing number of other ethnic groups. They traded on the Santa Fe Trail, they reached the Sod Frontier of Kansas (the great ballad of those range war times 'The Old Sod Shanty' was based on an Irish song), they penetrated to the California goldfields, but their contribution to Scots-Irish history was mainly the folk culture, music and religious and political opinions which they scattered across the receptive soil of the continent.

In assessing the musical contribution of the Scots-Irish to American culture one immediately comes up against the enigma of Stephen Collins Foster, author of 'Jeanie with the Light Brown Hair', 'Beautiful Dreamer', 'My Old Kentucky Home' and dozens of other immensely popular lyrics. Foster was born in 1826, exactly one hundred years after his great-grandfather arrived in Pennsylvania from Londonderry. In the intervening generations the Foster family lived in Scots-Irish communities and intermarried with other Scots-Irish families so that Stephen was as purely American Scots-Irish as anyone of his time. Despite this, there is no trace in his work of the influence of the virile balladry and folk music which his people brought to the New World. Where the Scots-Irish ballads like 'The Dark-Eyed Gypsy', 'The Two Brothers' and 'Our Goodman' are robust, often brutal and full of sexual humour, Foster's songs are gentle, sentimental and without a word to offend the most prudish ear, frequently only redeemed from bathos by his genius. He failed to draw on those rich resources at hand and turned instead to another ethnic group, the Negro slaves of the Southern plantations, for his material.

Foster's life was short and tragic. His marriage to 'Jeanie' (Jane McDowell) was not a happy one. He suffered continual ill-health and he had a massive alcohol problem. His death at the age of thirty-eight took place in New York, after he had been found with a gashed throat in a Bowery doss house. Looked at in the unsympathetic light of the twentieth century, his work would appear to have little positive to say on the subject of slavery but, despite this, its contribution to the Abolitionist Movement was considerable. Dean Root, a modern expert on Foster, says, 'He wrote songs which did as much in that medium as Abraham Lincoln did in politics or Harriet Beecher Stowe in novels and drama to create the ground swell of public opinion and the volition to do away with slavery'.

In 1915 Cecil Sharp, the English folksong collector, travelled through the Appalachian Mountains and came away with what he thought was a collection of transplanted English ballads. It was, in fact, a group of lyrics and narrative poems, most of which had come from Scotland by way of Ulster. Many of these were dark stories of fratricide, adultery

ABOVE *For the wagon trains crossing the Great Plains, the Rocky Mountains presented a final frontier where life reverted to the primitive.*

OVERLEAF *Yellowstone River painted by Thomas Moran. Even the crude and hard-drinking trappers were awed by the 'wild romantic splendor' of Yellowstone Falls. The Indians, on the other hand, regarded Yellowstone as an 'abode of evil spirits'.*

MORAN.
1893

ABOVE *The Scots-Irish 'capital', Pittsburgh, where God and Mammon coexisted successfully.*

LEFT *In the city's steel industry a powerful work ethic inspired Presbyterian masters and workers alike.*

and the supernatural originating in the Scottish Borders; a few were light-hearted with a dancing rhythm like 'Cripple Creek Girl'. They had the Scots-Irish trait of being anti-establishment: the high-born lady leaves her lord to live with the gypsies, the demon lover successfully challenges the sanctity of marriage, and that conventional figure of fun, the old and well-to-do peasant with the young wife, is cuckolded to the amusement of the community. It is hard to imagine how a skilled song collector could have mistaken for the products of an ordered rural society like that of southern England, the stark and bloodthirsty epics of the lawless Scottish hills.

The Scots-Irish strain is recognizable in the output of the modern music industry centred in the Great Smokies and eastern Tennessee. The narrative ballads are the raw ancestors of the saccharine story-songs of the country and western cult; the mountain music that was the direct forebear of bluegrass. Much traditional music, however, remains unchanged in the hands of expert performers like the Queen family of Jackson County, North Carolina. The Ulster fiddle was the main instrument of the eighteenth century, supplemented occasionally by the plucked dulcimer borrowed from the German settlers. The Negro banjo reached the mountains as the instrument of the travelling minstrel groups which sang the songs of Stephen Foster. The arrival of the guitar at the beginning of the nineteenth century sophisticated the music of the mountains, and the modern folk band was born. Mouth music, to which the early settlers danced their jigs and reels when no instruments were available, can still be heard, and buck dancing, another import from Scotland with a touch of the traditional Irish dancing gait, is performed not only at competitive folk festivals but also for private enjoyment. Much indeed of what is heard and seen in Appalachia today would be recognizable to an eighteenth-century immigrant.

Folksong was carried westward, and where the migrants from the Allegheny and Ohio regions met those from the Carolinas and Tennessee there was a blending of styles. A new and equally isolated folk culture arose in places like the Ozark Mountains of southern Louisiana. A tone of wry disillusionment, which is particularly American, came in with ballads like 'The State of Arkansas', the story of Charlie Brennan from Charleston who 'never knew what misery was till I came to Arkansas'. Although the old Scots-Irish songs like 'Barbara Allen' survived, the subject matter now became specifically American. The settlers' passage through the mountains into Kentucky is celebrated in the lively 'Cumberland Gap'. Religion too created its music; the white spirituals of the Southern uplands, like the revivalist hymn 'Am I Born to Die?', come from the little 'timber church' congregations of Scots-Irish Baptists.

The Scots-Irish of America were also fascinated by the spoken word. Jan Davidson, a leading folklorist in the Great Smokies, points out that there are two parts to this oral tradition: 'There is a strong tradition of telling the truth and a strong tradition of telling lies and both are equally important.' Telling the truth is the natural behaviour of Bible-ingrained Calvinists, no matter how much they may diverge from it in practice. The most obvious examples of the art of lying are the 'Jack tales', orally related stories of preposterously unlikely events, which have been brought from Scotland to Appalachia by Scots or Scots-Irish immigrants. On a higher plane are the great individual liars, word masters and lords of the imagination, of whom Davy Crockett is the supreme example. With him the art of lying passed into the realms of poetry, '... like a streak of greased lightning chased by the crocodiles of the Mississippi'. Crockett's finest hour came on the day which was so cold the earth froze on her axis. He saved humanity by greasing the axis with bear fat and giving the necessary push to get the diurnal motion going again.

James Bridger went into the Yellowstone region about twenty years after John Colter, but where Colter's truthful descriptions of the area made him the object of ridicule, Bridger's extravagant fantasies were widely believed. Bridger tried to shoot an elk which appeared to be close at hand, only to discover that there was a transparent mountain of 'volcanic glass' between them. He discovered streams flowing down inclines so steep that the water came out boiling at the bottom, and he fished in a lake where trout living in the cool waters at the bottom were cooked as the angler drew them up through the boiling water on the surface. Unfortunately for the Yellowstone tourist trade, no one has yet relocated the remote area where Bridger found 'petrified birds on petrified trees singing petrified songs'.

Traces of the Ulster immigrants can be found in many aspects of American life. In the western areas of Pennsylvania, Virginia and the Carolinas and in eastern Tennessee, Kentucky and Ohio the pattern of towns and older roads was decided by the first pioneers, largely Scots-Irish, though they in turn followed the much more ancient Indian paths. Many of the first surveyors were Ulstermen, like John Armstrong of Carlisle, and relatives and in-laws for whom he found similar jobs along the Allegheny frontier. Brendan Adams of the Ulster Folk Museum traced that special feature of Ulster Plantation towns, the central market place called the Diamond, to Pennsylvania where it turns up under the same name in a number of places, including Pittsburgh. In the terminology of Scots-Irish towns the Diamond is, inexplicably, square.

On a less tangible plane, the ghost stories of Ulster, the superstitions and omens, have appeared in several parts of the United States. (Travelling in the opposite direction, the wraiths of Irish emigrants have appeared to their families at home in Ireland weeks ahead of the letters announcing they had died.) A detailed study, from taped interviews of occult beliefs in the eastern Pennyroyal region in the Kentucky foothills has thrown up close parallels with the North of Ireland. The author of *Ghosts Along the Cumberland*, William Lynwood Montell, describes dreams and portents which foretell death, restless ghosts that seek justice, and beliefs connected with the dying and with funerals – a whole spine-chilling catalogue for which there are close parallels in the Irish countryside.

Scots-Irish studies received a bad name from the bombast that emerged from the Scotch-Irish Congresses assembled in various American cities in the 1880s and 1890s. There the middle-class descendants of the pioneers told each other about 'the patriotic spirit, the indomitable courage and the stern integrity' which characterized 'this noble race ever foremost in the march of Christian civilization'. Only in the second half of the twentieth century have scholars begun again to look seriously at the contribution of the Ulster Scots to the making of America. Much valuable and detailed work has been done by people like Richard McMaster, who has investigated the cattle drovers of the Valley of Virginia, or Bobby Moss, working on the Revolutionary War in South Carolina. Occasionally the area of research is very selective: Daniel Patterson has devoted years of study to the Bigham family of Scots-Irish stonemasons whose elaborately carved tombstones can be found from Pennsylvania to Mecklenburg County, North Carolina.

Modern scholars, specialized as they are, hesitate to pass overall judgements on the Scots-Irish; the summary condemnation by Arnold Toynbee in *A Study of History* – 'No better than barbarians' – is hardly worth consideration. Twenty years ago Estyn Evans offered a cautious verdict: 'If the Scotch-Irish played an important part . . . it is because they were well adapted pioneers rather than because they were endowed with superior qualities. . . .' The Philadelphia author and historian Denis Clark, taking an overall view, sees the Scots-Irish experience as a very contradictory one: 'Their successes when re-examined provide a much more tragic picture, a picture of frustration. This gifted group of high achievement was eventually eclipsed by the contradiction which its Calvinist code of religious and social behaviour represented in the free wheeling and casual life of America.'

Clark points out that in the late twentieth century, 'their remarkable record is hardly visible'. Apart from museums, historical societies and small dedicated communities like those around Staunton in Virginia, or at Greensburg, Pennsylvania, this is largely true. The Mountain Men and the millionaires, the politicians and the frontiersmen are remembered because they are part of American mythology, the mythology of success or the mythology of the self-sufficient loner, but the great mass of middle-class Scots-Irish who contributed so much in the nineteenth century are long forgotten. The network of second-rank politicians like Robert Breckinridge McAfee of Kentucky or Alexander Stuart of Virginia, who drew up the report on John Brown's epoch-making raid on Harper's Ferry; the hundreds of clerical leaders who created such a powerful religious infrastructure in the western world's most secular society; men with social consciences when such things were not in fashion, such as Gerry McAuley, highway robber turned evangelist to the down-and-outs of New York, 'Chaplain' McCabe who worked in the Civil War prison camps, and Robert Ross McBurney from Castleblaney, County Monaghan, the driving force behind the YMCA movement; many pioneering doctors, heirs of that versatile frontier surgeon Ephraim McDowell; ingenious educators in the McGuffey mould like the Rev. Thomas Smyth from Belfast and John Robert Gregg from County Monaghan, inventor of the shorthand system: all these people have vanished into the footnotes of history books.

Public awareness of the Ulster Scots as an ethnic group has also gone. How many who have watched James Maitland Stewart from Indiana in his delightful screen performances in pictures like 'The Man From Laramie', 'Harvey' or 'The Philadelphia Story' know, or care, about his Scots-Irish background dating back to the Carolina backcountry in pre-Revolution days? Today, if you travel through some of the original areas of settlement, such as the lands around the Octorara Creek in south-eastern Pennsylvania, you will come across living cameos of eighteenth-century life but it is not the Ulster Scots but their Amish neighbours who have survived and preserved a pioneer existence.

10 · HEARTS OF ULSTER

'a brotherhood of affection, an identity of interests, a communion of rights, and an union of power among Irishmen of all religious persuasions.'

From the oath of United Irishmen, 1791

> ON SATURDAY LAST Thomas Clingan was executed at Downpatrick pursuant to his sentence; when he hung for 28 or 30 minutes, (still shewing signs of life) the Sheriff ... perceived that it was impossible he could be so long dying if some extraordinary art had not been made use of; upon examination they found that he had a steel collar about his neck, which had straps to it that buckled between his legs; during the time the collar was taken from his neck, he recovered so well as to be able to walk up the ladder, and declare he had nothing more to say than what he had confessed before, which was that he was guilty ... The execution was then conducted with the greatest good order.

So the *Belfast Newsletter* of 19 May 1772 reports on the eventually successful execution of a Steelboy, a member of the Presbyterian secret society, the Hearts of Steel.

Thomas Clingan had been convicted two weeks earlier of stealing a gun, along with another Steelboy, Samuel Jameson, who had burned a neighbour's house. The readers of the *Newsletter* would have understood clearly the motives for the two crimes. The Hearts of Steel had been formed to resist the imposition of large fines for the renewal of farm leases on the vast estates of the Earl of Donegal in County Antrim. The fact that Lord Donegal needed the money to complete the Palladian mansion he was building on his English estates in Staffordshire did not make his Irish tenants any more anxious to pay. Another grievance was the increased rent being demanded by 'middlemen' holding Donegal estate lands, who speedily evicted any sub-tenant unable to pay. The methods of the Steelboys were to terrorize the landlords and their agents and to force their fellow peasants into compliance and silence by threats, arson and murder. Clingan was obviously collecting arms for the society and Jameson punishing a fellow tenant who had paid the rent increases, bought the farm of an evicted tenant, passed information to the authorities or otherwise fallen out of line with the Hearts.

Despite their moonlight rule, the countryside was largely in sympathy with 'the true harts of steel' led by such shadowy figures as 'Captain See Justice' and 'Captain Firebrand'. Their proclamation echoed the sentiments of the small farmers and the cottage weavers who combined farming with their trade. 'Betwixt landlord and rector, the very marrow is screwed out of our bones and our lives are even become burdensome to us, by these uncharitable and unreasonable men, that we do not care whether we live or die.' The plight of the tenants had been made worse by a series of bad harvests and

An Establishment view of Irish rural violence against landlords in the eighteenth century. The Right Boys of Tipperary closely resembled their Ulster contemporaries, the Steelboys.

many of them were starving: 'the poor are turned black in the face and the skin is parched on their back'. The phrase in the proclamation about not caring whether they lived or died was not idle eloquence. Dozens, besides Clingan and Jameson, died on the scaffold, often on the flimsiest of evidence. Steelboy leaders, usually fairly substantial tenant farmers, like John Blair of Donegore and his son John, were singled out as special targets by the magistrates: 'the hanging of father and son together would do more good than twenty others'. The counter-terror of the authorities increased support for the Hearts, and the executed men became folk martyrs. Middle-class liberals recognized the terrible social injustices which had caused the outbreak, and the Presbytery of Templepatrick, while not condoning the violence, roundly condemned the 'heavy oppression' which had sparked it off.

In January 1771 the *Belfast Newsletter* summed up the feelings of decent people to the absentee landlords who were racking the rents and draining the wealth from Ireland: '... we are informed there are no less than one hundred and thirty Irish families now at Bath spending the product of thousands of poor people here; besides vast numbers in other parts of England, France etc. Poor Ireland!'

The Steelboys were but one of several agrarian terrorist organizations in eighteenth-century Ireland. Earlier the Hearts of Oak operated in Tyrone, Armagh and Londonderry; their grievances were the increased county tax imposed by the grand juries for the building of roads and the new vigour with which the Church of Ireland was collecting its tithes. The tithe grievance had been exacerbated by the removal in 1735 of liability for tithes from pasture land, the large acreages grazed by well-to-do cattle farmers, that class who were described as 'the greatest graziers and cow keepers perhaps in the world ... too apt to attend to their claret as much as their bullocks'. This meant that small farmers raising arable crops were now carrying the burden of supporting the Episcopal Church. Another factor was the employment by rectors of 'tithe farmers' to collect their dues. These collectors were quite unscrupulous in extracting the last penny from tenants on the borderline of starvation, 'a species of wolf left behind by the shepherd to take care of the flock in his absence'. While the new roads would be a benefit to everyone, the Oakboys saw them only as a luxury for the landlords and magistrates who made up the grand juries. At the height of their activity the Hearts of Oak could mobilize thousands of followers at a time. In Armagh in 1763 they 'filled at least two miles of road and were formed into companies with each a standard or colours displayed ... drums, horns, fidles and bagpipes'.

In the South of Ireland the Catholic Whiteboys, who wore white shirts so as to recognize one another during their midnight raids, were considerably more ferocious. 'One of their usual punishments (and by no means the most severe) was taking people out of their beds, carrying them naked in winter, on horseback, for some distance and burying them up to their chin in a hole filled with briars, not forgetting to cut off one of their ears.' There was one important difference from the Northern societies. The Whiteboys had a strong political motive, believing that they were fighting for the lands from which their ancestors had been unjustly driven; perhaps because of that their organization was to continue into the middle of the nineteenth century and to be succeeded by others of a similar nature up to the present day.

The Steelboys organization spread into the counties of Down, Londonderry, Tyrone and Armagh, and what the magistrates described as 'a lawless, turbulent and dangerous Spirit of Insurgency' prevailed through 1771 and 1772, when throughout Ulster 'most gentlemen's houses' were fortified 'like garrisons'. They stormed a military barracks in Belfast to release a comrade, and at Gilford in County Down they fought a pitched battle and afterwards murdered a Presbyterian clergyman who had preached against them.

Troops were sent from Dublin against the Steelboys, although the Lord Lieutenant of Ireland, Lord Townshend, identified the rack-renting landlords as the basic cause of the trouble. Many Steelboys took the escape route to America, particularly to South Carolina, and the unsettled state of Ulster counties helped to make the years 1770 to 1775 record ones for emigration. In the homeland the stage was set for the great insurrection to come.

One of the regular features of market day in an Ulster town in the eighteenth century was the sea captain mounted on a barrel, touting for passengers for the New World. There would have been nothing extraordinary about his appearance, no parrot on the shoulder or patch over the eye; his speech would have been the ordinary dialect of Ulster (he probably came from the peninsula of Islandmagee in County Antrim or the Mourne country of County Down), and he would have used no colourful oaths for he would be a careful Presbyterian like many of his audience. The only thing to distinguish him from a better-off farmer or a small merchant would have been his rolling walk, acquired to counteract the rhythmic sway of his ship on the interminable Atlantic crossings. But what he would have had was a glib tongue and a ready imagination to paint a picture of America as a land of plenty, describing the voyage there as a short and even pleasurable experience.

As the captain would probably never see his passengers again after parting from them at Charleston or Newcastle on the Delaware, he could promise anything. A weaver showing signs of interest would be guaranteed the unheard-of income of £100 a year, a farmer would be told of land in Carolina which grew crops in abundance but not of the massive trees which had to be cleared first, nor of the malarial swamps and hostile Indians. Letters, often forged, from satisfied emigrants, extolling not only the new land but also the treatment they had received on the voyage, would be read out and the whole performance made both convincing and entertaining by the captain's confidential manner and ready wit. Soon he, or his agent, would be taking the customary guinea deposit from fare-paying passengers or signing up indentured servants and redemptioners.

Apart from the sea captains, a network of agents working for the merchants and shipowners who controlled the emigrant trade operated throughout the towns and villages of Ulster. This was backed up by advertisements in the *Newsletter* and the *Londonderry*

Journal. The authorities who believed that emigration spread like 'a contagious disease' did not recognize its highly organized nature or the business interests behind it. Two significant features of the movement of Ulster people to the American colonies were noticed by the English traveller Arthur Young. Writing of a visit to Ireland in 1776 he noted, 'The spirit of emigrating ... appears to be confined to two circumstances, the Presbyterian religion and the linen manufacture ... the Catholics almost never went; they seem not only tied to the country but almost to the parish in which their ancestors lived.' Twenty years earlier, before the defeat of Bonnie Prince Charlie at Culloden, the British authorities observed that the only Catholics who went abroad were young men being trained in the use of arms in Europe and returning to await a Jacobite uprising. The native Irish in the eighteenth century showed a much greater attachment to the soil of Ireland than the Scots-Irish, though this was to change significantly in the nineteenth century.

'Presbyterian religion and the linen manufacture': the linking of the terms had a wider significance than their stimulating effect on emigration. In many ways these were the factors which decided the climate of opinion and the political history of Ulster in the second half of the eighteenth century. It is clear that the fluctuation in numbers emigrating was tied to the frequent ups and downs in the linen business. The weaver usually also had a smallholding from which he supplied the family food, so that his trade earnings were in ready cash. In good years he lived well above the subsistence level of the small farmer but during a slump his standard of living could fall as low as that of a day labourer. He was often better educated than the average in a peasant society and that gave him access to newspapers, the columns of which were packed with advertisements and correspondence about emigration. Even in bad years the weaver often had enough money saved to pay his passage and avoid the ordeal of indenture. So several circumstances combined to make emigration an attractive option for the weaving élite of the linen trade. James McCullough, the diarist, is a good example of his class; his journal shows he could write, if not spell, that he had read books and newspapers and that he was able in 1745 to pay his own fare and that of his wife from Belfast to Delaware.

These connections through the linen industry were important in the political and economic history of both Ulster and the American colonies. At merchant level there were direct two-way links. Flax seeds from Pennsylvania were imported into Ulster from early in the century and on the return voyage linen cloth went to the colonies. It was these flax trade ships that provided passages for the first emigrants. Thomas Greer, a wealthy Quaker engaged in the trade, received a letter in 1773 from a fellow Quaker Thomas Wright, who had just emigrated, proposing to act as his American agent: 'Friend Thomas I believe it will be in my power to correspond with thee in the linen trade. By way of remittance I propose to send thee a bill for flaxseed next winter and expect linen for the same.' Dangerous ideas as well as goods, people and business letters crossed the Atlantic both ways in the next quarter century.

Linen had made Ulster prosperous. John Wesley, riding through Ireland from one emotion-charged revival meeting to another, observed, 'No sooner did we enter Ulster than we observed the difference. The ground was cultivated just as in England and the cottages not only neat, but with doors, chimneys and windows.' Weaving was a family business carried on in the cottages, with everyone in the family employed; the father and grown-up sons did the skilled work and sold the cloth, the women and children prepared the yarn and tilled the smallholding. Often there were up to three looms to a home, and the fact that everyone was contributing made the household comfortably off by the standard of the times.

The weaver sold his unbleached linen, 'brown cloths', at special markets, often going from merchant to merchant, and even from town to town, to get the best price. The dealing made him an alert and thinking man. Besides advertisements for emigrant ships he read political speeches and letters in the newspapers, and his journeys to market, even though they were confined to a radius of twenty miles, brought him into contact with new radical ideas. The linen trade became the conduit for revolution.

Psychologically his economic independence enabled him to shed the mental servitude imposed on his fellow peasants by centuries of tenanthood. He showed this in one way by copying the sports of the gentry. Arthur Young, in his Ulster tour, saw weavers hunting with hounds. Every weaver had his hound, 'and joining they hunt hares: a pack of hounds is never heard but all the weavers leave their looms and away they go after them by hundreds'. In the early nineteenth century that doyen of Northern Irish huntsmen and amateur jockeys, Squire Watson, saw a weaver bet up to twenty guineas on a race.

Ownership of bleach greens, where the 'brown cloths' were turned to white linen, enabled some to rise from primary manufacture to become small-time entrepreneurs; 'jobbing' or acting as agents for the big merchants also helped to create small pools of capital for individuals. All of this in the end was to help to destroy the radical society which cottage industry created. The bleach green owners would become exporters of linen, and from this class would emerge the rich Ulster merchants of the nineteenth century. The cottage industries would die. Factories would take over, and for the first time the Ulster Scots would be sharply divided into the 'haves' and the 'have-nots'. In the meantime, however, Ulster could present a picture of prosperity to Judge Edward Willes as he rode on circuit from one hanging court to the next: 'From Monaghan to Carrickfergus is the very picture of industry. The whole road for fifty miles is as it were, one continued village of neat cottages. Every cabin has a little orchard and spinning or weaving is going on in every house. T'is a fine sight to behold the great number of bleach yards; they look like white patches of unmelted snow.'

'The Presbyterian is happiest when he is being a radical. The austere doctrines of Calvinism, the simplicity of his worship, the democratic government of his Church, the memory of the martyred Covenanters and the Scottish refusal to yield or dissemble –

ABOVE *Wellbrook Mill, County Tyrone, typical of the small linen mills to be found in eighteenth-century Ulster.* BELOW *Nineteenth-century view of the bleach green and print works at Old Park, Belfast. By then much of the linen industry centred in Belfast and the Lagan Valley.*

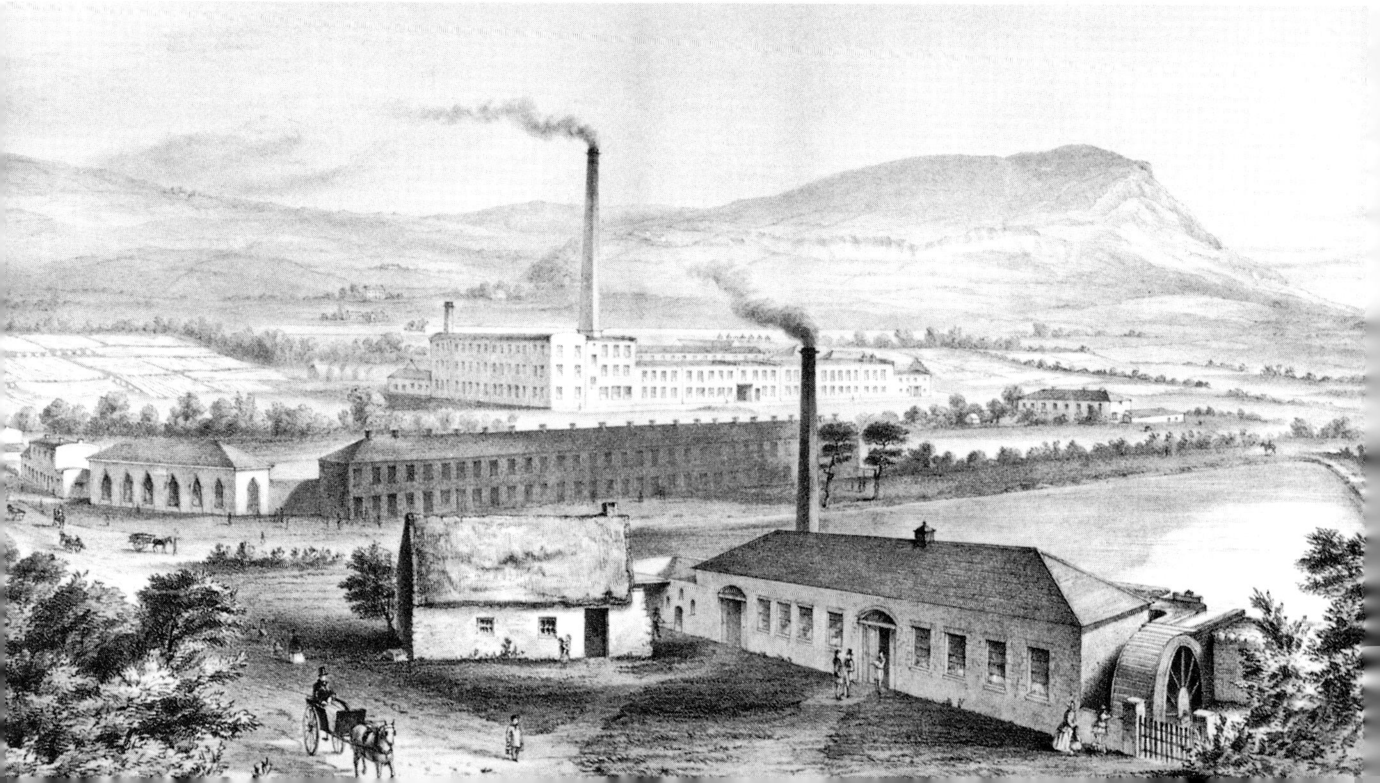

The philosopher Francis Hutcheson, whose political theories inspired Scots-Irish radicals in America and Ulster.

all these incline him to that difficult and cantankerous disposition which is characteristic of a certain kind of political radicalism': so A. T. Q. Stewart, in his classic study of Ulster's political history *The Narrow Ground*, defines a trait in the Scots-Irish make-up which was equally important on both sides of the Atlantic in the second half of the eighteenth century. This radicalism, growing from deep ancestral roots, affected every shade of Presbyterianism from the hard-line Covenanters to the liberal intellectuals of what was to be called the New Light, and it was to be one of the main causes of the tragic assertion in arms of Scots-Irish identity in the closing years of the eighteenth century. The other causes were the unrest arising from social oppression and the influence of two revolutions, the American and the French.

Parallel to this radicalism and deriving from it was the Presbyterian Church's tendency to fragment. In Scotland the Covenanters broke from the mainstream, claiming that they alone preserved in its purity the Reformation settlement; the Church of Scotland itself split over whether the practice of having church livings in the gift of a patron should be re-established. The Scottish breakaway groups collected adherents in Ulster, for the Scots-Irish Church was almost a mirror image of its mother church.

In the 1720s a major division appeared among Irish Presbyterians over the question of whether it was necessary for ministers to subscribe to the Westminster Confession of Faith, a document drawn up just before the English Civil War in an attempt to sort out the principles of Protestantism in those turbulent days. The argument between subscribers and non-subscribers was really an argument as to whether dogma, as in the Churches of Rome and Canterbury, or the ever-revolutionary principle of the supremacy of individual conscience, should guide Presbyterians. The Old Light subscribers were the conservatives of dissent; the New Light the tolerant and broad-minded liberals.

During this first subscription controversy emerged, perhaps, the most attractive and influential of the Scots-Irish race. Francis Hutcheson, whose influence on the American revolution has been discussed in Chapter 6, was also to exert immense influence on philosophy and political thought in Britain and Ireland. During his early years teaching in a Dublin Academy he was part of a robust intellectual circle which included Dean Swift. His Presbyterianism was leavened by the new culture which had blossomed in a Dublin that was becoming aware of its role as a national capital.

Hutcheson was appointed a professor at Glasgow University at a time when the rigid modes of thought and belief which governed the gloomy Calvinist world of Scottish academia were beginning to crack. This offered an opportunity to disseminate his new and gentler philosophy. He believed in the essential goodness of men, and taught that education and appreciation of the finer things in life would make people behave better, would make them live by that inner light which was the infallible guide. This, at a time when rationalism was destroying the comforts of revealed faith, offered a credible alternative to the dictum of John Hobbes that life was 'nasty, brutish and short'.

As a philosopher, Hutcheson has been called the 'Father of the Scottish Enlightenment', but it was in his political writings that he had the greatest impact on the history of the Scots-Irish. Politics he linked with morality and religion. God, said Hutcheson, was not on the side of rank and privilege, despite what popes and prelates might say. Tenants had a moral right to resist greedy landlords; oppressed peoples to overthrow tyrants; colonies to refuse to be exploited by the mother country. He thought deeply about the organization of society and as a realist recognized the vital role of money. He was contemptuous of the comfortable model of society which idealized the hardworking poor, happy in their place and in their poverty. It was common sense, he argued, that men were happy and made good citizens if they had enough of the world's goods; a property-owning people was the best guarantee of a stable democracy.

These ideas were a challenge to the principles by which the men of power ruled and lived, and the fact that they were expounded by a man of such charm, humanity and culture made them unforgettable to hungry young disciples, from the great economist Adam Smith to trainees for the Ulster Kirk. Hutcheson's devoted pupil Francis Allison carried his message, undiluted, to America where the master's words about 'oppressive laws ... made with respect to the colonies' and 'something unnatural in a large society ... remaining subject to the ... government of a distant body of men' must have sounded uncannily prophetic to the Philadelphia Revolutionaries.

Through Ulster friends like Thomas Drennan, ideas such as 'all power is vested in and consequently derived from the people ... rulers are their trustees and servants', reached the developing middle class of the province, and gave philosophical accreditation to notions already current that the political structure must be changed. These ideas were passed on to another generation which was to make its stand against tyranny in battlefields from Lexington to Ballynahinch.

If the Scots-Irish accepted Hutcheson's political theories, they found some of his other beliefs less palatable. For instance, his views on the rights of women and of animals belonged to the twentieth century rather than the eighteenth and must have seemed ridiculous to his compatriots, who were liberals in the political forum but despots in the home. Marriage he saw as an equal partnership, with the strengths of women in some areas counterbalancing the strengths of men in others. The fact that woman was a subordinate partner deprived by law of property and other rights seemed to him as unjustifiable as slavery. He also argued that animals, while their function was to serve men, had, at least, the right not to be ill-treated. The opinion of many of Hutcheson's co-religionists on his doctrinal stance is summed up in the probably apocryphal story of his early sermon in his father's church in County Armagh. After the sermon an elder sympathized with Hutcheson senior on his 'daft boy ... who has babblin' on this hour about a gude and benevolent God ... and not a word about the auld doctrines o' election, reprobation and original sin'. That true Presbyterian felt uneasy in church without the comforting proximity of hell's fires.

In the eighteenth century a concept emerged which today seems incredible, the concept of a Protestant Irish nation where the Catholics would continue to be Gibeonites, 'the hewers of wood and drawers of water'. Although these Protestant patriots envisaged some alleviation in the situation of Catholics (still without the right to vote or sit in Parliament, and suffering under many of the Penal Laws brought in after their defeat at the Boyne), the reality was that the Anglo-Irish gentry despised their Catholic servants and tenants. 'Nothing satisfies them but an unlimited submission', said Arthur Young. The Irish Parliament was completely subordinated to Westminster by a fifteenth-century law, and the first aim of the Protestant 'Patriot' Party was legislative independence, but this seemed remote until the Irish Volunteers came into existence.

When France (in 1778) and Spain (in 1779) declared war on Britain in support of the rebel American colonists, there appeared to be great danger that Ireland would be invaded (it had been invaded in past centuries by both French and Spanish troops). The Irish Volunteers were formed largely from the Protestant middle class and officered by the gentry. The Presbyterian Scots-Irish, particularly in Belfast and Armagh, joined in with great enthusiasm. For them this might appear a strangely ambivalent action, for they were, by and large, supporters of the American Revolution, where their brothers and cousins were fighting the British forces. 'The Protestant gentlemen ... of Tandragee [County Armagh]' toasted 'the martyrs that fell at Lexington.' The Yankee Club of Stewartstown (County Tyrone) sent messages of congratulation to Washington. But then the Volunteers were never quite what they purported to be, and they rapidly turned from a defence force into a political pressure group bent on wringing concessions from Britian.

The first demands were for an end to British restrictions on Irish trade, and when this was achieved the Volunteers campaigned to free the Irish Parliament from the crippling control of London. In 1782 the British Government, reeling from defeat in America, conceded legislative freedom to the Dublin Parliament. The Volunteers now turned to more controversial aims – the reforming of the Dublin Assembly to make it more democratic and the granting to Catholics of the right to vote and sit in Parliament. These objectives split the movement. The landowners who led them did not want Parliamentary reform, which would give middle-class merchants and even ordinary people a share in power. Many Protestants of all classes were afraid of what might follow if the franchise were extended to Catholics.

The Irish Parliament itself rejected the reform plan and the Volunteer movement lost its impetus. However, a new and far more radical organization was about to be born. In October 1792 a group of middle-class Presbyterians met in Belfast to create the first society of United Irishmen. Dr William Drennan, son of Francis Hutcheson's friend Thomas Drennan, defined the organization in a letter to a friend: 'A society having much of the ceremony and secrecy of Freemasonry. A benevolent conspiracy, a plot for the people. The Brotherhood its name; the rights of man its end. Real independence to Ireland and Republicanism its particular purpose.'

The Society of United Irishmen attracted men like the Rev. James Porter of Greyabbey in County Down, who had already exchanged his clerical coat for the scarlet of the

ABOVE *Henry Joy McCracken, the middle-class Presbyterian, who commanded the 1798 rebels in Antrim.*

LEFT *The eighteenth-century Irish Parliament, sitting in Dublin, achieved partial independence of Britain in 1782. At the same time, the Protestant Irish Volunteers (seen here at College Green outside Parliament House), led by the upper and middle classes, were demanding moderate political reforms. Unintentionally they fathered the revolutionary United Irishmen.*

Volunteers, believing that here at last was the citizen army which Hutcheson believed to be the best guarantee of democracy.

Many other of the more radical Volunteers now turned to the United Irishmen, and, because of the close association between the two bodies, the Volunteers came under Government ban. A branch of the United Irishmen was formed in Dublin with Drennan as its president, and from there the movement spread over much of Ireland.

The Belfast in which the United Irishmen first met was a Presbyterian town, cultured and radical in politics. The French Revolution was greeted with enthusiasm and the fall of the Bastille was celebrated with flags and parades by the Belfast Volunteer companies. Jacobin clubs modelled on the famous Revolutionary club in Paris to which Robespierre and Danton belonged, were formed and people in the remote parts of the countryside began to name their children after the French leaders.

About the same time middle-class Ulster Scots suddenly found a cultural identification with the land they had occupied for nearly two centuries. A great festival of native Irish harp music was held, and the Irish language was taught in Presbyterian schools. The Scots-Irish, in a truer sense than the Anglo-Irish a decade or so earlier, were tentatively feeling their way towards a sense of Irish nationhood.

The Duke of Rutland, Lord Lieutenant of Ireland, described the Northern Presbyterians as 'great levellers and republicans' and he, from the clearer viewpoint of his time, understood what those terms really implied. Today with vastly different definitions of Irish republicanism and Irish nationhood, such understanding is difficult. The nationalism of Drennan and Porter was not the chauvinistic tribalism of the modern variety; their republicanism reflected a vision of what could be achieved by the destruction of tyranny everywhere. 'To be a patriot', says A. T. Q. Stewart, 'was to adopt a wider, more cosmopolitan outlook, supporting the Rights of Man in opposition to the narrow self-interest of national governments.' Such a broad humanitarian viewpoint was to die with the Presbyterian rebels of 1798. After that Catholics had the monopoly of the name 'patriot'.

The Society of United Irishmen began as an open movement for constitutional reform, but the more extreme among the members wanted to separate from Britain and set up a republic on French Revolutionary lines. They campaigned strenuously for political rights for Catholics and in 1793 Catholics were given the vote. In the same year Britain went to war with republican France and the United Irish programme became treason. The association went underground.

For over two hundred years, County Armagh has experienced some of the worst sectarian troubles of any rural area in Ireland. The bitter and long-running conflict in the period leading up to the 1798 Rebellion illustrates the sad truth that religious divisions run deeper than any temporary political unity. It also underlines the fact that by no means all Protestants, or even all Presbyterians, supported the United Irish movement.

North Armagh was a densely populated area with more persons per square mile than any other piece of countryside in Europe. The linen trade dominated. The smallholdings of cottage weavers lined the roadsides, as described by Judge Willes; the towns lived by buying, selling and making up linen. Catholics were engaged in the trade but they were late entrants and they were restricted by tradition to certain less lucrative areas. There were few Catholic owners of bleach greens and few drapers. Their attempts to break into these restricted functions threatened the economic superiority of Protestants and led to market brawls, which developed into sectarian warfare. The first clash is said to have occurred when a Catholic intervened in a fist fight between two Protestants. True or not, it required only a spark to set alight the latent antagonism now fuelled by economic rivalry.

The Protestant group, the Peep O'Day Boys, so called because they attacked Catholic houses in the early hours of the morning and issued warnings to the inmates – 'Seamus . . . sell your things and go to Connaught or you will go to Hell' – were answered on the other side by the Defenders, whose original function of defence soon turned to counter-attack. The conflict degenerated from stick and stone fights, a traditional form of entertainment all over Ireland, to ugly clashes where firearms were used and lives lost. At the Diamond, near Loughgall in County Armagh, the troubles reached a climax on 21 September 1795. A large party of Catholics attacked a much smaller number of Protestants in Dan Winter's public house at the crossroads. The Catholics were beaten, and from that local victory the Orange Order, which in the nineteenth and twentieth century would wield immense political power, was born.

There is a widely held view that no Presbyterians were members of the Orange Order in the early days. Certainly the Presbyterian Church authorities did not look kindly on the Order; even the leading Conservative Henry Cooke wrote in 1834, '. . . out of 230 or 240 ministers belonging to the Synod of Ulster, not one-fiftieth part will be found even to countenance Orangeism'. But there is now little doubt that at peasant level some Presbyterians followed their Church of Ireland neighbours into the society.

Protestants were divided in their support for the United Irish cause. In predominantly Presbyterian areas, where Protestants were in the great majority, places such as South Antrim, North Down and Belfast, there was backing for the objectives of the United Irishmen, including giving Catholics more political and religious freedom. But elsewhere there was a good deal of hostility, particularly to the prospect that Catholics might be allowed to carry arms. Occasionally the differences among Protestants came into the open – radical Freemasons clashing with Orangemen.

What was more important to the situation in the 1790s was the takeover of the new Orange Order by the landed gentry. This not only gave it a status that other organizations of peasants and craftsmen lacked but it also meant that its members joined the newly formed Yeomanry and provided effective local forces to fight the United Irishmen.

The Chevalier De Latocnaye, an emigré French Royalist who walked round Ireland on the eve of the Rebellion, found on his inn door at Newtownards the military notice, 'If another shot is fired orders will be given to burn the town'. A few days later he found the people of Belfast 'in terror'. The Chevalier was seeing, from the comfortable position of a neutral, the repression which the British Government imposed on Ireland in response to the United Irish agitation. He would have felt less detached had he included Kilrea in his itinerary; these enthusiastic radicals were beheading cats and dogs on an experimental guillotine they had built in anticipation of the revolution.

Under military orders gatherings of people, even the traditional assembling of neighbours to bring in the harvest, were forbidden. No lights were allowed on in homes after nine o'clock and blacksmiths were warned by notice that if they made pike heads they would be hanged at their own doors. Dozens of liberals, both inside and outside the Society of United Irishmen, were arrested. The administering of the oath 'to forward a brotherhood of affection, an identity of interests, a communion of rights, and a union of power among Irishmen of all religious persuasions' was made a capital offence. The authorities actually had less to worry about than they believed. Catholics, since they had been granted the vote in the Catholic Relief Bill of 1793, had grown lukewarm towards their fellow conspirators and some, like Nicholas Maginn, a leader of the United Irishmen in County Down, were busy betraying them.

With the province terrified and the United organization in disarray, the Rebellion might never have happened but for one event. In 1796, William Orr, one of the most popular and attractive of the United leaders, was arrested and charged with administering an unlawful oath. After a year in jail he was tried and, after being convicted by a jury deliberately made drunk, was sentenced to death. On the day of his hanging hundreds of soldiers with cannon surrounded the place of execution. 'I die', said Orr on the scaffold, 'in the true faith of a Presbyterian . . . a persecuted man in a persecuted country.' The United Irish movement had been given the martyr it needed.

In December of 1796 a French army of 15,000 men attempted to land at Bantry Bay, in the south-west corner of Ireland. The landing was frustrated by heavy storms at sea, but rumours of a new French invasion spread over the country every month or so for the next two years. The Government were aware of the close links between the United Irishmen and the French Revolutionaries, although they must have been heartened by the fact that the Catholics in the hinterland of Bantry Bay gave every assistance to the British troops as they moved up to repel the landing. A search of Ulster by troops and Yeomanry uncovered over 5,000 guns; during the search the Yeomanry (largely members of the Orange Order) burned houses and summarily hanged and flogged suspects. A Presbyterian minister, Robert Magill, recalled years afterwards the floggings which took place in a field behind his father's house: 'I saw Samuel Bones of Lower Broughshane receive 500 lashes. I saw Samuel Crawford of Ballymena receive 500 lashes. The only words he spoke during the time were, "Gentlemen, be pleased to shoot me". I saw Hood Haslett . . . receive 500 lashes . . . he was only about nineteen years of age . . . I heard him exclaiming, "I'm a-cutting through".'

The apocalyptic element latent in the make-up of the Ulster Scot surfaced in the dark autumn of 1797. The country was full of rumours of supernatural happenings, all with strong political undertones. The antiquarian Samuel McSkimin, who was in his twenties at the time, described the phenomena:

> Visions were affirmed to have been witnessed ... and many persons reported to have had strange and prophetic dreams regarding the landing of the French near Belfast and their victorious progress ... at the dead hour of midnight lights had been observed in several ancient churches and that a person, more hardy than his neighbours on looking in at one of the windows, heard an angel read out of a green book the order for the extirpation of the English interest in Ireland.

The state of patriotic exaltation was heightened by Covenanters, who went from townland to townland quoting from the book of Revelations and foretelling the imminent destruction of Babylon (Britain) by the French and the coming in Ireland of 'the Holy City, the new Jerusalem'. The prophecies of the seventeenth-century patriarch Alexander Peden appeared to fit the Ulster situation and gave authenticity to the Covenanters' claim that the day of Armageddon had arrived. Emotive phrases like 'the springtide of plenty ... the poor shall be equal with the rich' found willing listeners in the oppressed Ulster villages. But even in such an emotional climate the earthy Scots-Irish humour remained to salt the verbal extravagances of the fanatics: 'May the skin of old Geordy [George III]' ran the current catch phrase, 'be stretched on a drumhead to rouse the republicans to arms.'

The United Irishmen, like most Irish conspiracies, was riddled with informers; the Government authorities in Dublin Castle knew more about their plans than any of the individual rebel commanders. The insurrection was planned to begin on 23 May 1798, but a few days before that deadline the military began arresting the leaders. In both County Antrim and County Down the commanders were taken into custody on the information of Nicholas Maginn, and in Dublin Lord Edward Fitzgerald, the nobleman around whom much of the plan was centred, was mortally wounded resisting arrest. Nevertheless, in the counties of Wexford, Wicklow and Kildare the Rebellion broke out with great fierceness.

In Wexford the rebels took over the whole county, but what started as a struggle against Government oppression turned into a sectarian bloodbath. A barn where about a hundred Protestants, with a few Catholic loyalists, were imprisoned was set on fire by the insurgents. Those who tried to escape were killed with pikes or driven back to die in the flames. In Wexford town there was a similar massacre of Protestant prisoners, and throughout the country fanatical Catholics told their Protestant neighbours that they must renounce Protestantism if they wished to live. James Beaghan, a rebel pikeman captured by the British, confessed before his execution that they 'thought it no more sin to kill a Protestant than a dog'.

The Southern revolt had already been crushed with great military brutality when the

Northern rebels took up arms, but even there the rising was not coordinated. The Northern commander was Henry Joy McCracken, a highly idealistic Belfast liberal whom one of his peasant soldiers summed up as 'a simple man with no devilishness in him'. McCracken addressed his untrained, half-armed force of farmers, labourers, weavers, clergymen and lawyers as 'Army of Ulster' and dated his communiqué '1st Year of Liberty'. In County Antrim the first attacks were launched on 7 June but in County Down, where the Presbyterian minister chosen to lead had been arrested, the insurrection did not start until a week later, when the Antrim rebels were already defeated.

McCracken's men assembled on Donegore Hill in the centre of the county from where, marching to the 'Marseillaise' and carrying a cannon which had been hidden in a local Presbyterian church, they launched an attack on the garrison town of Antrim. When they appeared to be on the point of victory, an unexplained panic set in among the United men and they ran away. McCracken was captured a few days later and hanged at Belfast market-house which his great-grandfather had given to the town.

A bald recital of the facts gives little idea of the rich colour of the '98 story in which comedy mixed with tragedy, great courage with very human cowardice. It is a great pity subsequent political changes have pushed the Rebellion into the background of Scots-Irish mythology, for its elements of restraint and mercy, of generosity and fidelity to friends showed this people at their best.

The 'turnout', as it was called, had farce mixed with a general feeling of celebration. Pikes were made only the night before the battle with the result that some men were so tired they were barely able to march; others, prematurely celebrating, were too drunk. Women baked oaten cakes and sewed up bags to carry three days' provisions, which was the time estimated to beat the British. When an East Antrim company of insurgents unexpectedly met a company of neighbouring Yeomen, each pretended not to see the other and went on their separate ways.

The weaver poet James Orr, who 'turned out' with the Ballycarry company, cast a cold eye on his fellow rebels. When the time came to march he wrote, 'Some hid, like hens in byre-neuks' (corners of cow sheds). Others, he noticed, slipped away on the march, 'lettin' on their burn to mak' (pretending they had an urgent call of nature), and when the rest reached Donegore Hill and saw the signs of battle they took off in a body, 'like a bee skip migrating'.

The sight of friends in green uniforms marching to pipes and drums excited Willie Nelson, who was at the impressionable age of sixteen. Armed with a pistol, he frightened the local squire's servants into giving him one of their master's thoroughbreds. On this he rode madly over the country all morning, carrying messages for the United commanders. When his first mount was worn out he commandeered another and went to the battle. Captured and condemned by court martial, Willie was brought on a cart, with his coffin beside him, to his mother's door and hanged on a sycamore tree.

Ironically, Ballymena, now the very heartland of Unionism, was the only place where the Antrim rebels were successful, holding the town for several days. Here occurred one of the few examples of bloodthirstiness on the part of the United men. After the capture of the Loyalist strongpoint in the town several prisoners were killed. Retribution by the authorities continued into the next year, when Robert Magill remembered 'the awful spectacle of human heads fixed on spikes and placed on the market-house'.

In County Down the revolt turned quite suddenly from initial success to disaster. This was at least partly due to the quixotic character of Henry Monro, the rebel leader. Monro was a Protestant shopkeeper and former Irish Volunteer whose political objectives were Parliamentary reform and equal rights for Catholics. He had been an early member of the United Irish Society, but, as he was not in favour of violent solutions, had taken no part in the preparations for the rising. When the arrest of the Rev. Steel Dickson left the insurgents leaderless he was persuaded, on the strength of his military experience in the Volunteers, to take over command.

After defeating the British forces at the village of Saintfield, the rebel army captured the strategic town of Ballynahinch. The letter of John Patton on the eve of the battle shows the mood of optimism which filled the rebel camp: 'Dear Father, I am afraid you will be troubled about me.... With God's help I hope there is no danger. Our army is about 5,000 commanded by General Monro. A part of the army went to Ballynahinch today and the soldiers ran before ours could get near them.... I intend to be home as soon as possible.' Such high hopes and such innocence were not the stuff to win battles.

British forces with artillery attacked Ballynahinch, and Monro withdrew his men to the heights around the town. The troops looted the town and during the succeeding night got extremely drunk on pillaged liquor. The officers of the United Army wanted an immediate night attack but Monro refused to take 'ungenerous advantage which this night affords ... we will fight them like men ... under the first rays of tomorrow's sun'.

When the rebels went into battle in the morning an eyewitness noticed that the Presbyterians wore their best clothes as if they were going to church; a sense of religious dedication was never far from the political causes of the Scots-Irish. They drove the military back almost out of the town, but when the British bugles sounded the retreat it was the inexperienced rebels who fled. In the cavalry pursuit that followed, hundreds of insurgents were cut down. Monro was captured and executed. The steward of the great local landlord, the Marquis of Downshire, wrote to his employer: 'Hanging and flogging have had a fine effect, and some more examples will show the scoundrels what they have to expect.' Over the County Down countryside in the next few months his expectations were amply fulfilled.

About twenty Presbyterian ministers and assistants, including Covenanters, were implicated in the rising and three died on the scaffold. The most intriguing of the clerics involved was James Porter, the son of a small farmer in Donegal. Porter took the traditional path to the ministry, 'starving' his way through Glasgow University. He emerged not a narrow Calvinist but a broadly cultured man with both literary and scientific interests. With a living at Greyabbey, he lectured to the young ladies of Belfast on 'astronomy, pnuematics Electricity ... Magnetisms and Opticks'. Had he stuck to scientific subjects he would probably have survived the Rebellion but he also turned out political satire for the radical newspaper *The Morning Star*, and lampooned the all-powerful Marquis of Londonderry. Whether Porter took part in the Rebellion is not clear but he was convicted on the evidence of a paid informer and hanged before his meeting-house in Greyabbey.

Other ministers were jailed for long periods and some, like John Glendy of Maghera, avoided execution by escaping to America. Glendy went first to the Shenandoah Valley and later became prominent as cleric and politician in New York. Many rebels, both lay and clerical, were offered emigration as an alternative to hanging. Sometimes whole families, like the Caldwells of Harmony Hill, near Ballymoney in County Antrim, were forced to emigrate because one or two members had been involved. It was almost as if the Government believed they could uproot radicalism by the wholesale weeding out of people.

After 1798 the Ulster Scots were a deeply disillusioned people. Their fellow Protestants had been massacred in Wexford, and in the north the Catholics had failed to give any real support to the Rebellion. The Presbyterians felt this double betrayal but there was also a deeper, more significant reason. The patriotism which inspired the Ulster rebels was a broad one, concerned with the rights of human beings and social justice rather than narrow tribal interests. It had nothing in common with the 'ourselves alone' approach of the later Catholic nationalism.

The '98 Rebellion in Ulster was ill-conceived, badly organized and ultimately pointless, but it sprang from generous hearts and the rebels died with hardly a blemish on their name. The Presbyterian community – New Light, Old Light, Seceder and Covenanter – gave some of their brightest and best in a cause that was only partly their own.

11 · COCKPIT CITY

'a party of about seventy men and women advanced down Wilson Street keeping up all the time an intermittent fire . . . I advanced my sub-division . . . wheeled to the right and fired at the mob.'

Report of British officer on Belfast riot, 1864

'while rioters do not mind the hottest fire, they object strongly to a cold shower of rain.'

Frankfort Moore, *c.*1886

This jewel that houses our hopes and our fears
Was knocked up from the swamps in the last hundred years.

SO MAURICE JAMES CRAIG, with ironic affection, sums up the mushroom growth of Belfast in the nineteenth century, an event that was vitally important in the history of the Ulster Scots. Belfast, in the last decade of the eighteenth century, was a town of 20,000 inhabitants, open, enlightened and, by the standards of the period, fairly humane and tolerant. Ninety years on it had become a crowded city of nearly 350,000, sectarian, claustrophobic and run by a small group of entrepreneurs whose exploitation of its workers was tempered by a hard-faced charity.

Victorian capitalism brought an extra dimension of misery to Belfast which it did not visit on other British cities, where it created equally bad, if not worse, social conditions. The geography of Belfast helped to breed the sectarian warfare which became endemic in the city; paradoxically it also fostered a spirit of self-help. Bounded by hills to the west, north and east, the town became a natural cockpit, where the frustration and hatred brought in by migrants from country districts, lacked space to dissipate. Poor people, crowded together in their wretchedness, fought with the unreason of animals in a cage; to get on top of the pile was the most important thing. It was an atmosphere which bred violence and enterprise, bigotry and business acumen.

Belfast in the eighteenth century was owned by the Donegall family, who despite their reputation as landlords during the Steelboy troubles were generous and easy going. Their patronage was responsible for most of the town's fine Georgian buildings. The White Linen Hall of 1783 was a symbol of Ulster independence; no longer would the linen trade, increasingly centred on the North, have to deal through the Dublin Linen Hall. Elegant and unpretentious, the White Linen Hall also spoke of the solid plebian virtues of the Scots-Irish. Facing the front of the new Linen Hall, a terrace of fine homes to house the gentry and well-off merchants was built by the architect Roger Mulholland.

Behind the elegance there was much bad housing, filth and extreme poverty, but the middle-class Presbyterians who dominated the town were great committee men with strong, if stern, social consciences. In 1774 the Belfast Charitable Society opened a poor house and infirmary, still the city's finest building. At the same time beggars' licences – badges with the financial incentive 'He that giveth to the poor, lendeth to the Lord' engraved on them – were revoked in anticipation of a final solution to Belfast's massive vagrancy problem. It was obviously better to view the symmetrical Georgian building from outside than to be entertained within. The diet was plain – 'This day's dinner is rice porrige' – and the discipline sharp; truant boys were 'severely flogged . . . and put in Solitary Confinement on a chain'. What happened inside the town's House of Correction, with its slogan 'Within Amend, Without Beware', is not revealed. Hospitals were also set up, in this case the Catholic doctor James McDonnell giving the lead to Protestant friends, and Belfast's famous medical school began.

The Ulster Scots placed a higher priority on education than did the Catholic Irish or the episcopal Anglo-Irish. Although Trinity College, Dublin, Ireland's only university, was opened in 1793 to Presbyterians, there was a growing demand in the North for its own university, particularly in view of the fact that a seminary for Catholic priests had been built at Maynooth, south of Dublin in 1796. But the Government, in the wake of the '98 Rebellion, did not trust Presbyterians and had no intention of creating a college which could well be a nurturing ground for sedition. In a magnificent display of self-help the Belfast community opened their own grammar school-cum-university, the Belfast Academical Institution, still functioning today as a public school with the prefix 'Royal' added to its title. Its university department consisted of two faculties, arts and medicine, and it offered a certificate of degree standard.

The Institution admitted students and appointed professors of all religions. The divinity school had teachers from Protestant faiths lecturing to students of their own denominations. The Catholic bishop refused to appoint a priest to teach divinity at the college, but in every other way he was friendly and cooperative towards the enterprise, and he allowed Catholic students, including trainee priests, to attend lectures. This was the most hopeful bid ever to solve that fundamental sectarian problem, divided education; liberal efforts at school stage today have not come nearly as far in achieving educational unity. 'For thirty-five years', says T. W. Moody, 'the Institution occupied a unique place in the cultural life of Ulster and in the esteem of educated Ulstermen, both Protestant and Catholic.'

A Government experiment along similar lines began in 1849 when three non-sectarian colleges were built in Belfast, Cork and Galway to constitute the Queen's University of Ireland. By this time a new reactionary Catholic line was being dictated from the Vatican which was readily received by Irish prelates: attendance at non-Catholic schools and colleges, they proclaimed, was detrimental to the faith and morals of the Catholic youth. Archbishop Crolly, who was a parish priest in Belfast in 1815 when Catholics there thanked their 'much esteemed Protestant and Dissenting Brethren' for putting up the money to build a new Catholic church, and who promoted his Church's cooperation with Belfast Academical Institution, urged consideration of the new university colleges. But after his death less liberal bishops banned Catholics from attending them. Not to be outdone in narrow-mindedness, a Presbyterian minority boycotted the Belfast College and founded their own sectarian institution, Magee College in Londonderry.

This era of Catholic-Presbyterian cooperation in education was also one of cultural activity. The Belfast Library and Society for Promoting Knowledge (today the Linen Hall Library) was founded; its first librarian, Thomas Russell, was hanged as a United Irishman. The Harp Society came into being in 1807 and the Anacreontic Society in 1814. The formation of a natural history society seven years later was followed by Belfast's first museum. A number of artists, such as Andrew Nicholl and Thomas Robinson, were producing talented – if not very original – work, and around the counties weaver poets, like William Orr, were publishing volumes in the style of Robert Burns. Such a modest achievement hardly qualified Belfast for the grandiose title bestowed upon it, 'the Athens of the North', (echoing the title given to the Edinburgh of the Scottish Enlightenment), but it was, for a Scots-Irish town, a praiseworthy effort.

In 1800 an event occurred which once again illustrated the paradoxical nature of Irish politics. The London Government, with judicious bribery, persuaded the Dublin Parliament to vote itself out of existence and put Ireland under Westminster control. Ironically, the conservative landed gentry and the Orange Order fought to keep Irish Home Rule, while the radical Presbyterians, who two years before had fought for independence, looked on with indifference. The idea of a united Ireland based on a triple partnership of Anglican, Catholic and Presbyterian had disappeared; the arrogance of Anglicans, the selfishness of Catholics and the suspicions of the majority of Presbyterians had ensured that. From now on it was difficult for the middle-class Scots-Irish to think of their future in an all-Ireland context, so for the moment they turned from politics to something at which they were supremely good – the art of making money.

Despite the long tradition of linen, Belfast's first mills were built to manufacture cotton. Because the raw material had to be imported, the cotton boom was brief, but it set Belfast on the road to becoming an industrial city. When Thomas Mulholland's large mill in York Street burned down he rebuilt it for the spinning of flax, and his success encouraged others to return to linen. With the breaking of the Bank of Ireland monopoly, the Northern Bank was opened in 1824, followed a year later by the Ulster Bank and the Belfast Bank; finance had arrived to oil the wheels of the new industry.

The new factories were first driven by water power and they grew up along the streams which flowed down from the Divis-Black Mountain range to the west of the city. This was to determine the alignment of the great roads of West Belfast – the Crumlin, the Shankill and the Falls – and the sectarian ghettos which they later became. Engineering was already strong in the town, and it provided steam power which put the Belfast textile

LEFT *Clifton House in Belfast, built in 1774, contained a poorhouse, an infirmary and a ballroom where the rich danced to raise funds for the sick and indigent.*

LEFT BELOW *Paupers eating outside a Belfast workhouse about the beginning of the twentieth century.*

BELOW *Children, who abounded in Belfast's slums, were licensed in 1903 to trade in the streets – this usually meant to beg.*

industry on a footing with that of English towns and cities, and far ahead of any other Irish centre. Belfast had been the third town in the island in terms of population, behind Cork and far behind Dublin. Now it outstripped Cork and although in 1835 it had fewer than 70,000 people as against a Dublin population three times as big, its exports that year, over half of them linen goods, were a million pounds greater in value than Dublin's.

The American Civil War, in which many transatlantic Scots-Irish were fighting some of the bloodiest battles of the century, was to their Ulster kinsfolk in the linen trade an unexpected blessing. When cotton supplies from the Southern states were cut off, the Lancashire industry virtually shut down and linen boomed. The numbers engaged in linen manufacture in Ulster almost doubled in ten years, and continued to rise until the last year of the century. But the benefits of the boom never reached the workers. Women in the Belfast mills were the lowest paid in the British Isles. By the beginning of the twentieth century the Belfast textile business offered a picture of 'long hours, violation of truck and factory acts and large profit margins'.

William Thackeray came to Belfast in 1842 and described the town as 'hearty, thriving and prosperous as if it had money in its pocket and roast beef for dinner', but there was little money and less roast beef for the workers in Belfast's chief industry. Even before the factory system took over, some weavers in cotton were virtually dying of hunger because of low pay rates. In 1815 desperate workers attacked the home of a 'starvation wage' employer and three were publicly hanged in the town centre. This contrasted with the old damask trade, surviving from the eighteenth century, in which workers could expect free housing and a pension.

Under the factory system the linen trade became a capitalist free-for-all in which the new Scots-Irish entrepreneurs behaved with a degree of moral and social irresponsibility comparable only to that demonstrated at about the same time by their American counterparts in Pittsburgh. Business was brisk and the linen magnates rapidly became millionaires. In the early years they showed a sound Ulster-Scots caution about revealing the fact: 'the profits of the York Street concern exceeded the dreamiest imaginings of the proprietors but like wise men they had the good sense to preserve perfect silence on a subject few can resist the temptation to talk about.'

Linen wealth was built on exploitation, particularly of women and children. In 1890, when production was near its all-time peak, 9 per cent of the labour force was under thirteen and 70 per cent of the workers were women. The young people were 'half-timers' who alternately worked a day and spent a day at school. They earned as little as two shillings and sixpence a fortnight, but in the factory homes of Victorian Belfast even this small amount of money was vital to the family economy. Old people in the 1950s recalled hearing the armies of weary children going crying to work through the early morning darkness.

As a result of philanthropic agitation in Great Britain, factory hours were reduced by law to ten a day. The small group of rich Scots-Irish business families who controlled the industry in Belfast bitterly opposed the changes. The *Belfast Newsletter*, having moved from its radical position in the eighteenth century to become the mouthpiece of Ulster capitalism, declared, 'our country is not in a position to bear this legislation. It will ruin our trade and perhaps, leave Belfast a forest of smokeless chimneys.'

Working conditions in the mills were appalling. In the steam-filled spinning rooms women spent ten or twelve hours in temperatures of 90° to 120°F, and a girl who started there at eighteen was unfit for work when she was thirty. Even worse were the carding rooms where the air was filled with minute particles of flax fibre, and the working life expectation was seventeen years. Dr C. D. Purdon, medical officer for the Belfast factory district, described a typical woman worker in the 1870s:

> She is forty years old, having commenced work at fourteen. After a few years she felt herself 'choked-up'. The attacks of cough and dyspnoea begin to come every morning and night ... when they come she has to lie across one of the cans in order to get relief and the paroxysm does not cease until she throws off the contents of her stomach and sometimes blood ... in this department the death rate from chest infections is very high.

Accidents were frequent because the employers took minimal safety precautions. Tired workers were accident prone. Typical was the case of Sarah Jane Quin who was tending a fast-moving carding machine when 'her head by some means got entangled in the machinery in which a greater part of the scalp was removed from the head'. As there was no workers' compensation law, serious accidents usually meant that the injured person spent the rest of his or her life on public charity. An Act of 1844, which provided for the fining of negligent employers, aroused even more opposition from mill-owners than the Factory Hours Act had done. After an injury to a thirteen-year-old County Tyrone boy, his employer was fined ten pounds for failing to provide adequate safeguards. The conviction was quashed on appeal and the leader writer of the *Belfast Newsletter* crowed with delight: 'It is but a false, mawkish and mongrel humanity which cares not though trade should go to the dogs lest an impudent little larking scamp should fail to get his cut fingers salved with a ten pound note.'

In 1846 the potato crop, the staple food of much of rural Ireland, failed, and thousands of the starving flocked into Belfast, expecting food and work or seeking a ship to emigrate. They came mainly from Catholic counties – Cavan, Monaghan and Leitrim – and the Catholic population of Belfast rose to over a third of the total. Even liberal middle-class Protestants were alarmed by this development and, as the refugees were poor, illiterate and often carrying cholera, working-class prejudice against them was extreme. The refugees, particularly those from County Armagh, brought with them from their widely spaced townlands to the confined ghettos of Belfast the tribal rituals of sectarian hatred.

Belfast at the time was expanding faster than any other town in the British Isles, but not fast enough to absorb without trauma the numbers wanting to settle there. West Belfast was growing around the Falls, Shankill and Crumlin districts. All three areas were Protestant, but because they offered work and living space they appeared preferable to the central area of the town which formed the Catholic ghetto. When Hercules Street was demolished to make way for the town's new Royal Avenue, the Catholics moved from there into the Lower Falls, their first gain in a long territorial war.

The dispute over actual territory was far less important to Protestants than the knowledge that Catholics were a political force to be reckoned with in the Scots-Irish capital. In Ireland as a whole, Catholics, for the first time in two centuries, had asserted themselves. A highly organized campaign, led by Daniel O'Connell, won Catholics in 1829 the right to sit in the Westminster Parliament, and this was followed by a mass agitation for the repeal of the Act of Union and the restoration of an Irish Parliament. Protestants, both Episcopal and Presbyterian, were deeply alarmed at the prospect of being ruled by an assembly with a large Catholic majority. That alarm expressed itself in Belfast in the shape of street violence.

In the second and third decades of the century Ulster Protestantism closed ranks in a way it had not done since the Williamite Wars. Paradoxically the opportunity for this was a new theological split among Presbyterians. The Old Light versus New Light controversy of the eighteenth century, that struggle between a conservative, formalized view of the Church's function and a personalized liberal one, reappeared with formidable leaders on either side. There were political differences also between the leaders; Henry Montgomery was sympathetic to full political emancipation for Catholics, and conservative Henry Cooke, although an advocate of joint education, believed that the granting of full parliamentary and civic rights, instead of limited ones, could lead to some form of Catholic totalitarianism such as was to be seen in Europe. To be fair, in this Cooke was voicing the misgivings held by earlier liberals such as the Irish Volunteer leader Flood.

In the great debate Henry Cooke was victorious, not only because he was a superb extempore speaker, with wit and the will to win, but also because public taste was swinging away from the intellectual religion of the eighteenth century to the evangelical enthusiasm which was to predominate in the nineteenth. This change was made evident in the replacement of Belfast's Georgian churches with new ones, the black Gothic spires of which stood for a simple view of existence, bright heavens above and lurid hells below. Montgomery and his associates withdrew to form the Non-Subscribing Presbyterian Church, and Cooke, who was always strongly motivated by political considerations, advocated an alliance between his own mainstream Presbyterians and the Church of Ireland: 'Between the divided Churches', he declared, 'I publish the banns of a sacred marriage.' Ulster's Protestants could now present a reasonably united front to resurgent Catholicism.

A political as much as a religious leader, Cooke mobilized Protestant opinion against Daniel O'Connell when he came to Belfast during his campaign for the return of an Irish Parliament, and O'Connell had to be protected by troops from a huge rioting crowd. By now street fighting had become a permanent feature of Belfast life, returning

The cottage linen industry employed every member of the weaver's family and brought a measure of prosperity and independence which had a profound effect on the politics of eighteenth-century Ulster.

ABOVE *Eighteenth-century agricultural scene: with high rents and constant rural violence, life for the Ulster tenant farmer was considerably less idyllic than suggested here.*

OPPOSITE *Contemporary romanticism inspired the Belfast artist Andrew Nicholl to make the Giant's Causeway much larger than life* (ABOVE). *There is, however, a strong element of realism in this distant view of Belfast as a cultured Georgian town with the countryside at its doorstep* (BELOW).

ABOVE *In the eighteenth century ships tied up in Belfast's High Street, now in the heart of the city.*

BELOW *By the nineteenth century, Belfast's new worldwide trade had crowded the River Lagan with masts.*

every few years like an epidemic. Political meetings, like the O'Connell rally, traditional marches, even sermons, provided the opportunity to fight. Sectarian violence seemed to offer relief from the monotony of work-filled lives controlled by the factory horn. It also provided the working class of either side with a convenient scapegoat for the wretchedness of their own existence.

Intemperate preaching, characteristic of the new evangelicals, whether indoors or in the open air, led to trouble. The Rev. Hugh Hanna, 'Roaring Hanna', minister of Berry Street Presbyterian Church, packed the streets with his violent rhetoric but told his excited listeners to leave a way through their ranks so that anyone who did not want to listen could pass through: 'Call that clearance "the Pope's pad [path]".' Catholics preferred to come in large numbers equipped with 'kidney' stones torn up from the pavement. An ironic bystander, Frankfort Moore, observed, 'Some of our more bellicose clergy ... had taken to preaching en plein air some highly seasoned Protestant doctrines condemning the errors of Rome ... passing members of that erroneous creed ... had the bad taste to respond with stones and missiles which are really in their own way quite as irritating as theological arguments.'

At the same time a Catholicism even more entrenched and obdurate was evolving. When the Vatican-trained Jesuit Paul Cullen was appointed Archbishop of Armagh in 1850, he represented the new aggressive spirit of Rome being directed in Europe against radicals. Immensely energetic, Cullen built schools, encouraged dynamic preaching Orders like the Redemptorists and the Passionists, nursing nuns like the Sisters of Mercy and lay social workers like the St Vincent de Paul Society. But his vision was of an exclusive, self-sufficient Catholic world run on strict disciplinarian lines. He set the priests apart by introducing the term 'Father' as a form of address and he did away with the lay committees which worked at parish level. The priest-dominated, inward-looking Irish Catholic society which resulted was possibly the greatest barrier to understanding between Protestant and Catholic in the nineteenth and twentieth centuries.

Protestant reaction was inevitable but ill-directed. The Rev. Thomas Drew, dedicated social worker and ardent Orangeman, preached a sermon in church to his brethren on the Twelfth of July 1857 in which he spoke of the 'Pope's prisons ... paved with the calcined bones of men and cemented with gore and human hair', and he linked these with America which had 'her black millions which she called slaves not men'. But whatever Drew's intentions, it was not the Pope nor the slave-owners of Georgia and Virginia who suffered as a result of his emotive diatribe. That the Pope's victims were much more likely to be free-thinking Italian liberals and Masons than Irish Protestants was lost on his congregation, and his uplifting view of a 'world regenerated' through liberal Protestantism, where all men would shed the chains from their minds and bodies disappeared in contemporary polemic. For ten days after the sermon Protestant and Catholic mobs hurled stones at each other in the city streets, and Frankfort Moore was able to observe 'the close connection since the martyrdom of St. Stephen between theology and geology'.

Daniel O'Connell, leader of the resurgent Catholic Irish, ranked with the Pope in the demonology of the Ulster Scots.

Revisionist social historians believe that exploited workers, like those of Victorian Belfast, did not feel their misery in the way that we feel it for them. Betty Messenger, in her scholarly study of the Ulster industry, *Picking up the Linen Threads*, argues that 'imbued with an ethic which exalted work well done . . . the linen workers, by and large, did not feel completely oppressed by these conditions'. She quotes retired workers looking nostalgically back at the comforting atmosphere of the work floor, the friendliness, the 'wonderful times, then in the mill'. This was probably true of the great majority, but the fact that people are not fully conscious of their degraded conditions does not in any way lessen the injustice when a much better existence is only denied them by the greed of others and the rigid adherence of the authorities to *laissez-faire* principles. The degree to which women were degraded in the conditions of linen mill life is illustrated by the savage sexual initiation rituals imposed by mill girls on young male workers.

Living conditions in the 'cockpit city' were mapped out graphically by the Rev. William O'Hanlon in his *Walks Among the Poor in Belfast*. He found 'two and even three families all occupying the same room – fathers, mothers, brothers and sisters all sleeping indiscriminately on the floor'. O'Hanlon was concerned with souls rather than bodies, the frequency of incest more than the squalor of home life. As he walked the narrow alleyways his ears were assailed by 'the frantic shouts of bacchanalian orgies'. But he was a sharp social observer and a realist who identified the social causes of immorality, and recognized that 'whiskey drinking and lewd singing relieve the monotony'.

The town fathers were well aware of the conditions in which the majority of their citizens lived. They were given the relevant statistics in successive reports by their medical officers: 'forty-five out of every hundred homes suffering from fever'; the life expectation at birth nine years; 'twenty-five thousand people without any form of sanitary accommodation'; the streets littered each morning with excreta. In 1848 Dr Andrew Malcolm came up with a suggestion which must have warmed their mercantile hearts. He pointed out that in London and Manchester this excreta was collected – by private enterprise, of course – and sold to farmers. In Belfast 'the sale of such could reach the sum of £1 per head per annum . . . we cannot but feel surprised that a money-loving people did not pounce on this mine of wealth before'.

The rise of the shipbuilding and engineering industries did much to lift the Belfast worker out of the cesspool of poverty. Belfast was an unlikely place to become either a great shipbuilding centre or a major port. It had no natural advantages of timber, coal or iron, and the River Lagan leading to its harbour was crooked, narrow and tidal. A great effort by the harbour authorities cured much of the port's physical disabilities, and the coming of skilled engineers like the Yorkshireman Edward Harland was of immense benefit to shipbuilding, but in the end the great success of both port and shipyard was due to the pool of industrious and innovative Scots-Irish workers.

By the late nineteenth century Belfast harbour was a bustling place with a global trade in linen and ships. From 1860 onwards shipbuilding had steadily increased, and, despite

ABOVE *Workers going home from the Harland and Wolff shipyard in Belfast. Shipbuilding brought prosperity to the city in the late nineteenth century.* BELOW *The* Titanic *under construction. The ship left the Belfast yard on 2 April 1912 and sank in mid-Atlantic thirteen days later.*

a slump in the early 1880s, Harland and Wolff had become the biggest shipbuilding firm in the world by the turn of the century. In 1870 Harlands had launched the *Oceanic*, whose record-breaking runs brought them into the lucrative transatlantic trade, and in the Eighties the Belfast yard was the first with steel hulls and twin-screw liners, which again were Atlantic record breakers. In the last year of the century Harlands launched the second *Oceanic*, the world's first luxury liner.

Workers in the new industries shared a little of the prosperity; wages at the shipyard and in engineering were three times as high as in the linen mills. Providing the kind of homes these artisans could afford to rent created a building boom. Smaller factory industries also grew as a result of the success of linen and ships. Belfast now had the world's largest ropeworks, and Davidsons, who made ventilation equipment, and Mackies, who manufactured textile machinery, became world leaders.

Presbyterians dominated most aspects of Belfast and Ulster life. They were invariably the best educated; at the end of the century only 2 per cent of Belfast Presbyterians were illiterate as against 3 per cent of Episcopalians and over 7 per cent of Catholics. Because of this the skilled craftsmen were largely Presbyterian, numerically an important segment of the population as Belfast had a far higher proportion of skilled men in its workforce than the British average. Most of the great merchants and industrialists were Presbyterian, though some deserted the Church of their birth for the social status conferred by membership of the Church of Ireland. In Pittsburgh Scots-Irish businessmen remained Presbyterian for precisely the same reason – to segregate themselves from their workers who had moved to the more exciting atmosphere provided by the Baptists, the Methodists and the small pentecostal churches. W. R. Rodgers, the Presbyterian minister who, swimming against the tide, became a poet, said of Belfast, his native city, that it 'never lifted its factory hat of fumes except to God on Sunday'.

On the high and healthy ridge of Malone that runs southwards out of Belfast, and along the Antrim Road to the north, the wealthy mill-owners and manufacturers built their mansions. Their upper managers and the well-to-do shopkeepers lived there too, in substantial red brick villas. Their Calvinist canniness made them chary of ostentatious display in their own homes but in their public buildings they lost that reticence. In 1888 Belfast had become a city, and in 1905 the City Fathers expressed the brash, confident mood of the new Edwardian era by replacing the White Linen Hall with a grandiose City Hall which celebrated in stone and marble the business success of the Scots-Irish. The rich ornamentation, the statuary inside and out – Queen Victoria on the front lawn supported by the symbols of empire and trade – this was the full orchestration of the new theme in Scots-Irish history, but the architect had to sue the Corporation to get his full fee.

For a few the long-sought Eden had arrived – a comfortable Eden with booming trade, cap-touching workers and a quiet Sabbath to talk to the Great Businessman above. Now, at last, it seemed safe to take a cue from the English (whom they were apeing in most other matters), to relax and boast a little.

Belfast City Hall, with its opulent interior of Italian marble and rococo plasterwork, was built on the site of the Linen Hall in 1905.

In 1911 the name of Belfast appeared in world headlines for the first time. Harlands were building the *Olympic*, a liner of a size never before seen. The *Belfast Newsletter* was lyrical: 'The men worked heartily on the graceful vessel which for almost two years has grown under their hand until she Babel-like looks down with majesty on her contemporaries. She is not built to fail. A higher destiny awaits her.'

A year later the even bigger *Titanic* set out on her maiden voyage. The journal *Shipbuilder* said she was virtually unsinkable. Five days later she sank in the mid-Atlantic with heavy loss of life. In the *Titanic* disaster, Scots-Irish pride had its come-uppance.

12 · THE SASH ACROSS THE SEA

Here am I a loyal Orangeman
Just come across the sea
For singing and for dancing
I'm sure that I'll please thee.

Traditional Orange ballad

'TODAY IF AN ORANGEMAN goes to Toronto City Hall in search of a job, he takes his chance like everyone else – there's not a single Orange member on the City council.' So Norman Ritchie, Secretary of the Grand Lodge of Canada, in 1985 summed up the demise of Orange Order power in a city where it once controlled every appointment from mayor to garbage collector. The emigrations from central and southern Europe after the Second World War swamped the Orange 'empire' which for over a century encompassed much of southern Ontario and which openly exercised much political power.

The first large-scale settlement of Upper Canada came when Loyalists – many of them Scots-Irish – fled from the United States during and after the War of Independence. A second wave of immigration, coming directly from Ulster, consisted of disbanded soldiers and small farmers hit by the agricultural slump which followed the Napoleonic Wars. It was these settlers who brought Orangeism to Canada, and for them their certificate of membership was a passport to jobs, to farm grants and to a friendly social life that eased the emotional burden of emigration.

In the Ontarian backwoods, the lodge at a crossroads was not only a social centre for the developing community but also provided religious services until a church could be built. It provided relief from the loneliness and backbreaking labour of pioneer life, and created an atmosphere with which recent immigrants were very familiar. The elaborate rituals of the Order were a form of escapism in the long monotonous snow-bound months of winter.

Orangeism also created a much-needed discipline for frontier life. The lodge imposed fines for civil offences, their ultimate sanction being to expel the offender from the Order. Expulsion was a very serious matter; the culprit became a social pariah and often had to leave the locality. The organization in the Perth area of central southern Ontario announced in 1827, 'As soon as any member of our fraternity is guilty of any disorder, or misconduct and satisfactory proof of his guilt is adduced . . . by Catholics or Protestants the offender is expelled'. The inclusion of Catholics as potential witnesses is significant for at the same time the Perth brethren made it clear that they were 'ready at all times to give the right hand of friendship to our Catholic fellow subjects'.

One of the earliest clashes between Protestant and Catholic Irish immigrants occurred around Perth. The town was one of the original strategic outposts founded early in the century to form a defence line against an invasion of Canada by the United States. Disbanded soldiers from the British armies which had fought Napoleon came here on free passage provided by the Government. Most were Scots but a few were from Ulster, and many more Ulster civilians came in the 1820s. In 1824 a large group of Catholic Irish immigrants from Cork, led by a philanthropist called Peter Robinson, arrived in the area. Tensions, as much created by the size of the new immigration as by sectarian feelings, led to fighting.

Irish Protestants began to see themselves in the role of defenders of British Canada from the threat posed by the Republican United States in the South, by the Catholic French Canadians of Quebec to the east and by Nationalist elements within the country. The situation was a complicated one, for the Orange Order assumed the role of defender of the rights of the new immigrants. As a substantial number of these were Catholic Irish, some Orange leaders felt that an alliance between themselves and the Catholics could create a strong power bloc for the protection of British interests.

In this there were many Catholics willing to forget the quarrels of the old land in order to make a success of life in the new. The Catholic Bishop of Kingston, Dr Alexander MacDonnell, who had served as a British army chaplain in Ireland during the 1798 Rebellion, 'received from the Orangemen unequivocal and substantial proof of ... friendship and generosity'. The Bishop responded with political support for the pro-British Tory Party against the Canadian nationalist Reform party led by William Lyon MacKenzie. The political links and the friendly sentiments expressed on both sides, however, did not prevent the Catholic Irish navvies who were building the Rideau canal from breaking up the Orange procession at Kingston on the Twelfth of July 1827, the first of many Twelfth riots in the history of the country.

Where the Irish Protestant and Catholic votes looked to be insufficient for victory, Orangemen armed with clubs discouraged the Reform voters from coming to the polls, and when MacKenzie, defeated at the polls, attempted to stage a *coup d'état* Orangemen flocked into the militia raised to defeat the rebels. Official rewards did not come, the authorities regarded the Order as 'a numerous and very troublesomely disposed class of person', too plebian and too independent to be trusted.

Canadian Orangeism, growing rapidly but with little organization, needed a leader, and that leader appeared in the shape of Ogle Robert Gowan from County Wexford. He was the son of a gentleman farmer and was already deeply versed in the Orange cult when he arrived in Canada in 1829. A year later he became Grand Master of the newly formed Grand Lodge of British North America. Gowan was strongly in favour of an Orange-Catholic alliance against the Reformers, 'a civil union between Protestants and Roman Catholics against the gloomy yankee faction'.

Gowan was essentially a politician and he wished to use the Order as a political force, but, because of the degree of independence which has always marked Orangeism, any union with a political party was always an uneasy one. When the Scotsman John A. MacDonald, himself an Orangeman, took over the leadership of the Conservatives, the

Climatic extremes made life harder for the Ulster settlers in Canada than it had been for their American compatriots a century earlier. In Ontario forests were felled for timber, rather than to clear land as had been the case in Pennsylvania.

Order gave its support but was in no way a tool of the party. Gowan himself, despite his aristocratic Irish background, had strong liberal tendencies and his clash with the right wing within the Grand Lodge split Canadian Orangeism for three years.

When thousands of Catholic refugees from the great Irish famine came in to Canada after 1846, Orange attitudes towards Catholicism hardened. Orange processions were temporarily banned, but at township level there was continual sectarian trouble. It was a period of swift growth: by 1860 there were 100,000 Orangemen in the country and there were lodges in Quebec, in the Maritime Provinces and Nova Scotia and as far west as Manitoba. But that increase, along with a parallel rise in numbers of Catholic Irish, meant an end to any alliance between them.

A number of external factors contributed to the deterioration in relations between Irish Protestants and Irish Catholics in Canada, the most serious of which were the Fenian invasions. The Fenian Brotherhood was a highly theatrical and relatively ineffectual Irish terrorist organization which had gained a good deal of support among Catholic Irish Americans in the Northern and Middle States. At the end of the American Civil War the Fenians recruited some ex-soldiers, and in 1866 they launched an attack across the Canadian border with about a thousand men. They had an initial success in a skirmish with Canadian militia but were soon chased back across the border by regular troops. Five years later they made another similarly unsuccessful incursion. Neither posed any serious threat but they caused great alarm among the Ulster Protestant immigrants, in whom fears of Catholic Irish aggression were inherent.

Social rather than sectarian reasons were responsible for the growth of Orangeism in Ontario; the lodge attracted new members because they provided conviviality, mutual self-help and a primitive form of social insurance. The movement spread inland from the St Lawrence and the northern shore of Lake Ontario. Places like Peel County, close to Toronto, which were heavily populated with Ulster Protestants, became strongholds. The heaviest concentration of lodges in Ontario was in the immediate hinterland of Toronto, around Peterborough and between Kingston and Ottawa. The Order also got a foothold in Quebec, the centre of Catholic French Canada, but, not surprisingly, it was highly unpopular and there were many clashes with the French-speaking *habitants*.

Second generation Scots-Irish from Ontario settling in Manitoba brought the Orange organization with them. Orangemen already there found jobs for newcomers or guided them towards the best farmlands. 'A great number of our Brethren coming here ... never dreamed of such a thing as an Orange Lodge in this priest-ridden country, but when they came and found sometimes 100 members in our Lodge it cheered their Orange hearts.'

The order was established in Saskatchewan and Alberta, again from the parent organization in Ontario. The first Twelfth of July in Alberta was celebrated at Lacombe, south of Edmonton, in the 1890s. While across the border in Saskatchewan the Orangemen of Moosamin took a commendable stand for 'the liberty of free-born subjects' by protesting against the local police trying to enforce the law against the sale of alcohol.

During the prairie settlements there occurred one of those events which indirectly increased animosity between Protestant and Catholic Irish. The Metis were a people of mixed French and Indian extraction who lived, largely by hunting, on the Canadian central plains. When new settlers, a large proportion of them Ulster Protestants, began to move into their hunting grounds on the Red River, the Metis took up arms and resisted. A young Orangeman, Thomas Scott from Toronto, was captured by them and executed by a firing squad for threatening their leader, Louis Riel. Scott's courage in the face of death, and the fact that his executioners were devout Catholics, made him a Protestant martyr and a symbol capable of provoking violence for years to come in townships a thousand miles from the Red River.

Orangeism took root in New Brunswick and Nova Scotia much earlier than in the prairie provinces. In New Brunswick the movement had begun with a military lodge in 1818, and civilian lodges followed through the efforts of James McNichol who came from Ireland in 1830. In the paternalistic mining companies of Nova Scotia the Order became almost a part of the structure. In Newfoundland the organization only developed strongly around the beginning of the twentieth century.

In the nineteenth century rack-renting and evictions still drove Ulster people to emigrate, though actual famine, except for a period in the 1840s, ceased to be a significant factor. Modern scholars, however, have detected a hidden motivation among emigrants – the desire to preserve in the face of large-scale industrial and agricultural change, their traditional way of life. Tenant farmers and self-employed craftsmen, threatened with absorption in factory-based industries or new large farms, chose to prolong their economic independence by emigration. R. Cole Harris, Pauline Roulston and Chris De Friestas, in their essay 'The Settlement of Mono Township', see these emigrants as conservatives in a period of dynamic change, seeking the right to exercise their individualism by retreating into the Canadian wilderness. They trace a hardening of Scots-Irish attitudes in the privations of early pioneer days:

> The work and isolation of pioneering, the round of material pre-occupations inevitable in establishing a farm, and the constant exposure to physical change intensified this individualism while giving it a particularly materialistic cast. For the land-hungry rural Ulstermen, the land of southern Ontario was a means of this conservative defence; that is why it was sought so eagerly, cleared so rapidly often damaged so irreparably.'

Mono township, which lies north-west of Toronto on the route to the Bruce Peninsula, does not appear from its folklore to have been a deeply materialistic place, but it provides an excellent model from which to study the life patterns of the Scots-Irish immigrants. Mono was no Eden, such as the Ulster people had found a century earlier in south-eastern Pennsylvania. It was heavily wooded, with poor sandy soils underlaid with gravel (today that gravel is a major source of rural wealth). A surveyor in the 1830s reported that the place was 'hilly and swampy and not fit for settlement'. The winters were long and snow-bound, and as the township lay between two large bodies of water – Lake Ontario and Lake Huron – windstorms were a constant threat; in 1985 a tornado cut a swathe through the woods of Mono, levelling ancient trees, power lines and shopping centres with timeless impartiality.

The surveying of Mono began in 1823. The second man to settle there, in 1825, was Robert Henry from the north of Ireland. Up to the late 1840s there was a steady flow of immigrants into the township, taking up land in one-hundred- and two-hundred-acre lots. Some of these, veterans of the Napoleonic Wars, were granted land in return for military service; others bought their land from speculators at their port of entry or at auction from the Crown. Prices recorded for Mono land in the 1840s were from five to ten shillings an acre. These Canadian settlers were less well adapted for frontier existence than their forebears in Pennsylvania and the Carolinas. A larger proportion of them were townsfolk, working in the small industries which had grown up with the coming of the Industrial Revolution to Ulster.

With the great increase in the eighteenth century in enclosed estates where timber and game were protected, few of the settlers had any experience of tree-felling and land clearance. The failure rate was much higher than with the eighteenth-century immigrants. Settlers who had taken jobs on arrival in the developing towns along the St Lawrence in order to raise money to buy their land often drifted back to those or similiar jobs, their investment gone and they themselves deeply disillusioned. Some even deserted their families in the outback. Despite this, there were 2,300 people in the township by 1850. Eighty per cent of these were Ulster Scots, or 'improved Scotch', as they were described.

The pioneers maintained the eighteenth-century Ulster lifestyle of one-family dwellings, but in Canada these were isolated in a way that was not possible in the homeland. Farm clearances in the early years consisted of small patches around the log cabin, and these were usually separated from neighbours by perhaps a mile of dense woodland. The family of one settler, Robert Henry, did not realize that they had neighbours called Turnbull until one of the Henry's cows strayed into the Turnbull holding. By the 1860s, however, farm advertisements show that in holdings of one hundred acres, sixty acres would be cleared for cultivation and the remaining woodland listed as a farm asset, ripe for exploitation. As the land came under cultivation, schools and churches were built and roads marked out. Villages grew up, usually around grist mills or provisions stores. With improved communications, social life began in the townships, usually based around the church or the local Orange lodge. As with the earlier frontiersmen, there were communal gatherings or 'bees' to clear land, to build houses or to bring in the harvest.

The terrors of the long winter isolation were eased once the settlers learned that travel by sleigh over the frozen tracks in January was easier than travel on muddy roads in spring or autumn. 'People like deep snow for it gives good slaeing and they drive like fury', wrote Joseph Carrothers in a letter home. Because of the greater availability of horses, travel was much easier than it had been in the early American settlements; people now went on purely social visits, as the diaries of the old Mono residents record. Pork was the staple meat diet although, of course, some deer and other game were shot. For the winter, pork was preserved in a brine of brown sugar and salt, but the most popular method of preserving meat was to fry it in steaks, put these in a large stone crock and pour the lard over them so that the meat was sealed inside. It could then be kept for months at a low temperature in one of the colder rooms or in an outside store house.

'We haven't any history here, just things that happened to people.' This sentiment expressed by an old inhabitant of Mono township sums up the Scots-Irish distrust of the abstract. Mono, with its early Ulster settlers, the McMasters, the McCutcheons, the Henrys and the Allens, was a place of 'happenings', memorable drinking bouts in Orangeville or Shelburne, elections where Orange and Green clashed, narrow escapes from bears or wolves, small tragedies that occurred in the dead of winter, to be discovered with the melting of the snow in late spring. The Scots-Irish propensity for storytelling has woven these events into folklore, preserving even the texture of witty tavern exchange of a hundred years ago: 'None of our family were ever in jail'; 'No wonder, the penalty for sheep stealing was hanging.'

In early pioneer days the wolves, still large in numbers, hunted in packs of thirty or forty and would tail a lone settler moving through the woods in the hope that he might stumble and give them the opportunity to attack. When neighbours gathered at a farm in the early fall to thrash the wheat crop they knew the wolf pack was waiting in the surrounding forest. In the evening the progress of each man going home could be traced by the barking of the accompanying wolves. Only at nightfall did they become dangerous. Jeremiah Phillips, caught by darkness a quarter of a mile from home, was surrounded by wolves and had to climb a tree to escape. All night he could hear his wife sounding a horn to guide him home, but he dared not answer lest she should come to meet him and fall victim.

There is a whole mythology about bears in the township. William Johnston, coming on a large bear beside a newly uprooted spruce tree, shot at it with his musket but unfortunately for him the shot only wounded the animal sufficiently to infuriate it. William, in his fright, dropped his powder flask, and for the next twenty minutes he dodged round the spruce tree followed by the bear until he recoverd the powder, reloaded on the run and shot the animal as its teeth were closing on the gun barrel.

Bears were particularly fond of hog meat and would shake a hog pen until the logs became loose enough to pull away. If hungry enough, they came boldly in by the door. Betty Agnew, who lived in Lot 15 of the Mono township, saw a bear enter her pig pen one evening. Her husband locked himself in their dwelling house, but Betty seized a handspike and when the bear emerged carrying a squealing pig she brought the handspike down on his spine. To instructions from her husband, shouted from behind closed doors, she finished off the bear.

The Ontarian winter was an experience more strange and terrifying for the settler

ABOVE *Many Ulster Scots were among the Canadian Volunteers who were rushed by train to the American frontier in June 1866 to repel an invasion by Irish Fenians from the United States.*

BELOW *The execution of Orangeman Thomas Scott, by Catholic French Indian Meti rebels, deepened the feud between Protestant and Catholic Irish in Canada.*

than anything else he experienced in the immigration process. The cold was lethal to anyone caught off guard. Jane White of Goderich, Ontario, wrote home to her friends at Newtownards, 'so many persons have been frozen to death this winter, if they fall down they never rise again'. In the Mono backwoods a family recently arrived from Ulster were attacked by cholera, probably brought from the emigrant ship. Cut off from his neighbours by deep snow, the father of the family watched his wife and children, one by one, sicken and die. At each death he took out the family Bible, and, reading to the dwindling number of survivors, held a funeral service. The body was then carried to an outhouse. One night he heard the wolves scraping at the earth to break in, and from then on he had to mount guard over the frozen corpses. As he sat with his dead family around him he carved wooden tombstones for them, and when the ground unfroze he single-handedly buried them in a plot at the edge of the woods.

There were, inevitably, sectarian troubles, but these are among the more light-hearted episodes in Mono folklore. Catholic children were taunted with

Titter totter, holy water,
Sprinkle Catholics everyone,
If that won't do,
We'll cut them in two,
And make them lie under the
Orange and Blue.

John Flanaghan, who had trained in Ireland for the Catholic priesthood, came to farm in Mono. A Protestant neighbour, trading on the ignorance of the celibate ex-student, sold him a cow which to the immense delight of the local Orange Lodge turned out to be a bull. Even the more tense points in Protestant-Catholic relationships had their element of the ridiculous. During the Fenian invasion threat, Protestant communities expected to be attacked by their Catholic neighbours; the folk memory of seventeenth-century massacres in Ireland still haunted the Canadian backwoods. The people of Mono, armed with guns and pitchforks, assembled at midnight on the border of the adjoining Catholic township of Adjala to repel the expected attack. Scouts on horseback were sent to reconnoitre Adjala but found everyone there asleep. The Mono defenders then repaired to the nearest tavern, opened the bar and, joined by some Catholics awakened by the midnight manoeuvres, celebrated the peace.

Letters of Canadian emigrants show an attachment to Ulster that was missing from eighteenth-century emigrant letters; they also show that mental attitudes survived the Atlantic crossing better in the 1840s than they did a century earlier. Joseph and Nathaniel Carrothers, who came from the Lisbellaw district of County Fermanagh to western Ontario, had this rural *pietas*, an inbred love of the soil, a trigger which constantly recalled the wet lands of west Ulster to their minds. Their letters are full of requests for plants and seeds from home as if they were trying to recreate the Fermanagh landscape on their farms near London, Ontario: 'Send me 4 of the scarlit Thorn. James Graham will show you them at my old dwelling'; 'Any seed that is on the marchmallows . . . and on the Queen Cups . . . send me a few grains.'

Distance concentrated the exile's memory and sharpened his affection. As letters from home announced the deaths of friends, Joseph Carrothers grieved for them: 'many of my old acquaintances removed to there last home'. Alexander Robb, in British Columbia, wrote to his sister, 'The only thing I regret . . . is leaving those I love behind me'. Alexander, who was glad to be gone from a country where he had paid, 'twenty pounds . . . per acre for lease to farm a patch of hungry ground from which one may be turned out by the mere caprice of a landlord', had a very practical way of solving his loneliness: 'Do you know', he asked his sister Susanna, 'of some decent girl you could send out? . . . a good wife would be the making of me. . . . She may be of any age from twenty to forty, long or short, fair or dark, money or no money, but I would like her to be industrious . . . and at least middling good looking.'

Although communications were improved, America was still a remote place where friends and relatives could disappear entirely from the ken of those left at home in Ireland. John Miller, recently emigrated from County Armagh, was in a hotel at Oswego in up-state New York, on his way to Canada, when 'an oldish kind of lady', recognizing his accent, asked him his name and if he had relatives in America. He replied he had a sister Mary who came out when he was a child but he thought she must be dead: 'The tears falled down hir cheeks and she got me in hir arms and said you must be my brother John.'

The Orange or Masonic networks, or the help of relatives already established in Canada, smoothed the way for many emigrants; the journal of Wilson Benson is particularly interesting because he had none of these advantages. Benson was eighteen when he emigrated with his sixteen-year-old wife Jemima, and he was totally innocent of the ways of the world. The Bensons went headlong into every possible misfortune which awaited the inexperienced, and also had more than their share of bad luck. Trouble began just after their ship, the *Sarah Stewart*, left Belfast for Quebec: 'A storm arose and during the next three days was every moment expected to go to the bottom. A sum of five hundred sovereigns was raised amongst the passengers and offered to the captain if he would return to Belfast, but he declared that he dare not do so for any consideration, although we were up to the knees in water on the lower deck.' When the storm abated, cholera broke out. Wilson and his wife watched a shark follow the ship for the two days between the death and burial of a passenger. Then when the corpse went overboard the fish disappeared. As the *Sarah Stewart* lay becalmed in miles of dense fog off the Newfoundland Bank, a vessel without rigging or masts appeared through the murk like a ghost ship. After this encounter the brutal Captain Lowe went mad, and, taking the ship's carpenter into the hold, tried to scuttle the vessel.

On arrival at Brockville on the St Lawrence the couple had all their money and clothes stolen. Jemima took a job as a live-in maid and Wilson slept in the town graveyard. He tried a number of jobs, baking, shoe-making and working as a cook aboard a river steamer, none of which proved successful. While on board the steamer Wilson saw, to his surprise, a savage fight between groups of Catholic Irish navvies: 'Two men had their brains beaten out ... the wives and children of the murdered men rending the air with their piercing shrieks while the bloody butchery was being enacted.'

After some years Wilson discovered that he could make large profits by selling whiskey on the frontier. With this money he bought a farm in Amaranth township, south of Mono. He brought his first wheat crop to the neighbouring village of Orangeville, where the grist mill was owned by Mick McLaughlin, an Irish Catholic. When the flour from the grain mysteriously disappeared, all Wilson's Ulster prejudices were confirmed: 'the relative fairies of the McLaughlins had followed them from Ireland ... and spirited away my flour.' That fall he was awakened one night by the squeal of one of his pigs. Rushing out of the house he saw, 'a huge bear with a pig in his arms, making his way out of the pig-sty'.

Disheartened by their experiences, Wilson and his wife moved northward through Mono to the virtually unexplored area of Artemesia. Here he saw pioneer life in the raw – the first years of a settlement, when there was not enough food grown to keep a family at subsistence level: 'In the early summer wild leeks, cow cabbage, wild nettles etc were a substitute for a more substantial meal.... As soon as potatoes were the size of musket bullets they were carefully extracted from the root without damaging the stalk.'

An accident at a threshing mill left Wilson unfit for farm work. He sold his farm and moved into the village of Markdale where he opened a store. When he was in his mid-fifties he published his life story to guide the reader 'clear of the shoals upon which I ran aground'. As a storekeeper he must eventually have prospered for he is buried under a large marble tombstone in Markdale churchyard.

The commercial drive of the Ulster Scot showed itself in the phenomenal expansion of Toronto; from a small village in 1803 it became Canada's largest city and the port through which much of her wealth flowed. Until the middle of the twentieth century it was controlled, though by no means exclusively populated, by the Scots-Irish. Though its physical situation is quite unlike that of either Pittsburgh or Belfast, it resembled both cities in its rate of growth and the mercantile philosophy which inspired its citizens. It resembled the other cities too in its insistence on strict observance of Sunday. In the 1890s there was a bitter debate in the city as to whether streetcars ought to run on Sundays. But the singular feature of the city was the predominance of the Orange Order, in business, in politics and in everything related to the day-to-day running of the municipality. The City Fathers were almost entirely Orangemen. In fact the composition of the council was decided at the Order's headquarters and the list of approved candidates published before the election in the *Evening Telegraph*, the mouthpiece of Orangeism; it almost invariably proved to be the final make-up of the council elected a few days later.

ABOVE *Craigvale Orange Lodge, Simcoe County, Ontario, c. 1915.*

RIGHT *Orange parade in Toronto, c. 1905–10. The Orange Order virtually controlled Toronto in the late nineteenth and early twentieth centuries, and the Twelfth of July was as important there as in Belfast.*

No one could be mayor unless he belonged to the Order and the same was true of lesser office-holders. Paid jobs at City Hall, from city treasurer downwards, were doled out through Orange patronage. The police force and the fire service were controlled by the local lodges. Maverick Protestants who felt that 'riding the goat' – joining the Order – was too high a price to pay for a civic job, probably suffered more from the system than Catholics, who could often reach arrangements with Orange officialdom.

Orange power was at its greatest in the early decades of the twentieth century, but even then in terms of national politics it was no more than a powerful pressure group: 'We could stir up a hornet's nest', said Orange official Norman Ritchie, 'but we could not defeat a national government.' Often, too, the public face belied the private attitude. When an Orangeman, Thomas Hackett, was murdered in Montreal on the Twelfth of July 1877, there was a massive turnout of brethren at his funeral and the Grand Master declared, 'Woe betide this city if we have to come again.' But the following year, when the Twelfth parade was banned in Montreal, the Orange leaders responsibly withdrew from a confrontation which could have led to bloodshed.

Sectarianism was not created by the Orange Order on the Protestant side nor by the Ancient Order of Hibernians on the Catholic; bigotry was deeply ingrained in the men and women of both denominations. Jane White, a well-educated immigrant, could write of Catholics in a purely social context, 'I never liked any I ever knew ... they are so bigotted and uncharitable'. Nor did the Orange Order represent the extremes of Protestant feeling. There was a brief flirtation with the Ku Klux Klan who tried, with some success in Saskatchewan, to create a common anti-Catholic front. But such virulent extremism as the Klan's was ill-suited to a broadly based movement like Orangeism. In the second half of the nineteenth century the Orange oath was rewritten to include a clause forbidding Orangemen to marry Catholics. This, however, was mild compared with the strictures against mixed marriage placed on Catholics by their own Church.

Outside of the Order, Orangemen formed themselves into associations at local level to resist the encroachment of Catholics into Protestant areas. In Cavan township near Peterborough, the 'Town Line Blazers', a Canadian version of the Peep O'Day Boys, threatened Catholics attempting to settle in the township and burned the homes of those who had the temerity to ignore the threats. There is no doubt that this movement had the support of the local Protestants; no witnesses to the outrages came forward and no warrants were issued for the arrest of the perpetrators.

To the average Orangeman the lodge was a place of companionship, an all-male refuge from womenfolk and family. Despite what might be believed outside, more time was spent drinking punch than plotting against the Pope. (Later, as the temperance movement grew strong in the Protestant churches, more and more lodges banned alcohol.) Only one verse of the Orange theme song, 'The Sash My Father Wore', is devoted to the Order's political stance; the rest is about pride in regalia, meeting old friends and singing and dancing. Lodge meetings, with their atmosphere of secrecy and their elaborate rituals, provided excitement, and progression through the degrees of Orangeism gave a sense of achievement to thousands whom the expected rewards of emigration had eluded.

The Order declined dramatically from the middle of the twentieth century. The Twelfth of July could no longer compete as a folk festival with modern forms of entertainment; the lodge could only attract older men. Even those coming out from Ulster did not take up membership in Canada, possibly because they wanted to forget the troubles of their native province. The more nationally-minded Canada became, the less relevant Orangeism – with its pledge to maintain the British connection – was to Canadian life. But most important of all, the Scots-Irish in Canada, as they had much earlier in the United States, became absorbed by succeeding waves of immigration and lost their coherence as a people.

13 · PROMISED LANDS DOWN UNDER

'Rank and title have no charms in the antipodes ... Great family connections and ancestry would only provoke, to any who should parade them, the remark that "he was like a potato: all that was good belonging to him was underground".'

G. Butler Earp, *The Gold Colonies of Australia*, 1852

THE SCOTS-IRISH experience in Australasia differed in a number of ways from that in the United States or Canada. In the first place, the emigrants left Ulster in the mid-nineteenth century largely for private and personal reasons; there was no major economic or religious cause creating a mass exodus, as in the 1720s and 1770s to North America. A family might emigrate because their Ulster farm offered them only a subsistence, but their poverty arose from their own individual circumstances. Many of their neighbours would be immune to the lure of 'the best country under the sun' because they were already comparatively prosperous in their own land. Tithes were now less of a burden than an irritant and the 'Ulster Custom', which enabled tenants to be paid for improvements which they made on a leased farm, created a source of capital for any prepared to be hardworking and thrifty.

A far greater proportion of those emigrating were middle-class professional people – doctors, teachers, lawyers, engineers. Part of the reason for this increase in the middle-class percentage was the cost of the fare, which was three and sometimes four times greater than that to America; part was the surplus of educated people which the developing professional classes in Ulster produced in the nineteenth century. These people quickly took commanding positions in the political and business life of the colony, and were vital in Australia's incredibly rapid development in urbanization, in agriculture and in commerce.

A third factor creating a difference in Scots-Irish pioneering attitudes in Australia and New Zealand is something which may have happened to them on the voyage out. Patrick O'Farrell, in his *Letters From Irish Australia 1825–1929*, sees the long journey as 'a strange time-warp across the lives of those who experience it', which 'dissolved or weakened the fabric of organized, church-oriented religion ... the Catholics seem to have best survived'. O'Farrell offers convincing evidence of a process which was the direct opposite to the American, where the Presbyterian Church became a unifying bond – at least until such times as frontier life and the excitement of the Baptist and Methodist creeds weakened it. But if formalized religion was the primary casualty of that 'strange time-warp', it is equally true that a large proportion of both the Catholic

Irish and the Ulster Scots brought with them to the antipodes that suspicion and dislike of each other which seems to be a basic ingredient of Irish religion. Sectarian politics, which vanished in the American melting pot, were carried to Australasia not as contraband but as an openly declared part of the emigrants' luggage.

The voyages of the notorious 'Fleets', which in the closing years of the eighteenth century brought to Australia her first white – and convict – population, were an important but separate component in the make-up of the Australian nation. No convicts came directly from Ireland in the First Fleet in 1788, or the Second in 1790, but the Third had one ship which sailed from Cork and carried convicts from all over Ireland, including some from Ulster, such as John Armstrong from Monaghan and Mary Davidson from Armagh.

Life aboard the Fleets certainly compared in hardship with the Atlantic voyages. Discipline was harsh. Months in chains with short rations killed off seven of the Irish prisoners in the Third Fleet, and left the rest in such a weakened condition that a year after arrival only fifty of the male convicts were still alive. It was little wonder that a group from the Irish party 'absconded from the settlement with the chimerical idea of walking to China'. Some of the fugitives were killed by natives, some died of exposure and the rest were rounded up, hungry and dispirited, to face the penalties.

Frequent floggings were a feature of all the convict voyages, and on one a man was executed at the yardarm. Aboard the *Britannia*, in 1797, six men died from flogging. What the authorities had begun on ship, they continued on land. H. C. Allen, in his *Bush and Backwoods*, draws attention to the amount of 'blood drawn by the lash in Australia', and to the victims with 'swollen, gangrened backs stuck to their shirts'. Added to the official cruelty, there was the exploitation by private employers to whom the prisoners were hired out, and who regarded them as more expendable than slaves. Anglican clerics aboard the convict ships were identified with official repression and what appeared to the convicts to be religious hypocrisy. After arrival many became magistrates and earned a further unenviable reputation as 'flogging parsons'.

Men, women and children were transported for trivial offences. A County Antrim man, William McKeown, received a seven-year sentence for stealing two and a half yards of cloth; Tom McKibbin, also of County Antrim, was given twice that sentence for attempting to pass a forged banknote. Boys of twelve and under were sent to the penal colony for pilfering, and women, often with infants or small children, merely for 'being vagabonds'.

In addition to the physical torments of these so-called criminals, there were also the deep emotional ones of separation. Alexander Boyce, who had been transported from Belfast, heard nothing of his wife and family for three years. 'I am surprised at your neglect and silence', he wrote, appealing to her to join him in Australia with his 'beloved children', and promising, 'a salubrity of climate equal to the garden of the world'. Next March, he told her, he would be as 'free as the air' and ready to take up a Government land grant. Sarah Cramsie, transported for her part in a violent robbery in a Belfast alleyway, but ten years later 'most respectably married' in Australia, begged for news of 'a boy child' whom she had left behind her in a city workhouse. 'She is most anxious to get him out to her, if living, as she is well off.'

Immediately before and after the 1798 Rebellion, numbers of what today would be termed political prisoners were transported, though in that period of Government panic the definition was broad enough to include those caught away from home during curfew. For the actual rebels, after the first fury of drumhead courts martial and immediate executions had died down, transportation seemed to those in authority an ideal solution. 'All United Irishmen who were in on treasonable practices are only indicted for a lesser offence so as to come under transportation,' according to one Ulster magistrate. The colonial government looked less favourably on this wholesale export of seditious persons, fearing that, with the number of transported Whiteboys and other agrarian terrorists, there could be a revolution in the making in the southern continent.

The voyage to Australia is much better documented than the early transatlantic crossings. By Victorian times the keeping of journals and the writing of lengthy descriptive letters had become a habit. Reading these, perhaps the first thing that strikes one is the vast improvement in the passengers' diet.

> Each man gets daily half a pound of meat, fresh meat twice and salt meat five times a week. We get a pound of flour daily and bread is baked by the baker four times a week. We get porridge five times a week and soup five times, cheese three times and rashers [bacon] three, 12 oz of sugar each, plenty of tea and coffee and other things such as spices, pickles and molasses and any amount of biscuits, always plenty of water.

Samuel Shaw, to whom we owe this description of the ship's menu, was a steerage passenger from Belfast to Sydney in 1877. John Sayers, sailing two years earlier, commented, 'Excellent fare ... Irish stew made with preserved mutton for dinner and some tart or Sweet cake and plaice for tea.' Elizabeth Anketell, a cabin class passenger in 1865 and a chronic complainer, recorded in her journal, 'Wretched cooking, pork, pork every day now for weeks which does not agree with me'. Less privileged passengers found the meals compared favourably with the potato-dominated diet they had left behind: 'I am stronger and a good deal fatter since I left.' Certainly it was a vastly different culinary experience from that of John Smillie aboard the *Sally*, bound for Philadelphia in 1762.

Storms were still a hazard, even for the larger and better-equipped ships of the antipodes route. Bessie Macready, sailing to New Zealand in 1828, encountered a 'perfectly appalling gale. It screamed as if the ship's sides would be driven in ... the sound was like that of a cannonball ... the bows of the ship dipping into the water and throwing it over the deck in a magnificent waterfall ... the ship was filled with water and remained sometimes on one side before it could right itself.' Oliver McSparran,

ABOVE *The settler's letters home, with glowing and often exaggerated descriptions of life in Australia, frequently persuaded others to emigrate.* BELOW *Joe McKinney (centre), who prospered on an Australian sheep ranch, on a visit home to his family at Sentry Hill near Belfast.*

from Feeney in County Londonderry, who sailed to Victoria in 1859, had a terrifying experience shortly after entering the Southern Hemisphere: 'our vessel was struck by lightning. It fractured the main mast and ran down a chain to the coppering of the bulwarks. It tore it up on some places and melted it in others and made its way out through the bulwarks and into the water . . . if a thousand cannons had been fired in one volley it would not have been as loud.' At the height of these fierce storms, Mrs Flemming, a Methodist lady from County Donegal who was travelling cabin class, could hear the Catholic peasant women down in the steerage, 'screaming, and praying and confessing their sins'.

Something approaching naval discipline, though without the ferocity of the convict ships, was maintained aboard. James Dempsey, sailing from Londonderry in 1838, discovered that, 'if anyone is found pilfering . . . or giving insolence . . . or refusing to clean their births or sweep upper and lower decks . . . when they arrived at Sidney, will be given up to the government and punished in proportion . . .'. No doubt his landlord's son, to whom the sycophantic Dempsey ('your kind and affectionate servant until death') addressed his letter, heartily approved. Samuel Shaw witnessed a court martial on board: 'one of the married men would not take his [fire] watch so they gave him a month scrubbing the deck'. During the voyage of the *Minehaha* in 1858 a man who disobeyed the mate was, 'handcuffed for two days . . . and fed on bread and water'.

Boredom affected mainly the middle-class passengers. Elizabeth Anketell, from Aughnacloy in County Tyrone, was a very refined, very pious Protestant who enjoyed 'Miss Sharpe's nice book, *Wandering over Bible Lands*', but kept 'Mr Pollock's *Sermons* . . . for an especial treat on Sunday'. When not reading uplifting literature she was deeply bored: 'A more monstrous, horrible life could not be: the night shut up in a close cabin smelling of oil paint and with the noise, tramp, tramp, overhead.' Her only comfort, outside of the works of Miss Sharpe or Mr Pollock, was the company of two nice gentlemen: 'a great protection as the steerage passengers are allowed quite too much liberty in coming up on our deck'.

For the less refined there were amusements, mock auctions, various traditional nautical romps and plenty of opportunities to play practical jokes on pompous fellow passengers. The ceremony of initiating those 'crossing the line' for the first time was observed aboard the *Queen of Australia*, to the disgust of Elizabeth Anketell:

> I cannot enjoy these nasty jokes – the victim is placed on a stool, held by two men blackened all over to represent negroes; Neptune and his wife dressed up in the most hideous manner, sit in front. A large brush, dipped in pitch and tar is put all over the face and into the mouth if possible . . . he is rolled down into a tank of sea water and nearly smothered by the two negroes. . . . I had to pay a fine of three shillings and kiss Mrs Neptune – this I certainly did not calculate on.

On the other hand, John Sayers, a Belfast Methodist, thoroughly enjoyed the buffoonery, including the 'dead horse', a pantomine animal which was ridden about the deck by the sailors, then hoisted to the yardarm and set on fire.

William Bates, an earnest young Presbyterian clergyman from Strabane in County Tyrone, experienced at first hand the effect of O'Farrell's 'time warp' in religious observances. 'Our young men seem indifferent to religion . . . they crowned the sabbath evening's impropriety by closing Mr Bowman [a fellow cleric] in the water closet, tying the doors together with a rope.' Indeed the whole of shipboard life seemed to indicate to Bates a sudden inexplicable decline in spiritual values, whether it was gambling, drinking or the sailors singing 'a very wicked song, the chorus coming every four lines was, "And hell to your soul is it tea you want"'. As far as poor Mr Bowman was concerned, the customary Irish respect for clerical cloth seems to have completely vanished. Some of the younger passengers climbed to the mizzen topmast and began pelting him as he lay reading, 'with rotten cabbages and turnips'. For Elizabeth Anketell, another symbol of the hierarchical world they had left behind, the jokers of the *Queen of Australia* reserved more subtle torments, making her believe 'by squeaking and scratching that rats are coming down the air pipe', and they violated her Victorian sense of propriety by hoisting some clothing she put out to dry, 'to the highest mast on the ship'.

For everyone, from the cabin passengers paying fifty pounds to the steerage emigrants paying fifteen, the voyage was full of strange, even unheard-of things. 'Imagine', wrote Daniel Gardner to his wife Rosey, 'a piece of ice three miles long and 350 feet high floating in mid-ocean.' Samuel Shaw saw his first porpoises, flying fish and whales off Madeira. He and his fellow passengers, oblivious of the fate of the Ancient Mariner, devised a particularly cruel way of catching albatrosses: 'all that is necessary is to put a piece of meat on an ordinary fishing rod, they catch at the meat and swallow the hook'. Around the emigrant ships the winged fishes were 'flying about the way sparrows does at home', while the porpoises were 'snorting like horses'. Even the bored Miss Anketell had to admire 'such numbers of beautiful birds'.

There was a theatrical quality about shipboard life; everything that the emigrants experienced, the unusually good food, the marine life, the frightening storms, the sudden short quarrels, all had a compression and a heightened intensity not to be found in the slow-moving life ashore. By and large, sectarianism had been written out of the script and for an interlude the majority of the passengers were Irish together. Down-to-earth people like Samuel Shaw, son of a tenant farmer, recognized the common disabilities that linked lower-class Protestant and Catholic. If trouble threatened, they were the peacemakers: 'We nearly had a row this evening between the Roman Catholics and one of the married men who was laughing at them at mass. They all came on deck vowing vengence but the matter was hushed up.'

In contrast, Charles Elliot, a gentleman from the politically tense area of Scarva in Armagh, needed to distance himself, for social as well as sectarian reasons, from his Catholic countrymen. Elliot was a snob and a bigot, eager to record the shortcomings of Catholics who 'at what they called their prayers . . . were hardly off their knees till they

Hill End (ABOVE) *and Home Rule* (BELOW), *two typical goldmining towns in New South Wales photographed in the late nineteenth century. The Irish – Catholic and Protestant, farm labourers and gentlemen – joined the rush to the goldfields.*

had a hard box among themselves – a most infernal lot of blackguards are the dirty Irish papists'. Shaw messed with Catholics, 'but we have agreed very well' and when 'the greatest fight yet . . . between a Scotchman and an Englishman' occurred he and the rest of the Irish, irrespective of denomination, sided with the Scot. Mrs Hemmings, who sailed in the *Fearnought* in the 1870s, was also 'thoroughly sick of the English, their abominable jargon sounds hateful to my Celtic ears and whenever I hear an Irish accent, North or South, it seems like music . . .'.

When gold was found in New South Wales in 1851, the Scots-Irish were no more impervious to the lure of quick riches than any other people. Ulster Scots, already in Australia, gave up their jobs and moved to the goldfields; back in the Irish homeland the excitement was almost as great as gentlemen's sons and farm labourers vied with each other for places aboard the clippers bound for Sydney. Disappointed miners from California, Scots-Irish among them, crossed the Pacific to try again in Australia. The population of the continent rose from half a million in the year of the gold find to over a million eight years later. In the new shantytowns of the goldfields prices soared – water 15 cents a bucket, milk 20 cents a quart, butter 30 cents a pound, a dollar a night for a flea-ridden bed in a doss house; the prospectors' money quickly disappeared and they were forced to take jobs serving the newly arrived who still had cash in their pockets.

A surprising number of Ulster prospectors were middle-class or minor gentry. Noah Dalway, who belonged to one of Ulster's original planter families – Dalway's Bawn, near Carrickfergus, is still a showpiece of Plantation architecture – invested his total savings in a mine but found no worthwhile gold. He was soon living on bread and water and sleeping rough. Eventually, an Ulster friend found him a job but by that time he had decided that it was not his 'lot to become a fortune finder . . . I am quite sick of this horrid colony'.

John Steele Nicholson, originating from Bangor on the opposite shore of Belfast Lough, belonged to the same gentry class. He had some initial success, quarrying about one hundred pounds' worth of gold at Dimolly, in Victoria, but discovered that below the surface his gold reef petered away to nothing. Steele Nicholson could afford to be cheerful for his family, unlike Dalway's, still had money, and he found the antipodean blood sports exhilarating, if somewhat different from the hunts of North Down. 'I was at a fine kangaroo hunt last week; that's the fun; the devil a ditch or fence but at it just as fast as your horse can carry you.'

The Lawrence brothers, also from a well-to-do family in Coleraine, tried the Victoria fields without much success. Charles Lawrence died in poverty in Melbourne but his brother Sampson, partly supported by a small private income from Ireland, hung around the diggings for years, long after other miners had given up, a lonely man, sustained by the eternal hope of a rich find and by the correspondence he kept up with relatives at home. Although the other miners were 'his best friends', Sampson Lawrence never forgot he was a gentleman, paying 'the wife of an old Dublin seaman' to wash his 'fine shirts' and expressing horror at the depths to which his countrymen, such as 'the bushranger Kelly who I am sorry to say are sons of Irish parents', could fall. Gold mining, however, hardened others to the crudities of frontier life. Lewis Twigg, son of a solicitor in Cookstown, County Tyrone, recorded without disapproval an incident on New Zealand diggings, 'I saw one chap wipe his backside with a £5 note.'

To some Ulster people their close family ties were more important than the chance of a large fortune. James Getty from the Ballymoney district of Antrim had tried the Australian diggings and failed. His brother John appealed to him to return and share the family farm. 'Mother cries come home and Mary wishes you were home and I wish you were home ... I fear you will encumber yourself with houses and work and affairs that you will never get rid of.' So strong was the pull of kinship that it was almost as if the absent one's wraith could cross ten thousand miles of water in response to these impulses of love: 'Your mother will dream of you sometimes and thinks she hears you at the window and rises to let you in.'

Twenty years after the first gold finds the whole character of the diggings had changed. The hopes of overnight fortunes, along with the rampant exploitation and the squalor, had gone. George McLean, writing to a friend in Richhill, County Armagh, noted that companies had replaced individuals in prospecting: 'Very few miners ... except Johnny Chinaman.... Gold digging is both dangerous and uncertain.... Store keeping is a much shurer game.'

Possibly because of the country's origins as a penal colony, the folk heroes of Australia are its bushrangers. As early as the 1840s, Van Diemen's Land (Tasmania) recognized that its 'historical great man' was a desperado called Michael Howe. The scaffold speech of the notorious outlaw Jenkins, hanged in 1834 – 'If you take to the bush, shoot every tyrant you come across' – was quoted with relish in bar rooms throughout the continent. Though Ned Kelly, who came of Catholic Irish stock, was the most famous and most admired of these highwaymen, it was the Scots-Irishman Andrew George Scott who became the model for 'Captain Starlite' in Rolf Boldrewood's classic novel *Robbery Under Arms*.

Scott was born in 1842, at Rathfriland, County Down, where his father was the local Anglican clergyman. As a youth Scott was described as 'dark, handsome, active and full of spirits ... but known for impulsive acts of violence'.

Before he began to figure in official records it is difficult to distinguish fact from fiction in Scott's life. He claimed to have studied engineering in London, his student career abruptly terminated when he seduced the wife of a leading businessman; to have served with Garibaldi in the liberation of Italy (in his outlaw days he wore a red shirt in memory of the great Italian) and to have marched in the American Civil War with Sherman, 'from Atlanta to the sea'. It is known that he arrived in New Zealand with his family in

1861; there his father took up a post in Christchurch and his brother was ordained a parson. Scott became a schoolmaster, joined the militia during the Maori Wars, and, after a shadowy period when it is possible he was a quartermaster in Sherman's army, he arrived in Australia in 1868.

Scott had fine manners and was charming and plausible. Everywhere he went he made a point of ingratiating himself with the higher ranks of the Anglican Church, and was known and well regarded by a network of bishops and clergy. The Bishop of Melbourne appointed him a stipendiary lay reader at the Church of the Holy Trinity, Bacchus Marsh, where he drew full congregations by his colourful sermons, spiced with anecdotes from his 'military career'. After a year he was sent to Egerton, near Ballarat; there, bored with months of preaching, scripture reading and taking tea with respectable ladies, he put on a cloak and mask one evening and, armed with a revolver, robbed the Egerton bank.

His bravado in leaving a note signed 'Captain Moonlite' brought suspicion on him but he managed to avoid arrest and, quitting clerical circles, moved to the very secular society of Sydney. He lived in a grand manner on the proceeds of the robbery and when they were finished began passing worthless cheques. Such was the position he created for himself among the wealthy that he was able to buy a large yacht, and was about to embark for Fiji when arrested for fraud. After serving a twelve-month sentence he was re-arrested on the bank robbery charge. He conducted his own defence and kept the courtroom amused by scoring off witnesses, opposing counsel and judge alike. Despite, or perhaps because of, his remarkable histrionic talent, he was given ten years.

In jail Scott was a violent and recalcitrant prisoner, but after his release his chameleon-like character underwent yet another change and he began a campaign of lectures for prison reform. To his extreme annoyance – for Scott craved recognition above anything else – the newspapers ignored his campaign, preferring to fill their columns with the exploits of the newcomer Ned Kelly.

Motivated by envy as well as admiration, Scott recruited a gang from jail friends and fellow customers in brothels. One ingenuous young man answered an advertisement placed by Scott for a 'lecturer's assistant'. With his men, Scott took over the Wantabadgery sheep station, holding the family and workers at gunpoint for two days. He now openly called himself 'Captain Moonlite' and exulted when his gang drove off the police troopers in the gun battle at Wantabadgery. Soon afterwards they were surrounded in a small homestead where they had taken two children hostage. A constable and a bushranger were killed and 'Moonlite', resisting to the end, was overpowered.

At his trial in the Supreme Court in Sydney, on what he believed to be his penultimate stage, Scott played his wide range of parts: the strong and fearless leader appealing for mercy, not for himself but for his friends; the compassionate enemy sorry for the policeman he had killed; the true follower of Christ reminding the Pharisees in authority of the hollowness of their Sunday bells; the witty highwayman flirting with the ladies in the public gallery. On the day of his hanging he asked if there were reporters present, and on being told there were not went silently to his final drop. Had he read one journalist's summing-up of his career – 'Brave to the verge of recklessness, cool, clear-headed and sagacious and with a certain chivalrous dash . . . the beau ideal of the brigand chief' – he would probably have thought it was all worth while.

It would be wrong to suggest that 'Captain Moonlite' or gentlemen prospectors like Steele Nicholson were typical of the Ulster Scot 'down under'. The true blossoming of Scots-Irish endeavour came in the careers of men like 'Bullocky' Sam Wilson, from the townland of Ballycloughan in the very heart of the Scots-Irish lands of mid-Antrim, or Wilson's nephew, the genial sheep rancher Sam McCaughey, or Joseph McGaw from the fertile ridge of Mallusk which runs north from Belfast; these were the pastoralists, the Australian 'squattocracy' who rapidly gained control of vast areas of the continent.

The ownership of land was the Grail of the Scots-Irish quest, and reluctance to pay for it was a feature of their pioneering, whether in the Juniata Valley of Pennsylvania or on the Murray River of south-eastern Australia. But, unlike the Ulster settlers in colonial Pennsylvania, many of the land-hungry men who came to Australia or New Zealand had already acquired some capital in the more prosperous farming conditions of nineteenth-century Ireland. Such capital was necessary not to buy land – at the frontier 'the land is everywhere', to be squatted on, not paid for – but to clear it and provide the fencing required for the control and protection of sheep. It was the possession of cash, often in relatively small amounts, which gave the pastoralists a chance to carve out 'bush empires' encompassing hundreds of thousands of acres, to stock them with sheep and to break into the lucrative wool market.

The pastoralists pushed the frontier westward, at the same time acquiring enough political power to protect their interests from the encroachment of smallholders. In 1838 the low 'upset price', established by the Government to prevent squatters from acquiring vast tracts of free land, was raised, with the deliberate object of preventing workers becoming owners and thus reducing the labour supply necessary for the sheep ranches. Even when the Crown Land Acts, designed to allow the ordinary settler to 'freely select' smaller blocks of land, came into force the big ranchers found ways of rendering this democratizing process ineffective. Professor Allen, in *Bush and Backwoods*, points out the similarity between the methods used by the graziers of the American Midwest – with their strong infusion of both blood and tradition from the cattle-droving Scots-Irish – and the pastoralists of Australia in using 'dummies' to buy up adjoining plots created under the American and Australian Land Acts. By 1850 more than 70 million acres of Crown lands were in the hands of fewer than two thousand squatters.

Two features marked the Scots-Irish squattocracy; they usually possessed capital or had access to it, and they were part of a family chain of emigration. Henry Osborne sold his farm in County Tyrone for £3,000 and went in 1829 to New South Wales, where he was helped by two brothers already settled there. His first two land grants in the Wollongong area were worked with convict labour. He then moved westward and squatted on a much larger area, between the Murrumbidgee and the Murray rivers, to which he received retrospective rights. The Government could make laws aimed at a fairer distribution of land but in reality could do little to restrict the buccaneering activities of people like Osborne in the bush.

Like others in this group of Scots-Irish, Henry Osborne was an opportunist. He recognized that livestock was more valuable for breeding than for meat, and drove his surplus animals over the mountains to the newly established colony of South Australia. The New South Wales meat market, depressed by low population numbers and the lack of export facilities, received a tremendous boost from the influx of immigrants in the gold rush period, and Osborne made a large fortune within a few years. With the sharp nose of the true entrepreneur, he scented the sudden growth of native industry only a decade or so away, and moved into coalmining in time to meet the new commercial demand for fuel. Henry Osborne died in 1859 the wealthiest man in the country.

Like Osborne, Sam Wilson followed his brothers, already squatters with considerable holdings, to Australia in 1852. He had some success in the gold diggings, then managed one of the family sheep stations. Having sold his property in Ireland, he bought a ranch and began acquiring more and more land at advantageous prices as drought or a market slump hit other pastoralists. As well as business acumen, Wilson brought engineering skills to outback farming and devised irrigation schemes which greatly enhanced the value of his property. Aware that he and his fellow pastoralists were Australia's first aristocracy, Wilson created for himself 'a princely estate where Victorian squatting life was seen at its best', but, somewhat out of character with his fellow Scots-Irishmen, he eventually retired to live as a gentleman in the south of England.

Wilson's nephew, Sam McCaughey, was the son of a large farmer and linen manufacturer, but this affluent background did not prevent him, when he went out to join his Wilson uncles, from walking the two hundred miles to their up-country station in order to save money. McCaughey followed the same business pattern as other Ulster squatters, building up his land holdings piecemeal; at one point he owned 3 million acres. He had that, not unusual, Ulster combination of thrift and warm-hearted friendliness and became well known as a philanthropist. His most notable financial donation, however, went to buy guns for the Ulster Volunteers during the Home Rule crisis.

Across the empty stretches of the outback a Scots-Irish network operated, finding jobs for friends and relatives and providing loans to start a newcomer off in the ranching business. Joseph McGaw, coming out from Ireland, was put in charge of a station by a fellow County Antrim man; Ulster blood counted for more than experience. McGaw obviously handled his convict workers with skill, for six years later he was managing an even larger undertaking with '34,000 sheep lambing in paddocks'. He earned large amounts from profit-sharing, sold his part of the family farm at Mallusk and joined John Cochrane from Coleraine in buying the Burrabogie station for £110,000. Returns on capital were high; McGaw estimated he earned 20 per cent a year on his investment.

LEFT The Moonliters; *oil painting by Patrick William Marony, 1894. Captain Starlite, hero of Rolf Boldrewood's classic novel* Robbery Under Arms, *was closely modelled on the real-life bushranger Andrew Scott who was known as Captain Moonlite, the leader of the Moonliters gang. Scott was the son of a County Down clergyman.*

RIGHT ABOVE *Life in the bush, 1840. There was little in the spartan surroundings of the squatter's first home to indicate the potential millionaire.*

RIGHT BELOW *A farm belonging to Alexander Riley in New South Wales from Joseph Lycett's* Views in Australia, *1824. Of farming in New South Wales, the County Armagh emigrant George McLean wrote, 'the soil is very rich ... Indian corn grows well and oats ... and splendid wheat'.*

After twelve years he bought out his partner and before retiring owned a third of a million acres.

There is a certain sadness about the squatter preoccupation with success. Unlike the pioneers of Appalachia, they hesitated to marry lest the cares of a family interfere with the business of making money. Joseph McGaw wrote home to his sister, 'bespeak me a sweetheart to be ready in two or three years time but not too young as I am now getting greyhaired'. Joseph, like his Biblical counterpart, was cautious, and another twelve years elapsed before he settled on a bride from Ulster.

Dr George Hill Adams, coming out on a visit to a brother and sister ranching in the Grampian district near Geelong, noted the indifference of his relatives to the magnificent mountain scenery around them. 'Not one of them even visited the ranges till I did ... there is nothing almost in any settlers' heads but ... sheep, wool, bullocks, drays, servants, horses ... that is the eternal, never-ceasing lingo, day and night, summer and winter. It is horribly boring....'

In contrast to the large fortunes made by the squatters, ordinary station hands often had difficulty in earning enough to live. William Cherry, writing home to Lisburn, complained that his wages were 'very low' and prices in the outback were 'exorbitant ... a pound at home would go as far as three here'. Moving two hundred miles inland from Melbourne, Cherry found himself at the mercy of the station owner, without the money to pay his bill at the store or the fare back to the coast. Labourers like him were often arbitrarily paid off and marooned hundreds of miles from the prospect of new work. Only at lambing and shearing time could they be certain of employment. Cherry moved every few months, usually with just enough money to take him to his next job.

Unlike the Adams family, who were obsessed with sheep and money, Daniel Gardner was interested in all he saw around him. Going deep into the bush he found only 'huts of a very primitive nature and here and there a herd of cattle or a flock of sheep ... grazing amongst the trees'. A squirrel, he estimated, could travel from tree to tree all the way from Melbourne to Sydney. He saw the itinerant 'swagger' with his possessions on his back, living in a tent made with blankets and sticks: 'He also carries his victuals, bakes his bread and boils his billy.'

Gardner recognized the hard economic realities beneath the picturesque: 'I see plainly that squatting is the most profitable business on the land – but capital is required in commencing.' The selector – a poor settler allowed to pick land from unallocated Crown territory – acquiring a farm under the Crown Land Acts usually lost out to the squatter: 'Selector ... is poor as a mule, and in the end the squatter buys his land when he, the selector, cannot make a living on it.' Money was the key to success but the immigrant must also be shrewd enough to hold on to it: 'an unconcerned sort of fellow will soon be relieved of his cash'.

James Milliken, who came to New South Wales from Islandmagee, believed that even the smaller farmer could 'make a very good living out here', but he was bitter about the squatters: 'there has been a land bill that is a great barrier to the setteler; it is in favor of the squatter; their is a great many of them in power so the[y] make the laws to suit themselves like the landlords of Ireland. . . .' Milliken's daily life, like his sentiments, resembled that of the early American colonists. He cleared his land, burning off the timber where possible, ploughed with bullocks and planted potatoes and grain. He had banked some money but he remained dangerously close to subsistence farming.

Australian colonial life was a great leveller, education no guarantee of success. Frank Robb 'met hundreds of fellows who have got splendid educations working their hard days work with an axe or a shovel . . . I would not advise any young fellow without capital to come to this country'. Robb himself thought that life in the bush was 'the happiest existence for a man in this world' but he doubted if he could 'make it pay well enough'.

It is interesting to compare the relationships of the Australian settlers with the Aboriginals and those which existed between the Scots-Irish frontiersmen and the Indians of the American Old West. Both ended in extremely harsh treatment of the native populations. The attitude of the Appalachian pioneers towards the Indians ranged from close friendship to murderous hatred but was always mixed with respect, while their Victorian cousins regarded the Australian natives with a condescension usually reserved for the lower animal breeds. Alexander Crawford, from Belfast, took a slightly more humane view than some of his compatriots, who shot or poisoned Aboriginals as 'vermin', but he too enjoyed a 'niggerhunt'. In May 1882, writing from his sheep station on the desert frontier of Western Australia, he described just such a hunt to his fiancée. Having heard that some natives were killing sheep in the vicinity, Crawford went off by night with his native tracker, Monkey, to capture them. 'The following morning . . . we came on some tracks . . . soon Monkey pointed out something but I could see nothing. He said "gallop" which I did in the direction he pointed and I saw a black fellow run and try to hide under a bush. I made straight for him.' Crawford then wheeled and saw two more natives, 'one fitting a spear into his Woomera to throw at me'. He shot the spear carrier and clubbed the other with the revolver butt. All three were chained to a tree by the neck and the following day one, who eventually admitted sheep-stealing, was flogged.

Crawford found it hard to understand a people whose ways of thought were so totally alien to Scots-Irish culture. 'They never eat anything if there are others about without sharing it, sometimes giving it all away and going without. . . . They have no religion nor idea of God they are afraid of an evil spirit they call Gingie . . . some odd times they indulge in cannibalism but not often and they only eat black fellows that's one consolation.' On his station he kept 'about 20 niggers, some I only keep and feed to keep them from killing the sheep'. He saw nothing unjust in sentencing these simple people for terms of up to nine years' hard labour for killing sheep on the land where for centuries they had lived by hunting. One night in 1883 he was severely injured, trying single-handed to apprehend thirteen natives, but blamed his reversal on the darkness. 'In the daylight I consider myself a match for thirty or more niggers . . . I'll teach them a lesson once and for all that they will remember to the end of their days.'

The Crawford parents back in Belfast, who were deeply religious Methodists, deplored their son's conflict with the Aborigines: 'your Aunt Matty says kindness goes far with them'. Alexander's fiancée, Elizabeth Matthews, reproved him for sneering at the speech of the natives as 'having no words, tenses etc. . . . Why Alick how do you know they haven't? You know very little of their language. . . .'. A devout Christian, she condemned the manhunts: 'It is a dreadful thing to be continually hunting down one's fellow creatures . . . when really in your heart you cannot blame them for taking the sheep.' With a foresight remarkable for an ordinary young woman in the high noon of empire, she knew it would all end badly: 'the whites will have a deal to be answerable for some day'.

The Scots-Irish found it easier to accept Australia as a predominantly English settlement than did the Catholic Irish immigrants; the reverse had been largely true in colonial America. In Australia, however, the influential men among the Ulster immigrants were prosperous and had no economic reason to rebel against the mother country. Also, in the first generations of settlement they had no feeling of Australian nationality, and they were at the same time totally alienated from an Irish Nationalism which had become largely sectarian and tribal.

Because the Scots-Irish were comparatively few in number, and spread evenly among other English-speaking immigrants, they were easily assimilated. They became Ulster Protestants again only in response to some perceived threat from a much more cohesive Catholic Irish population. While the majority of Irish Catholic immigrants came with the hope of a better and freer life, it was unfortunate that the educated and articulate among them were often strongly segregationalist Catholics or belonged to the extreme republican fringe elements of Irish Nationalism. Such sentiments, religious or political, were bound to provoke a Protestant reaction.

The problem began when the autocratic system of the Irish Catholic Church was exported to Australia. Minor popes, like Bishop Quinn of Brisbane – who claimed that anyone criticizing him committed 'a most gross and sacreligious act' – drilled their immigrant flocks into obedience. They enthusiastically endorsed the anti-liberal pronouncements of the Vatican Council of 1870 and began a long struggle for exclusive, segregated education for their flocks. Australian Protestants, particularly those from Ulster, were confirmed in their view that the Catholic leadership did not in its heart believe in the democratic process and was manipulating the Australian political system to circumvent or destroy it.

When Fenianism became a disruptive and dangerous element in Ireland, and in English cities with large Irish populations, the British Government, with its usual insensitive handling of an Irish problem, sent a large group of convicted Fenian prisoners to Western Australia. The prisoners themselves created no trouble, but in the minds of the settlers in that most isolated colony they were part of a worldwide conspiracy of subversion and murder – a fear which was fomented by the loudmouthed supporters of Fenianism in American cities and which was transmitted to Ulster Scots and other Protestants throughout the Australian continent.

In 1868 an incident occurred which seemed to confirm this fear. Henry James O'Farrell – whose entry in the *Australian Dictionary of Biography* lists what appears to be his occupation as 'paranoic' – shot and seriously wounded the Duke of Edinburgh, Queen Victoria's second son, during a royal visit to Sydney. O'Farrell was what in Irish Catholic terminology is called a 'spoiled priest', one who has dropped out on the road to ordination; his diary, seized by the police, revealed strong Fenian sympathies and a corresponding desire to stir sectarian strife – 'Oh that the Orangemen would rouse up the apathetic Irish of these parts'. All the circumstances caused bitter anti-Catholic and anti-Irish feeling in New South Wales. Despite his obvious mental derangement, and the efforts of his royal victim to save him, O'Farrell was hanged and an Irish Australian 'martyr' created.

Orangeism never reached the position in Australia which it held in certain Canadian provinces. There were lodges and Twelfth of July processions but little of the political influence which the Order wielded in Ireland and in Canada. This may have been because so large a proportion of the Scots-Irish immigrants were the offspring of reasonably well-to-do farmers, merchants and professional men, people who felt little need of the assistance of the Order in their working and social life and may have wished to distance themselves from their fellow countrymen who worked on their sheep stations or in their shops. What was probably a much stronger factor was the independent, critical nature of the Ulster Scot, which was cautious of organizations and which, away from the claustrophobic atmosphere of an Irish parish, reasserted itself in the wide spaces of Australia.

John Maxwell, who came from North Down, epitomized that independent spirit. He believed that 'Orangemen were a great hinderance to the advancement of civil liberties of people at home', and he blamed the Irish aristocracy, 'who use them with great dexterity to suit their own ends'. John Maxwell and his brother Hugh were both interested in the politics of their homeland. Home Rule in Ireland, Hugh realized, 'would be a bad thing for Protestants if it was to become law'. John commented on the Ulster habit of mixing politics and religion and drew a parallel between Ireland and Australia:

> Regarding Home Rule, it is most extraordinary how people differ at home from people out here or rather how they are situated and how they act. . . . Every man votes for the candidate who he believes will look after his interest, irrespective of religion (save the Catholics who are greatly influenced by their ecclesiastical dignitaries as they are in Ireland). . . . It is a grevious thing to think that Irishmen's bigotry should stand between men and their own interests.

Such an admirable analysis of the malaise in Ulster politics must have been echoed by many of the Scots-Irish who merged with such comparative ease into a pluralist colonial society.

Clashes on St Patrick's Day or the Twelfth of July; death threat letters – 'You Orange dog ... the sun will not shine on your Orange body in August till we quarter you and burn you like a damned heretic dog....'; the rantings of 'reformed priests' or 'escaped nuns' at ultra-Protestant meetings: none of this would have survived long under the Southern Cross had it not been for the ethnically orientated policy of the Australian Catholic Church and the work, in particular, of one man, Archbishop Daniel Mannix.

Mannix came from a comfortably off farming family in County Cork, and combined reactionary Romanist Catholicism and extreme Irish Nationalism with a ruthless determination to have his own way. As Bishop of Melbourne from 1912, he organized a long and eventually successful political campaign to obtain Government funding for the private Catholic school system, thus bringing to Australia the most divisive element in Irish inter-denominational relations. Protestants, who saw no reason why, within their democratic Australian society, they should pay taxes to support a religious faith which in their eyes owed its allegiance elsewhere, reacted strongly. When Mannix gave public support to the Sinn Fein Rebellion in 1916 and engaged in fund-raising for the Irish Republican Army in America, he gravely deepened the sectarian divide in Australia.

> The climate is everything one could desire; not too hot by day even in the middle of summer and the evenings and nights then delightfully cool ... in mid-winter we have a light frost which those who rise very early in the morning may see but when the sun ascends to the meridian, we have what the people at home would call a beautiful summer day ... sixty-six thousand acres ... a large proportion is flat and rich and most beautifully watered.

The first idyllic reports by Ulster settlers from Katikati on the Bay of Plenty in the North Island of New Zealand made it seem as if that almost-forgotten dream of an Eden specially created for Ulster Protestants had been realized. Fertile land, a temperate climate, natives no longer effectively hostile, no other settlers with whom to quarrel, Presbyterians and Episcopalians working together in harmony – surely this at last was the Promised Land?

The Katikati expeditions in 1875 and 1878 represented the last organized exodus of the Scots-Irish, but in some ways it resembled their first arrival in Ulster. The leader, George Vesey Stewart from Ballygawley in County Tyrone, was not only of Ulster planter stock but also in his methods and his social rank – he was a substantial landowner and gentleman – he closely resembled the Scottish undertakers or lords who came to mid-Ulster at the beginning of the seventeenth century. Like the original planters, he wanted some guarantee that the people he brought in would be successful pioneers, 'not clerks, drapers' assistants or broken-down tradesmen ... no person should join my party with a capital of less than £3 to £5 an acre ...'. He asked for two classes, 'capitalists and well-to-do farmers', but not 'young gentlemen with soft hands'.

As in the Ulster Plantations, Stewart had to give undertakings, subject to a penalty, to fulfil the conditions laid down by the New Zealand Government. He had an opportunity, not given by James I to his undertakers, to pick the land he wanted to colonize, and spent several months travelling around before choosing Katikati. The reasons for his choice were purely practical: the land was generally good, it had already been cleared of most of its timber by its original Maori population, and only required the burning off of fern and other secondary growth, and it was close enough to the goldfields at Waiki to provide a market for the settlers' produce.

Returning to Ulster, Stewart began recruiting tenants. He spoke at public meetings, he canvassed Orange lodges and he used the Ulster newspapers to publicize his scheme, which in the end was over-subscribed. The first group of settlers, two hundred and thirty-eight tenant farmers, sailed from Belfast in June 1875; the second party left three years later and included some rather unlikely pioneers: 'Two Generals, a Major, two or three Captains and Lieutenants, a Canon, a Doctor, no end of pretty girls. ...'

It is obvious from the records of Katikati that this New Zealand party did not need to fend for themselves in the way the American frontiersmen were compelled to do. Where the Appalachian pioneers cut timber from the forest to build their homes, the Katikati settlers, despite the thick forest on the Kaimai range which backed their valley, bought timber in Auckland or the nearby town of Tauranga. Why did they ignore the abundant standing timber when the material they bought in Auckland had to be brought in by the expensive sea route? Probably because in the long period since their forefathers had cleared Ireland's native forests, the art of felling and dressing timber had been lost.

The Ulster families settled quickly. Before the beginning of winter they burnt the fern and tutu shrub from the land, ploughed in the ash fertilizer and sowed grass seed. Wheat, maize and potatoes were planted, and within the first eighteen months most settlers had an orchard and garden. The fruit trees were not grafted from wild stock, as in Pennsylvania, but supplied, along with roses and ornamental shrubs, by nurseries in Auckland, emphasizing that this was not the wild frontier but cosy Victorian countryside. Stewart also suggested that each family bring out a pair of songbirds, and he considered introducing the Irish hare. In fact, his object seems to have been to recreate County Tyrone in a better climate.

Nature, however, turned sour. Plants like blackberry and gorse, introduced by the settlers, ran rampant through their crops. The friendly hedges of the homeland, planted in the more vigorous climate of New Zealand, got out of control and smothered what they were supposed to protect. After the first few crops had been harvested the poorer soils of the hilly land reverted to scrub through lack of fertilizer. The tutu plant proved deadly to livestock, and many cattle drowned in the creeks and swamps because of inadequate fencing.

The harmony of the early years turned to rancour. Stewart was a generous and philanthropic man but he was also an autocrat who wanted to rule 'in the patriarchal fashion of a Highland chief'. Many of his people, who still had enough of the old Scots-Irish independence to reject his paternalism, left their farms for more congenial settlements. Vesey Stewart continued to live in the grand manner at Mountstewart, with its ballroom and cricket ground, and its staff of cadet farmers drawn from good Ulster families and paying one hundred and fifty guineas a year to learn colonial farming. In 1884 he entertained Te Kooti, the most feared of Maori leaders, with a hundred armed warriors, to tea on the lawn. Up to a year before his death at the age of eighty-eight he continued to hold all the principal public offices in the Katikati district. By 1950 only twenty of the original Ulster families still had descendants in the area.

Much of the Australian experience of transplanted Irish conflict was paralleled in New Zealand, following a pattern of Irish Nationalist activism and Protestant reaction. Fenianism gained considerable support among the Catholic Irish immigrants, a support which first expressed itself in fund-raising among the country's goldminers. When three Fenian activists were executed for killing a policeman in Manchester in 1867, a funeral ceremony headed by a priest wearing a green sash over his vestments was held in memory of the 'Manchester Martyrs'. Such displays, at a period when a Fenian bomb had killed twelve innocent people in Clerkenwell, London that year, increased tension between Protestant and Catholic immigrants. There was widespread suspicion of organized political action by Catholics, and, given the sympathy professed by Irish Nationalist leaders with the Maori cause, this was compounded by some vivid imaginations into an Irish-Maori plot to take over the country.

Orangeism, lacking in New Zealand the social *raison d'etre* which gave it impetus in Canada, made a slow start but in response to demonstrations of Catholic solidarity the Order began to flourish. The first lodge had been formed in 1858; there were eighteen lodges by 1876 and ten years later the North Island alone had forty-seven lodges. Twelfth of July celebrations were held in Dunedin and Christchurch as early as 1873.

Lecture tours by former priests and nuns exposing 'the vices of the Romish system' were then popular throughout the Protestant Anglo-Saxon world. These were usually lurid and highly entertaining and thousands flocked to them to be enjoyably shocked and scandalized. Unfortunately, they also raised sectarian temperatures on both sides, and, when a particularly scurrilous ex-priest, Charles P. Chiniquy, toured New Zealand under the protection of the Orange Order, mobs of Irish Catholics set upon Orangemen, severely injuring a number of them. The pattern of inter-denominational relationships began to look ominously like that prevailing in Ireland.

Two Ulster Scots, John Ballance, who was Prime Minister from 1891 to 1893, and William Ferguson Massey, who held office intermittently between 1912 and 1925, were major figures in the development of native New Zealand politics, but throughout their careers the divisions of their Irish homeland complicated their political lives. Ballance, who was born in Glenavy, County Antrim, was a radical with high humanitarian ideals and, although he had taken part in the Maori Wars, favoured a conciliatory policy towards the native population. Like the Liberal Party to which he belonged, Ballance advocated Home Rule for Ireland, but when he also came to believe that the Catholic Church in New Zealand should be given State aid for its schools, he failed to convince Liberal colleagues dedicated to the ideal of free secular education.

William Massey, who had emigrated from Limavady, in County Londonderry, led the right-wing Reform Party and at one time was Orange Grand Master. His conservatism was a complex thing which probably sprang from the souring pioneer experience of his father, whose 'dreams of freehold independence died in the scrub-covered hills of Puhoi'. There was a fine Scots-Irish ring about his election slogan in 1896: 'Every man his own landlord'. As W. J. Gardner says in his paper 'The Rise of W. F. Massey, 1891–1912', 'his instinct was to see political opinions and the men who held them in an Irish manner, if not through Irish spectacles'. His radical attitude on land ownership was married to a strong opposition to Irish Home Rule, and he blocked attempts to have a motion favouring it put through the New Zealand Parliament.

As New Zealand politics was a question of personalities, so also was the broad Scots-Irish experience in the country. Whatever temporary unity was created by opposition to the Catholic Irish, the Ulster immigrants never achieved cohesion. There were many men who were remarkable and dedicated in their own fields: Ballance and Massey in politics, the great jurist James Livingston Macassey, the horseback missionary John Macky, the educationalist Edward Mulgan Ker. Some displayed recognizable Ulster traits; others, like Rutherford Waddell, who awakened the social conscience of New Zealand to the sweated labour conditions in Dunedin in 1888, or Henry Montgomery (nephew and namesake of the Ulster Presbyterian divine), who opposed the introduction of the Bible into New Zealand schools, belonged to broad inter-racial traditions of humanitarianism and rationalism; their membership of the Scots-Irish race was incidental to their achievements.

14 · CONTRACT AND COVENANTS

The dark eleventh hour
Draws on and sees is sold
To every evil power
We fought against of old
Rebellion, rapine, hate
Oppression, wrong and greed
Are loosed to rule our fate
By England's act and deed.

Rudyard Kipling, '1912'

CLOSE TO THE ULSTER family home of the Australian millionaire squatter Joseph McGaw, at Mallusk just north of Belfast, his brother-in-law William McKinney lived and farmed. The story of the McKinneys illustrates the political change which occurred during the nineteenth century among Scots-Irish families. The McKinneys (originally 'McKenzies') came from Scotland at the beginning of the eighteenth century. Unlike most Scots-Irish, they were Highlanders, and had been forced to leave because of their Jacobite sympathies. William McKinney's two grandfathers were United Irishmen; one was the horseman sent to rouse the country on the eve of the Battle of Antrim, at which McKinney's great-uncle was killed. Throughout his life William McKinney was a staunch Presbyterian; in politics he was a Liberal and no friend to the Anglican establishment. Yet, despite this radical, Nonconformist background, he remained resolutely against Home Rule for Ireland and signed the Ulster Covenant in 1912. Behind the volte-face in political attitudes of William McKinney and many like him lies not a major revolution but a series of gradual political and social changes interspersed with violent, though not particularly bloody, events.

Rural Ulster during McKinney's lifetime was physically as well as politically transformed, the two processes being closely interlinked. A phenomenal rise in population over Ireland as a whole caused thousands of acres of waste land to be brought under cultivation. In the hills of County Antrim cultivation was 'gradually creeping up to their summits, as far as their steepness and climate will allow'; today traces of this can be seen in what are called 'famine ridges', lines of spadework long turfed over and visible only from a distance in the low light of the setting sun. In the drumlin region – the succession of glacial hillocks which dominate the centre and west of the province – drainage also added hundreds of acres of crop-bearing land. By the mid century the overall amount of arable land was rising by more than one per cent a year. Although the better-intentioned landlords did much to help, it was the efforts of the tenant farmers which brought about the change, efforts stimulated by the Ulster Custom which guaranteed the tenant compensation – if he quit his farm – for the improvements which he had made.

Despite such earnest industry, rural Ulster did not present an attractive picture. The Marquis of Dufferin and Ava, an extensive landowner in County Down, toured his estates in 1846 while still a student at Oxford and remarked on the undeveloped state of agriculture: 'bare country studded thickly with the gables of ruined houses and dotted over with low black cabins, without a hedge or tree, but intersected with rugged blue stone walls, and flooded with black bogs or dull steel-coloured sheets of water ... you have a picture of what most of my estate consists of.' Perhaps this was an exaggeration by a young man accustomed to the orderliness of the English countryside. Nevertheless, over the two centuries since the Plantation, strip cultivation and the wholesale removal of forest had given Ulster a bleakness of landscape which, happily, the rising optimism of the tenant farmers was to alter dramatically in the next few decades.

Whitethorn hedges, hitherto common only in the hinterland of Belfast, began to appear over most of Ulster, dividing the cultivation and pasture strips into a pattern of small sheltered fields. The clachans, or family group dwellings, gave way to individual farmhouses scattered haphazardly over the countryside. Emigration to Belfast, to the British cities and abroad, had reduced the rural population to such an extent as to make these changes possible. Standards of living rose and stone-built homes replaced cabins of rubble and mud. The province, which had been virtually unchanged since Plantation times, was given the appearance which in general it wears today.

The physical transformation did not take place in other parts of Ireland. A traveller entering the Northern province from the South in 1843 recorded his amazement: 'everything was as suddenly changed as if struck by a magician's wand ... the dirty cabins of the roadside were succeeded by neat, pretty, cheerful-looking cottages. Regular plantations, well-cultivated fields, pleasant cottage-gardens and shady lines of trees met the eye on every side....' The fact that the improvements in Ulster were not to be found in the rest of the country points even more strongly to the motivation provided by the Ulster Custom of tenant right.

Tenant right was a traditional and not a legal obligation and, from 1830 until the Land Act of 1881, there was a continuous conflict between landlords trying to erode the privileges conferred by the Custom and tenants trying to legalize them. The great British politician Lord Palmerston, himself an Irish landlord, defined the establishment point of view: 'Tenant right is landlord's wrong.' The struggle crossed religious barriers and created some unity among tenant farmers of all creeds, but it eventually brought bitter sectarian division.

The Presbyterian Church reassumed its role as champion of the oppressed when it backed the campaign to legalize the Custom. The Orange movement too gave some support, John Ellison Macartney, an Orange-backed politician, proposing a tenant right Bill. A 'League of North and South Tenants' was formed to extend the Ulster Custom to the rest of Ireland, and Catholic priests and Presbyterian ministers shared the same platform. At Banbridge a young minister called Rutherford maintained that, as Ulster-Scottish pioneers had brought the land 'from a state of primeval barreness to its present fertility', they should pay no more than the original rent paid by their forefathers for the unimproved land. Landlordism, he claimed, had no sanction in the Bible, 'a fact illustrated by the division of the Promised Land among the children of Israel'. The old religio-economic argument, which had been the doctrine of justification among the Scots-Irish in frontier Ulster and frontier America, was still alive in nineteenth-century County Down. The alarm felt at all this by the landowning classes was betrayed by the *Belfast Newsletter* when it described the Tenant League as 'that monstrous coalition between the Romish priesthood and the communism of other creeds'.

1879 was one of those years when the weather took a hand in shaping Irish history. In west and central Ulster, as well as many other parts of the island, the harvest was devastated by phenomenal rains. First near-starvation, then eviction for non-payment of rents faced hundreds of families. In the South of Ireland the mainly Catholic Land League, led by Charles Stewart Parnell, had worked out an effective policy of social ostracization to fight evictions, a system which was later to give the word 'boycott' – from its principal victim, Captain Cunningham Boycott – to the English language. Recognizing that the Ulster situation was ripe for exploitation, the League began to organize there, but this was to prove, as so often with interference from the South, a tactical error.

Protestants willing to cooperate with their Catholic neighbours against the landlords found the Home Rule politics of the Land League unacceptable. Orange Lodges were instructed to mount counter-demonstrations whenever League meetings were announced. In Fermanagh the Grand Lodge called on its members to prepare for armed resistance. Landlords, including justices of the peace, took over control of the Orange demonstrations and provided transport to areas with League meetings. Not for the first – or last – time, Protestant-Catholic solidarity at peasant level was wrecked by the insensitivity and intransigence of Irish Nationalism and the hot-headed reaction of some Protestants.

The series of Land Acts which went through the British Parliament from 1881 onwards cured many of the ills of the Irish tenant farmer. The three 'Fs' – fair (meaning fixed) rent, fixity of tenure and freedom to sell his tenancy – became law, and a Government loan scheme enabled tenants to buy their farms outright, repaying the loan in annuities over a number of years. The Ulster Scot, like his fellow countrymen, achieved his objective of land ownership, but for him especially it had a political significance.

Reading the diaries and letters of William McKinney and comparing them with similar ones in the eighteenth century, one sees a subtle change. The Ulster Scot's relationship to the land had been an economic one, a matter of survival on the best possible terms; now it acquired an emotional dimension. It is significant that Brian Mercer Walker subtitles his book on the McKinneys 'An Ulster farm and its family'. The main question in Ulster had not been political dominance or religious independence but possession of the land; the long struggle to achieve this had forged a new bond between the farmer and his new possessions. As Walker says, 'every field had a name. As well as the Crossland and the Far Hill, there were the Pea Hill, the East and the West Fauld ... and many others.' The land was a living presence, an extension of the family. After two and a half centuries in Ulster the Scots-Irish had achieved a *pietas*, a devotion to the country in its physical aspects which was to be more solid than any vanished form of nationalism.

Perceptions of 'the other sort' – people of the opposite religion – have done much to shape the course of Ulster's history. As the nineteenth century wore on, Protestants began more and more to view Catholics as a body and less as individuals. A similar narrowing and blurring of the vision occurred in the reverse direction. The demography of the religious groups became more sharply defined. Catholics lived in Catholic townlands or urban ghettos, Protestants in Protestant ones. Physical communications improved. Railways linked the remoter Plantation populations in Fermanagh and Tyrone with the heartlands, north and south of Belfast. By 1860 all the major Plantation towns, Londonderry, Enniskillen, Omagh, Coleraine and Portadown, had rail connections. At the same time the psychological connections across the sectarian divide worsened. Ironically, the joining of Belfast and Dublin by rail was delayed because of the difficulty of crossing the Boyne.

The Victorian temperance movement brought about a great change in the social habits of the Scots-Irish. Drinking alcohol became a moral evil and the mark of low social standing. At the same time there emerged a strong tendency to identify strong drink with Catholicism, although there was at the same time a temperance movement being conducted inside the Irish Catholic Church. Total abstinence from alcohol was something new among the Ulster Protestants, and attempts to dissociate themselves from drinking ignored their recent past. In frontier America the making and drinking of homemade whiskey was almost the identifying mark of the Scots-Irish. On both sides of the Atlantic, clergy as well as laymen drank spirits; the Rev. Robert Huey was tried at Hanna's Town not for drinking but for being obnoxiously drunk. Brian Walker, in his book on the McKinneys, cites a dinner for the ordination of a Presbyterian minister at which fifty-one bottles of wine were consumed.

Both Catholic and Protestant communities in the early years of the nineteenth century were awash with liquor. Drink-selling licences were cheap and, says the Report of the Revenue Commissioners, 'the whole country ... is deluged with low, inferior establishments'. There were also many unlicensed houses; in County Down they 'abounded to a fearful extent'. Many of these, like G. K. Chesterton's 'Flying Inn', kept on the move: 'numbers of portable shebeen houses are taken to every market, fair or funeral'. Few of the shebeens sold legal or 'Parliament' whiskey, except as a front. Not only was the illicit spirit tax free but customers preferred it: 'superior in sweetness, salubriety and gusto to all that machinery, science and capital can produce in the legalized way'.

These Revenue reports from the early part of the century give the impression of a community dedicated to the production, distribution and consumption of 'poteen', or home-distilled whiskey, to such an extent that it invaded the ordinary activities of farming, trading, praying, getting married and dying. The liquor was manufactured in churches and in cow byres. It was moved across the country under loads of turf, in coffins and in dummies made of tin, and dressed to look like the farmer's wife riding to market behind her husband on the family horse. The excisemen were so stretched that the clandestine distillers were less worried about them than about neighbours who took advantage of the tradition of hospitality during poteen-making, 'every idle blackguard . . . drops in for a taste', thus seriously eroding the profit margins.

The whiskey business occupied a great many Northern Irish peasants of all denominations, either as drinkers or as sellers. The act of forgetting their part in this Dionysian past by morally and socially improved Protestants necessitated a clear psychological break with their Catholic co-participants, who for economic reasons were still deeply involved.

The ether-drinking epidemic, which affected much of central Ulster from 1865, and which has been exhaustively charted by the historian Kenneth Connell, provides an example of how each community was anxious to shift the responsibility for indulgence on to the other. Absorbing ether was, according to French imbibers, like getting drunk on champagne, and such was its popularity that in towns like Moneymore and Cookstown the market place, the railway station and even the bank smelled of it. Within a diamond-shaped area, which took in County Tyrone, north Fermanagh and the southern third of County Derry, 17,000 gallons of ether were drunk every year.

Though ether-drinking was denounced by Catholic and Protestant clergy alike, there was the suspicion in each community that the habit belonged predominantly to the other. In *Irish Peasant Society* Kenneth Connell quotes the catch phrase 'Smell a man's breath and tell his religion', and shows how the perceptions of neither side matched up with the truth. It was 'darkly hinted' that ether-drinking was a vice associated with Romanism, but an English observer found 'enough and to spare of Protestant ether tipplers. The habit prevailed as much in Protestant Tobermore [in County Tyrone] as in its Catholic vicinity.'

A more offensive misconception was the widespread belief among Catholics that the sexual morals of Protestants were less strict than their own. Such a view was stimulated by the frenzied preaching of Catholic missionary priests who, perhaps because of their celibacy, seemed obsessed with the subject. One wonders if the lurid sermons, with their veiled references to the alleged sexual laxity of nubile Protestant girls, preached to a congregation with a large percentage of virile young men (children were barred from these 'special' occasions and old people discouraged), could be anything but counterproductive. Of course, the truth was precisely the opposite: Presbyterians, especially, were even more sexually puritanical than Catholics. But, unfortunately, such myths being, unlike political or religious ones, the matter of everyday gossip, they helped to enhance the feeling of 'otherness' which existed in the relationship between the two creeds.

The faction fights which took place from time to time in rural Ulster are celebrated in rousing ballads. As the best of these are Orange ballads, they commemorate Protestant victories. The most famous is 'Dolly's Brae', remembering a hill in the middle of County Down where, on the Twelfth of July 1849, Catholics attacked the Orange procession and eight people were killed. Much the same pattern of events occurred at Glenoe in west Tyrone on 13 July 1829, when five were killed, and on the same day at Macken in south Fermanagh, when four of the Orange marchers were killed. The so-called Battle of Garvagh, however, had a more interesting and complex genesis.

Garvagh, as the historian Aiken McClelland demonstrated, was a frontier village – 'the fertile lowlands to the north and east were planted by English and Scottish settlers, while the high ground to the south and west was largely in the possession of the original inhabitants'. This classic battleground between Planter and Gael had already been fought over during the 1641 Rebellion and just prior to the Battle of the Boyne.

At the Garvagh fair on 23 May 1813, Alexander Purviance, the local magistrate, noticed among the market crowd 'some disposition towards riot', and called his four constables into action, only to be confronted with 'near three hundred cudgels, all up'. The Catholic 'Ribbonmen', being far more numerous, gave the Protestants a severe drubbing, Mr Purviance and his men wisely staying out of the way. At the June fair the Protestants, having had time to prepare, reversed the result. With the July fair came the decider (so far the worst that had happened were a few broken heads) –

The day before the July fair
The Ribbonmen they did prepare
For three miles round to rack and tear
And burn the town of Garvagh.

The official report estimated the Catholic force to be four hundred; the ballad-maker, possibly for the purposes of scansion, put the figure at 'thirteen hundred Ribbonmen'. The Protestants, again outnumbered, had some armed yeomanry among them who at first fired over the heads of the Catholics, hesitating to shoot at people they probably knew. But, as the Ribbonmen came on, the yeomen fired into the crowd, killing several. At that the Catholic force disintegrated and fled.

The Battle of Garvagh, a miniscule event, even in the history of Ulster, nevertheless proves McClelland's point that a physical frontier situation existed two centuries after the Plantation. It also illustrated certain modes of warfare that derived from the early seventeenth century. The Catholics still believed in a spontaneous tribal rally which could win by weight of numbers; after the Garvagh shooting William Hamilton saw on the road leading south from the town, 'the crowds of retreating glensfolk'. The Ulster Scots used militia in the encounter, as had been their habit from their first arrival in

Ulster. This form of defence began with the musters of armed tenantry on the first plantations; Nicholas Pynnar, the King's Surveyor, reported having seen on a Tyrone estate in 1618, '38 men armed, having taken the Oath of Supremacy'. This phrase is repeated, with varying numbers, from estate to estate throughout Pynnar's tour. In 1641 tenantry assembled at Comber, County Down, 'armed with scythes, cornforks, staffs and a few pikes'. In the Williamite Wars a highly successful citizen force was raised at Enniskillen, which still exists in the British Army as the Royal Inniskilling Dragoon Guards. Whether these fighting units were regarded by the authorities as a law-keeping force or a dangerous nuisance depended very largely on the state of the country. Just after the Garvagh affair a judge sourly described the Protestant forces as 'Orange Yeoman' who 'frequent fairs and markets with arms in their hands . . . inviting the attacks of the Ribbonmen'. In the British view, the 'B' Special Constabulary of the twentieth century changed within a few months from a useful arm of the police to a sectarian force which must be disbanded. But whether they were accurately or harshly judged, these were in essence the typical militia of the frontier, alike in many respects to their buckskin-clad cousins in Appalachia.

Twelve men were charged with murder as a result of the Garvagh affray, but the Grand Jury, comprised of Protestant landowners, reduced the charge to manslaughter and in the final event no one was punished. As the ballad frankly says,

> Our thanks are due to Sir George Hill,
> The Beresfords befriend us still,
> And Sir Harvey Bruce of Downhill,
> They cleared the boys of Garvagh.

Irish conceptions of justice were not British ones. The Ribbonmen appeared to have accepted that the Grand Jury were performing no more than their proper function as interpreted by the Irish peasant world when they gave their protection to the culprits from their own side. At the next assizes, as the prisoners were discharged, it was announced that the two sides 'had mutually agreed to a reconciliation, to forget all former animosities and to live for the future in peace and harmony'.

The other, conspiratorial, mode of warfare employed by the Catholic Irish alarmed Ulster Scots because they did not understand it. The Fenian movement offered no serious threat to them but many were convinced it did, believing, quite absurdly, that it was part of a worldwide conspiracy commanded by the Pope and officered by disguised Jesuits. This was in spite of frequent condemnations of Fenianism by the Irish Catholic hierarchy, including Bishop Moriarty of Kerry who pronounced on the organization, 'God's heaviest curse, his withering, blasting, blighting curse.'

The Fenian society was a secret, revolutionary one, a mixture of romanticism and bungled terror. There was an oath which, at a time of unchallenged British rule, spoke of 'the Irish Republic now virtually established'; there were purely mythical 'Fenian regiments' and a complicated organization of 'circles' and 'centres', a fair percentage of the members of which were British spies. Occasionally an outrage like the Clerkenwell bomb gave a spurious reality to this shadowy world, but in the long run there were only two significant facts about Fenianism. It gave continuity to what was in nineteenth-century Ireland a thin tradition of revolutionary violence. The tradition began with the Young Irelanders, an extreme Republican organization whose attempt at revolution in 1848 was Gilbertian in concept and reached an appropriate finale when its leaders, realizing the lack of popular enthusiasm for their cause, surrendered ingloriously to the police in 'Widow McCormack's cabbage patch'. Its continuation in the Fenians' own attempt at revolution in 1867 ended almost as soon as it began on the night of 5 March with troops and police pulling the rebels from snowdrifts. But in seaboard cities of the American northern states Fenianism, in the shape of its American counterpart Clann na Gael, took root and has flourished to this day. To the Ulster Protestant the Fenian bogey loomed large and kept a sharp edge on sectarian bitterness.

While much of the political life of the Ulster Scots was a reaction to the general Irish situation, the people themselves were evolving in the process of history from a divided and poverty-ridden society in the eighteenth century to a prosperous and virtually united people in the early twentieth. Religion had split them from 1660 onwards; by the 1860s it was a unifying factor. Henry Cooke proclaimed, a little prematurely, the 'marriage' of the Anglican and Presbyterian Churches. In 1818 the two branches of the Seceding Presbyterian Church united, and in 1840 joined the mainstream of Irish Presbyterianism to form the General Assembly. Covenanters on the one hand and Non-Subscribers on the other stood apart, but the centre ground of Nonconformism was occupied by a single Church, though this, too, was later to have its confrontations, political and doctrinal.

For the mass of Protestant people in Ulster the unifying event concerned neither theological points nor Church government; it was that strange phenomenon known as the '59 Revival. To some the 'reviving wind of the Lord', to others 'mass hysteria', this wave of religious enthusiasm moved rapidly across much of Ulster, leaving no town or village untouched. People were seized spontaneously with a desire to seek salvation. A man converted while working alone in a turf bog 'jumped some height from the ground'. Those affected experienced a deep anxiety and depression, followed by elation. William McKinney 'felt as if enveloped in a cloud of horrid darkness and a terrible weight pressed upon my head . . . suddenly a sound came into my ears and I felt quiet, light and happy'. In the town of Comber, 'great numbers were unable to attend to their usual vocations, but gave themselves almost unceasingly to the study of the Scriptures, singing and prayer'. In a Coleraine school, pupils left the classroom one by one to kneel in the playground; 'Their silent grief soon broke into a bitter cry. As this reached the ears of the boys in the room, it seemed to pierce their hearts as by one consent, they cast themselves upon their knees and began to cry for mercy.' The whole town was so affected that the new town hall had to be opened to accommodate 'groaning, weeping, praying penitents', and on the fair day the public houses did not have a single customer.

In the normally stolid and undemonstrative Ballymena there was a complete transformation. 'They fall with a deep groan – some with a wild cry of horror.... The language and the looks and the terrible struggles ... tell convincingly they are in deadly conflict with the old serpent ... Some pass through this exhausting conflict several times ... many will eat nothing for a number of days.' All over the province the Twelfth of July that year passed 'without banners, ribbons, drums or music', and stalwarts of Sandy Row were heard declaring brotherly love for Catholics with whom, at that time of the year, they would normally be exchanging volleys of paving stones. Catholic priests were less than gratified when some of their flock deserted to the evangelical movement, but Protestant clergy – Presbyterian, Anglican and Methodist – as a whole cooperated; some 'did not get to bed till morning' with the rush of conversions. In Coleraine a committee was set up to help the town's now workless prostitutes to emigrate.

But the Revival had its critics. The Rev. Isaac Nelson, a Belfast Presbyterian minister, dubbed it 'The Year of Delusion'. The *Lancet*, taking a less than clinical approach, spoke of 'a temporary unsettling of reason among the duped and a high degree of rascality among the knaves who encouraged the evil'. The Presbyterian controversialist J. B. Armour was both puzzled and shocked: 'I cannot understand the sleeping cases at all, some say they get a vision from the other world and that they see Christ.... Another dreadful imposture is practiced in this town; girls painting on their breast the words "Jesus Christ" and saying it came there while they were in their sleep.' The cynical Frankfort Moore, author of that neglected classic *The Truth about Ulster*, believed that the stigmata on the neck and arms of a mill girl were caused by Revival counsellors pinching her to accelerate her conversion. There were rumours of easy sexual conquests on the fringes of the Great Awakening rallies, and of couples, fresh from conversion, rousing resting cows in damp summer meadows to provide a dry couch on which to consummate their kindled emotions. When Frankfort Moore put these rumours to a Revival veteran years afterwards, he did not deny them. Satan as well as God was at work, he said. After all, it was the Devil's 'last chance'.

The Orange Order increased in strength as the century wore on. It had been almost exclusively Church of Ireland in its membership; now it appealed to a much wider section of the Protestant population, increased its membership enormously and acquired a number of able political leaders. For a time there was a challenge to its innate conservatism. William Johnston of Ballykilbeg, perhaps the outstanding leader of Orangeism, came to prominence when he defied a Conservative Government ban on processions and led a Twelfth of July march. 'For thirty years', he told his Orange followers, 'you have sent these lords and gentlemen to Parliament and I think it is time you put them through their catechism.' Johnston's view of Ulster life as one of tradition and ritual allowed for cooperation, at the right time, with Catholics. Opening the Working Men's Institute in Belfast, to which both Catholic and Protestant paraded under their various banners, he declared, 'The working class of Belfast have set an example – each of you holding earnestly to his own belief in religion and politics ... have united here'. In 1903

Tom Sloan, a militant Protestant worker, defeated the Conservative candidate for a parliamentary seat in Belfast and as a result was expelled from the Orange Order. In defiance, he set up the Independent Orange Order, which had a working-class base and strong Presbyterian support in north Antrim.

As industrial jobs drew away the young to Belfast and the manufacturing towns, there was a sense of loneliness about the countryside. This was enhanced by the now isolated homes in which farming families lived, and by the social divisions which a fully money-based economy produced in the villages. For a hundred years or more the racial boundaries – Irish Quarter, Scots Quarter – which had marked out the Plantation towns were disappearing and there was a healthy mingling of populations. In the nineteenth century the process went into reverse. People congregated in their own religious groupings; parishes, villages and areas of towns took on a sectarian character. In this new situation Orange lodges were widely established in Protestant areas and became the focal points of social life, much as they were doing at about the same time in Ontario. The Order gave Protestantism a structure which cut across class divisions; the aristocratic landowners, the middle-class politicians, the farmers and the factory hands had a common ground on which to organize political and, if necessary, military action. The radicalism of people like Johnston and Sloan did not break the unity of Orangeism but rather emphasized that it was capable of challenging authority when that challenge was needed.

In 1883 Tim Healy, a Home Ruler from Bantry on the southern shores of Ireland, a lawyer with a glib but irresponsible tongue, won a by-election in County Monaghan and proclaimed 'the invasion of Ulster'. No other phrase could have better authenticated for Ulster Protestants the view they had of Home Rule. 'All Ulster is ours', said Healy, and it was plain that this was no marginal victory in the knockabout of Catholic-Protestant politics but a breakthrough into Scots-Irish territory by the land-hungry 'Celts'.

The threat became more immediate after the British General Election of 1885, which left the two major parties, Conservative and Liberal, relying on the support of the eighty-six Irish Nationalists to form a government. The price of such support was likely to be Home Rule for Ireland, and when William Ewart Gladstone, the Liberal leader, gave that commitment, excitement among the Catholic Irish population was intense. There was a widespread assumption that Home Rule would mean the greatest eviction that Ireland had ever seen – the turning-out of the Scots-Irish from their lands, their factories and their homes. Ulster was filled with rumours of Protestant property being raffled at Catholic churches in anticipation. 'Lots were drawn', says Frankfort Moore, 'for certain houses, with the grounds, timber and livestock.' In Belfast, people living in the more prosperous part of the city 'were surprised to come suddenly upon strangers measuring their lawns and examining their fences'. One householder politely asked an intruder what he was doing; 'The man replied with equal civility, that he had merely come to have a good look at the place, as he had been fortunate enough to win it in the raffle ... by the Nationalist club.' No doubt the impracticalities of an immediate wholesale expropriation of Ulster-Scots property – a reversal of the Plantation settlement – was realized at the higher levels of Nationalist leadership, but within the Catholic rank and file the expectation was there.

Not since 1641 had so many spectres stalked the Ulster landscape. A British Prime Minister was preparing to sell the Ulster Protestants for a handful of parliamentary votes. They would be ruled by a Catholic administration in Dublin, with Catholic judges and a Catholic police; they would lose the industries which had made Belfast a great city (the chairman of the Belfast shipyard said he would move his firm to Scotland if Home Rule came about); and looming very close to them now was the menacing figure of the now infallible Pope whom they – and many Catholics – believed would be the real ruler of Ireland.

The Ulster Scots were not without friends in Britain. Lord Randolph Churchill, father of Winston, came to Belfast 'to play the Orange card' and assure anti-Home Rulers of the support of 'those of position and influence in England'. The Protestant people, now united, were prepared to resist a Dublin administration by force; 'Advertisements for the supply of twenty thousand Snider rifles and for the services of competent drill instructors appeared in the Ulster papers.' But, in the event, the precautions were unnecessary. Enough of Gladstone's Liberals voted against his Home Rule Bill in June 1856 to defeat it, not because of the bloodshed its implementation would have brought about in Ireland but for the purely chauvinistic reason that it might lead to the disintegration of the British Empire.

Until the Home Rule Bill of 1886 the British Liberal Party had considerable support in Ulster, mainly from Presbyterian tenant farmers and from families whose fathers and grandfathers had fought the rebels in 1798. To these people Gladstone's espousal of Home Rule was a betrayal, and at a convention in Belfast in March 1886 they voted by an overwhelming majority against the proposed Bill. William McKinney, who was secretary of his local Liberal Association, attended that meeting and sent a letter of protest to Downing Street. After 1886 people like McKinney became Liberal Unionists, as determined as their Conservative neighbours to maintain the union between Britain and Ireland.

The Scots-Irish have always had an obsession with agreements – covenants with God, contracts with men. In the 1760s they believed they had a contract with the government of Pennsylvania for protection from Indian attack; the 'Remonstrance of the distressed and bleeding Inhabitants' addressed to Governor Penn was based on the existence of such a contract. Thomas McKnight, who edited the Belfast Liberal newspaper the *Northern Whig*, and who is one of the few Englishmen to have written with real knowledge about Ireland, defined the compact which the Ulster Scots perceived to exist between themselves and Britain: 'When the Ulster settlements were made, there was an implied compact that they who crossed the Irish Sea on what was believed to be a great colonising and civilizing mission should not in themselves, nor in their descendants, be abandoned to those who regard them as intruders and as enemies.'

Failure to fulfil the terms of the compact absolved the other party from obedience, allegiance and matters usually implicit in any contract between ruler and ruled. The Pennsylvania colonists made this plain when they marched on Philadelphia. Frank Wright, in 'Protestant Ideology and Politics', shows how, over the relatively minor matter of the proposed disestablishment of the Anglican Church of Ireland, some Ulster Protestants were apparently prepared to break the link with Britain: 'We shall be forced to regard the Union as virtually dissolved.' The *Belfast Newsletter*, in a rare flash of percipience, saw the connection between Ulster Protestants threatened with Home Rule in 1886 and the embattled New England colonists in 1774: the Massachusetts patriots 'did not contemplate separation from the British Empire. They sought no more than the preservation of their ancient liberties.' The American actions from Bunker Hill onwards deserved the 'careful consideration of the Loyalists of Ulster', said the newspaper leader. This message was to be sent at various times from Belfast to London in the late nineteenth and the twentieth centuries. More importantly, the Ulster Scots showed that their continuance as a people independent of Dublin rule was by no means reliant on the continuance of such a contract; in the phrase Lord Randolph Churchill had coined for them, 'Ulster will fight and Ulster will be right'.

While the British Liberals were out of power after the defeat of the 1886 Bill, Home Rule was a dormant issue, but in 1893 the Liberals – with the support of the Irish Nationalists – came back to power and Gladstone introduced another Home Rule Bill. This was passed by the House of Commons but defeated in the House of Lords. Anticipating the measure, the Ulster Unionists had, the previous year, brought together in Belfast a vast and superbly organized anti-Home Rule convention, at which they made their intentions, in the event of Home Rule, absolutely clear. The threatening gestures, however, were less important than the unity, organization and control displayed by the Unionists, which contrasted strongly with the sad disarray of the Irish Nationalists since the death of Parnell.

Paradoxically, when the Liberals returned to power in 1906, the fact that they had one of the largest majorities in the history of the British House of Commons put Irish Home Rule 'into cold storage'. No longer needing the support of the Irish members, the Government turned its attention to more pressing British affairs. But the Home Rule Bill of 1893 had reminded the House of Lords of their constitutional power, and they continued to frustrate Liberal Government legislation. By 1910 the Liberal majority was again reduced to the point where they needed Irish Nationalist support and again the price was Home Rule for Ireland.

The Unionists were fortunate in their leaders. Edward Carson, a Dublin Protestant and the most brilliant lawyer at the English Bar, took over the leadership in 1910. Carson had prosecuted Oscar Wilde with devastating effect and he had successfully defended young Martin Archer-Shee, the cadet who was accused of stealing a postal order for five shillings from his naval college, and on whom Terence Rattigan's play *The Winslow Boy* was based. He brought the passionate conviction with which he argued legal cases into

ABOVE *Carson reviews the Ulster Volunteer Force, the military arm of Unionism.*
BELOW *Unionists gather at Belfast City Hall in 1912 to sign the Covenant.*

politics; the charisma which exuded from this tall, gaunt, eloquent man inspired his Ulster followers.

Captain James Craig, a whiskey millionaire who, while Carson advocated the Unionist cause in London, organized the resistance in Northern Ireland, looked like Colonel Blimp. He was big, red-faced, with a flattened nose and staring eyes, but no appearance could have been more deceiving. Craig had a sharp mind and a quick wit and he possessed superlative ability as a manager of men. Neither Carson nor Craig were bigots, but there was enough and to spare of those among their followers.

One of the oddest failings of Southern Irish and English politicians in dealing with the Ulster question has been their unwillingness, or inability, to look squarely at Unionism. They hearken back to 1798 as if the politics of McCracken and Drennan still had relevance; they profess to believe that Ulster Protestants are being deceived by their leaders, ignoring the fact that the grassroots rapidly unmakes any leader who steps out of line; they industriously pursue the 'white blackbird', the Ulster Protestant who is also an Irish Nationalist. The Rev. James Brown Armour, one-time Moderator of the Presbyterian General Assembly, is the best example of that particular quarry.

Armour, the son of a tenant farmer in north Antrim, was born five years before the Great Famine, and his political outlook was shaped at an early age by seeing a neighbour standing in the falling snow and begging a cigar-smoking landlord not to turn him out of his home. 'I vowed', he said, 'that if God gave me the opportunity, I would use what little strength was mine to drive a nail into the coffin of a system which ... so battered the moral qualities out of men that they could not look their fellow mortals in the face without their hat in their hand.' Armour did not support the first Home Rule Bill but by the time of the second Bill he believed in a parliament for all Ireland which maintained a link with Britain through the Crown. Throughout the crisis, which began in 1911, Armour attacked his fellow Protestants for following 'the prancing colonels, the blustering captains ... the circus riders of the Tory hippodrome'. Armour allowed his well-founded hatred of the Ulster landlord class to deceive him about the sincerity of his fellow Protestants in opposing Home Rule. He and the half-dozen who were like him never had any possibility of attracting support in the Protestant community and were irrelevant to the problem.

The Ulster Liberal Association, to which J. B. Armour belonged, organized a Home Rule meeting in Belfast in February 1912. The venue they chose was the Ulster Hall and their guest speaker was Winston Churchill, then a prominent Liberal politician. It was a tactless choice. In that hall, twenty-five years earlier, Winston's father had dedicated himself to the cause of Unionism. The Unionists booked the hall for the night previous to the Liberal meeting and announced their intention of staying there. The meeting was switched to a football park in the Catholic area of West Belfast, but Churchill, from his arrival at Larne Harbour until he reached the Nationalist ghetto, had to be protected from thousands of Protestant demonstrators. After the meeting he was smuggled back to England.

Ulster Unionism had now reached what Rudyard Kipling termed its 'dark eleventh hour'. There seemed no hope that Home Rule would be stopped by constitutional means. When another great rally was organized on the outskirts of Belfast at Easter 1912, it was addressed by the Conservative leader, Andrew Bonar Law, who although Canadian-born came of Scots-Irish stock. Law was well aware that Craig and Carson were talking of 'a Provisional Government of Ireland, having regard to the interests of Loyalists', and in his speech Law himself drew his imagery from that great example of Ulster Scots resistance in arms, the seige of Derry. It was plain that resistance from now on would be extra-Parliamentary; was it possible that England would divide into armed camps of Tory and radical as it had in 1642 against a similar background of an insurgent Ulster?

The Home Rule Bill was passed, a very reasonable amendment to exclude the four Ulster counties with Protestant majorities being rejected. Irish triumphalism exacerbated a bad situation in Ulster, and a disgraceful attack by an adult Catholic crowd on a holiday excursion of Protestant children led to brutal retaliation on Catholic workers in Belfast. Unrestrained and bloody mob warfare appeared to be at hand.

The compacts made with men had been betrayed; it was now time to turn to God. So ran the thinking of the Ulster Unionist leadership in the wake of the Home Rule Bill. A Solemn League and Covenant – what heroic memories the title evoked – was drawn up for signature by all Ulster Loyalists. It pledged resistance to a Dublin parliament, 'relying on the God whom our fathers in days of stress and trial confidently trusted ... and using all means that may be found necessary....' God gave every indication that Unionist prayers were being answered. Covenant Day, 28 September 1913, was one of those brilliant summer days that come seldom in Ireland. Carson marched under a banner said to have been carried before King William at the Boyne; its authenticity may have been doubtful but the timing of its reappearance was superb.

Many thousands signed with Carson at Belfast City Hall, some using their own blood to do so. Others signed in their own towns and villages; in all over 400,000 signatures were counted. No doubt among the signatories were bigots, fanatics and people who scarcely knew what they were signing, but the vast majority were people like William McKinney of Mallusk who saw no other course open to them if all they respected and lived by was not to vanish, as they believed, overnight. The great Liberal journalist J. L. Garvin, who watched the scene, wrote, 'No one for a moment could have mistaken the concentrated will and courage of these people. They do not know what fear and flinching mean in this business, and they are not going to know. They do not, indeed, believe it possible that they can be beaten, but no extremity, the worst, will ever see them ashamed.'

In Ulster the frontier is never far away.An old law designed to enable the earlier settlers to protect themselves, and still unrepealed, provided the Ulster Scots of the twentieth century with the opportunity legally to raise a citizen army. Under the law two justices of the peace could license the military training of civilians in their area. Taking advantage of this loophole, the Ulster Unionist Council began to recruit an army, which was to be called the Ulster Volunteer Force and which would have divisions, regiments, battalions and companies based on areas of the province. A framework for the recruiting existed in the Orange lodges and Unionist clubs. Many of the potential recruits already had experience with firearms in the gun clubs which sprang up after the 1893 crisis.

A. T. Q. Stewart, whose *Ulster Crisis* is the definitive work on this exciting period, describes the enthusiastic response to the appeal for volunteers:

> After a hard day's work in the fields or in the factories men walked for miles to attend parades and drills; the accent was on self-sacrifice and the clear call of duty, so familiar to, and so well understood by, hearts set in a Calvinist mould. Social distinctions were forgotten in the volunteer ranks; the gentry cheerfully took orders from their tenants, and company directors from their employees.

Over 90,000 men were recruited, and as they drilled – usually with wooden rifles – in the demesnes of the Unionist gentry, they must have recalled to anyone historically minded those first defence musters when 'the wolf and the woodkerne' were the enemy. The recruiting, the military training, the marching displays for the benefit of visiting journalists, all were strictly controlled from the top. Carson told them, 'I am responsible for everything . . . what circumstances you will have to come into action you must leave with us.' British newspapermen were impressed. 'There was certainly nothing of the mock soldier about them', wrote the reporter from the *Yorkshire Post*. Led by 'keen, smart-looking officers, they marched past in quarter column with five swinging steps, as if they had been training for years'.

Lack of arms was the one serious drawback the Ulster Unionists faced. The County Antrim Volunteers complained to Carson and Craig that they had only 200 rifles for more than 10,000 men. Money, however, was plentiful. A fund, set up to finance the resistance and compensate Loyalists who might suffer, and subscribed to by the wealthy men of Ulster and by expatriates like Sir Samuel McCaughey, raised more than a million pounds. A gun-runner was found in Major Fred Crawford, a Boer War veteran and brother of Alexander Crawford, the Western Australia pioneer who clashed with less formidable natives in the shape of Aborigines.

Crawford came of impeccable Scots-Irish stock – a long line of Presbyterian ministers including the caustic-tongued Andrew Stewart who had designated the first planters, both Scots and English, as 'generally the scum of both nations'. The patriotic Major Crawford omits his forefather's comment from his book *Guns for Ulster*.

From the time of the second Home Rule Bill, Fred Crawford had been organizing small-scale arms smuggling and training potential resistance fighters. At one point he conceived a scheme to kidnap Prime Minister Gladstone and cast him away on a deserted Pacific island. Now given the job of finding weapons for the Ulster Volunteers, he ordered rifles from Germany but was let down by the first firm he dealt with; they informed the British Government about the transaction. Finding a Jewish arms dealer in Berlin who, for the sake of business, could be trusted to keep his mouth shut, he

Guns for the Ulster Volunteer Force, shipped into Larne despite British vigilance, were rushed away to hiding in a highly organized operation.

managed to bring in several shipments before the authorities uncovered the operation. An attempt to import Italian-made guns ended in seizure at a London warehouse. The customs tightened their controls and seized several more consignments in Belfast. The gun-runners were forced to drop the arms in containers into the sea off the north Antrim coast, to be recovered after nightfall.

Civil War now became a very real threat. Southern Irish Nationalists organized an Irish Volunteer Force and began drilling, though without the dedication and expertise of their Northern counterparts. Arms were smuggled in and – ill omen for the future – control of these weapons and the people training to use them gradually passed from the responsible political leaders. A tragic clash during the Southern gun-running, which resulted in British troops killing three people in Bachelor's Walk on the Dublin quayside, put power further into the hands of the Southern extremists.

The Ulster Covenant was extended to England, and sympathizers there included the two laureates of imperialism, Rudyard Kipling and Sir Edward Elgar. In Canada, as might be expected, there was strong support for the Ulster cause. At mass meetings in Ontario, Manitoba, Alberta, Saskatchewan and British Columbia solidarity was pledged with the Unionists, and there was a scheme to raise a Canadian brigade to fight in Ulster. In Johannesburg, too, there was a call for volunteers for Ulster, while in Pittsburgh, Philadelphia and other Scots-Irish centres there were demonstrations on behalf of the Unionist cause. More than 100,000 in Australia signed a petition against Home Rule, and both there and in New Zealand money was raised to help arm the Ulster Volunteers and send fighting units to the province.

The organization of the Ulster resistance was a model of efficiency. A Provisional Government, under the leadership of Carson, was set up and a military committee was created. Sir George Richardson, a recently retired Indian Army officer with a distinguished career on the North-West Frontier, was hired to command the resistance. He came to Belfast and 'soon ... was as completely at home with the Ulster volunteers as with the tribesmen of the Tirah and Zhab valleys'. Richardson put his force well ahead of its time by giving it an integrated motor corps with dispatch riders. Overall strategy in the event of Home Rule being implemented was laid down. Rail communications, telephone and telegraph links and arms depots in the province were to be taken over and power would be seized in 'a sudden, complete and paralysing blow'.

There were equally extensive plans on the part of the British Government to bring the Ulstermen into line. British troops, including cavalry, would move northwards from their main Irish depot at the Curragh of Kildare, and, simultaneously, infantry battalions from Scotland would land on the Northern Ireland coast. In all 25,000 men would encircle the main areas of Ulster Scots resistance. Offshore, strong naval forces would be cooperating, and Bangor would be seized as a naval and supply base. For the first time since the days of Cromwell, military force was to be used within the United Kingdom to implement a political decision of Parliament. The British military of those days was about as capable of keeping secrets as the intelligence services in the 1940s and

'50s and, consequently, Ulster Volunteers headquarters knew every planned move in detail.

As the Home Rule Bill was moving through its closing stages in Parliament there were rumours that the Government was about to arrest the Ulster leaders. Carson made a dramatic speech to the House of Commons in which he challenged the Government to 'come and try conclusions with us in Ulster'. Then he stormed out of the chamber, telling a reporter, 'I go to my people.'

Throughout all this tension there was a remarkable degree of coolness among both Unionist leaders and people. In Belfast there was no rioting, as might have been expected, and the Volunteers maintained a high degree of discipline. Military moves were anticipated daily, and, while the Ulster force would probably have resisted fiercely, the outcome, given their shortage of arms, was never in doubt. At that point a respite came with help from an unexpected quarter. A group of senior British officers at the Curragh resigned rather than lead their troops against the North. The Government capitulated and gave the officers a guarantee that they would not be used to enforce Home Rule.

Meanwhile, Fred Crawford, in disguise and operating under his favourite persona of an American businessman, was in Germany concluding a major arms deal. He bought 20,000 of the finest German and Austrian rifles, which would make the Ulster Volunteer Force better equipped than the British Army. To bring the weapons to Ulster he purchased a Norwegian collier, the *Fanny*, hired her skipper and 'sold' him the vessel so that she could sail under the Norwegian flag. Such was Crawford's nature that he could not resist complicating operations with various kinds of subterfuge, including changing the names of the ships he used. In an earlier gun-buying episode he asked for the instruction manuals to be printed in Spanish to give the impression that they were intended for a revolution in Mexico.

A second ship, the *Clydevalley* – she was soon to become the *Mountjoy* – was bought in Glasgow to rendezvous at sea with the *Fanny* – now the *Bethia* – and bring the arms on the last stage of their journey. A third ship created a diversion by arriving in a suspicious manner at Belfast and holding up customs with arguments about whether she should be searched. The *Mountjoy* slipped through to Larne, where she was met by Volunteers and the weapons carried off by night to safe hiding places under the floorboards of churches, the thatch of innocent-looking cottages, in byres and in turf stacks.

Edward Carson is usually represented as narrow and intransigent, and photographs of his statue, which stands in front of the former Northern Ireland Parliament building, with its strong-jawed, forbidding face, are used to illustrate the point. This is a harsh judgement on a man who up to a point looked for compromise. He withdrew from rejection of Home Rule for Ireland as a whole to a position where he sought only to preserve the present six counties of Northern Ireland from inclusion. An offer by the British Government to allow these counties to remain outside the Dublin jurisdiction for six years he turned down as a 'sentence of death with a stay of execution'. While still pressing the Unionist case, he generously wished success to a future Southern Government, and spoke what was on his own mind about the future as plainly as he could at a time of such extreme tension: 'it might be even for the interests of Ulster itself to move towards that Government and come in under it and form one unit in relation to Ireland'.

In the high summer of 1914, war in Ulster seemed inevitable; by August it had broken out elsewhere. 'The parishes of Fermanagh and Tyrone faded back into the mists', wrote Winston Churchill. With the coming of the World War, the Act giving force to Home Rule was placed on the statute book, not to come into operation until the war was over. There was an additional condition that Parliament must make provision for Ulster in amending legislation. By the time a settlement was reached, events in Southern Ireland had left Britain with no alternative but to exclude the six counties.

The Ulster Volunteers joined the British armies in France as the 36th (Ulster) Division, and on 1 July 1916, which because of the change from the old calendar was the exact anniversary of the Boyne, they went into a battle in which they lost more than twice the total lost at the Boyne, at King's Mountain and at Ballynahinch. Like the Boyne, the Battle of the Somme was fought on a day of brilliant sunshine. After a supporting artillery bombardment the Ulstermen went over the top in lines, 'with rifles sloped and the sun glistening on their fixed bayonets, keeping their alignment and distance as well as if on ceremonial parade, unfaltering, unwavering'. Some wore their Orange sashes. By ten o'clock they had captured the first three lines of German trenches, but their casualties had been appalling. Of the 700 men of the West Belfast Battalion only 70 were left. Their drive had pushed deep into the German front but, as the attack on either flank had failed, it was a useless and indefensible gain. The Germans counter-attacked but the Ulstermen held out until nightfall in the captured trenches, without reinforcements, food or water. The 36th Division lost 5,500, killed, missing and wounded. Four of its men won the Victoria Cross. Tom McKinney, grandson of William McKinney, died of wounds after the battle. 'One of the finest displays of human courage', wrote the war correspondent Philip Gibbs; 'I would rather be an Ulsterman than anything else in the world', said an English officer.

Two months before the Somme a small group of extreme Nationalists, using the Irish Volunteer organization, had staged a rebellion in Dublin against British rule. This was crushed within a week but with heavy loss of life and the destruction of much of Dublin city centre. Unionists were inclined to treat the rebellion as a comic opera in line with the Young Irelanders' and the Fenian revolts. Had they paid attention to the speeches of the rebel leader Patrick Pearse – 'Bloodshed is a cleansing and sanctifying thing' – they would have known that the chances of a peaceful compromise in Ireland were vanishing. It is worth noting how closely Pearse's phrase 'Life springs from death' parallels the theme of the Spanish fascists, 'Viva la muerte', when they launched the Spanish Civil War.

The execution by British firing squad of fifteen of the rebel commanders in Dublin

ABOVE *1 July 1916: the 36th Ulster Division 'go over the top' at the Somme.* BELOW *Their ambulance men, seen here parading in Belfast a few months earlier, had to cope with thousands of casualties.*

RIGHT *Tom McKinney on his last leave home before he died of wounds at the Somme.*

swung public support in Southern Ireland away from the Parliamentary Nationalists to the new Sinn Fein Party, who were demanding nothing less than an all-Ireland republic totally independent of Britain. In the 1918 elections Sinn Fein won a landslide victory in the South, almost eliminating the old Nationalist Party, and set up an assembly in Dublin which claimed to legislate for the whole of Ireland. The Unionists, not unexpectedly, declined an invitation to attend, but had they come they would not have understood what was going on as the whole proceedings were conducted in Irish, spoken only by a tiny percentage of the population of the island.

Nothing was resolved. The British Government did not recognize the Dublin assembly, and, in the year after the World War ended, fierce guerilla fighting developed between the military wing of the Dublin Assembly, the Irish Republican Army and the British forces. Ambushes, attacks on police stations, the burning of the homes of Protestants, and assassinations of police officers and public officials brought reprisals from the British forces, the destruction of Nationalist property and the execution of captured IRA men. This ended in 1921, when a truce, followed by a treaty, set up the Irish Free State.

After the war the British Government, realizing the impossibility, particularly in a climate of violence, of cajoling or coercing Ulster Unionists into a Dublin Parliament, passed a Government of Ireland Act under which there would be two Irish Parliaments, one for the six counties sitting in Belfast and a Dublin Assembly for the rest of Ireland. When the Anglo-Irish Treaty of 1921 confirmed that settlement, there was further pressure on Unionists to join the new Free State, but the new militant complexion of Irish Nationalism had made that totally impossible.

A Northern Ireland state with a two-chamber Parliament, whose powers were strictly limited, its own legal system and police force, came into being; the first Parliamentary session was inaugurated by King George V in June 1921. From the outset Nationalist politicians were determined to wreck the new state, which they said would lead to 'irretrievable chaos, a mass of blackened ruins and bleaching bones'. For a time their prophecies looked like coming true. The fighting in the South had its reverberations in the six counties. Inflamed by IRA murders, Protestants expelled Catholic fellow workers from the Belfast shipyards. IRA men and Protestant gunmen sniped from the rooftops into each other's ghettos, killing whoever came within their rifle sights. As Protestants got the upper hand in the rioting, thousands of Catholics were driven from their homes.

James Craig became the first Prime Minister of Northern Ireland and set about a policy of conciliation towards Catholics, but he was met by their leaders, both religious and political, with outright rejection. The IRA began a campaign of large-scale attacks across the border from the Free State; at one point British artillery had to be used to repel them. For over a year the pattern of violence which had affected the South was repeated in the six counties. The Ulster Scots had achieved what they had not sought, a state of their own, but they had not found the 'peacable kingdom'; the frontier would not go away. What was the problem now, asked a puzzled English journalist – was it politics, religion or just the weight of past history? As that formidable old Anglo-Irish woman Lady Gregory commented, surveying the scene from a position both detached and involved, 'It is hard to say where history ends, and where religion and politics begin; for history, religion and politics grow on one stem in Ireland, an eternal trefoil.'

CEMENTED WITH LOVE
ER
GOD SAVE THE QUEEN

SURRENDER
REM. 1690

OPPOSITE ABOVE *Orange arches are as much a part of folk life as they are statements of a political stance.*

OPPOSITE BELOW *Loyalist wall painting portraying William* III – *another important part of folk culture.*

ABOVE *Friends in Orange regalia chat on the Twelfth – the subject is unlikely to be the Pope or the threat of Dublin rule.*

POSTSCRIPT

FOR FIFTY YEARS the Ulster Scots, as the ruling Unionist Party in Northern Ireland, virtually controlled their own destiny and that of their Catholic Irish fellow citizens. It was not on the face of it the most creditable period in their history: soon after taking office they abolished the existing proportional representation system of voting which favoured the minority and they engineered a series of electoral manipulations, the most notorious of which was the gerrymandering of Londonderry in 1936. These were pointless exercises as there is little doubt that the Unionist Party would have remained in power under any system.

Government and public authorities practised active discrimination against Catholics in housing and jobs. By 1939, all the top ranking officers and 90 per cent of the Northern Ireland Civil Service were Protestant, as were the great majority of judges, magistrates and senior police officers. Sir Basil Brooke, third Prime Minister of the state, recommended his fellow Protestants, 'not to employ Roman Catholics, 99 per cent of whom are disloyal'.

But Protestant actions must be seen against a background of Catholic intransigence. Cardinal Logue, head of the Catholic Church in Ireland, rejected an invitation to attend the opening of the first Northern Ireland Parliament and elected Nationalist MPs refused to take their seats. Catholic society rolled itself into a ball like a hedgehog, priests actively discouraging social contacts between their flocks and Protestant neighbours. The Ne Temere decree, issued by the Vatican in 1908, sought to compel the Protestant partner in a mixed marriage to agree to bring the children up as Catholics, and was rigorously enforced by Irish clergy; the pressure brought on young couples caused much heartbreak, marital breakdown and subsequent sectarian bitterness. Religious teaching in Catholic schools led children to look down on Protestants as spiritually and morally inferior and the Catholic Archbishop, Cardinal MacRory, declared that Protestants were 'not even part of the Church of Christ'. This more subtle and largely low-key bigotry was in the long run more divisive than the Protestant brand.

Edward Carson had cautiously expressed the view that Ulster might eventually come in under a Dublin government but there was little to attract a Unionist looking southwards. The standard of living was low, even in comparison with the North where nearly 30 per cent of the working population was out of work. The Free State's political situation was unstable: there was armed intimidation at the polls and some newly elected deputies went with revolvers in their pockets to the Parliament chamber. Blueshirted fascists, led by the fanatical Eoin O'Duffy, who had once threatened to shoot his way into Northern Ireland, marched and rioted. The militant Catholic organization Maria

Duce maintained a violent verbal campaign against Protestants and Jews, and the Irish Prime Minister Éamon de Valera, whose features were distinctly Semitic, was forced to deny in Parliament that there was 'a drop of Jewish blood' in his veins. Ulster Scots reasoned that if a small, cooperative and quiet minority such as the Irish Jews could arouse animosity, a large and belligerent Protestant one in a united Ireland could expect no less.

The Second World War brought a degree of harmony, along with considerable prosperity, to Northern Ireland but it also brought destruction and death, unexpected in a place so far from even what was then called the 'Home Front'. In a single spring night in 1941 German bombers flattened much of the area around Belfast harbour and killed nearly a thousand people, the worst single raid on a British city outside London. The wartime neutrality of the Irish state since 1937 called by the Gaelic name Eire, deepened the divide between North and South. The Ulster Scots, involved in the war effort, felt themselves British and were intensely proud of the five army commanders – Alexander, Auchinleck, Alanbrooke, Montgomery and Dill – who belonged to Ulster families. It was not, however, these essentially Anglo-Irish soldiers who represented the true military genius of the Scots-Irish – the spirit of Daniel Morgan or Sam Houston – but one reckless guerilla fighter of the Western Desert campaign, Col. Blair Mayne. Mayne, one of the eight founder members of the Special Air Service, won four DSOs and the Croix de Guerre in raids against Rommel's supply lines and after D-Day in enemy-occupied France.

In 1948 Eire, which until then had belonged to the British Commonwealth, declared itself an independent republic with jurisdiction over Northern Ireland. The situation was a typically Irish one: the new republic had neither the power, nor perhaps even the will, to exercise all-Ireland sovereignty. Britain replied by giving the Ulster people, who had stood by them during the war, a guarantee that, as long as they wished, they would remain British. This British guarantee is frequently quoted as the main obstacle to Irish unity and the central cause of the present troubles. It is, in fact, no more than political window dressing: one has only to examine the events of early 1974 to realize that the Protestant people themselves have the power to maintain their independence of any Irish state. Within a few days in February 1974 and, by Northern Irish standards, with a minimum of force, the Protestant majority destroyed the power-sharing Executive set up as a result of the Sunningdale agreement with the blessing of the London and Dublin Governments, and backed by the resources of Whitehall. Oddly enough no historian at the time recalled the parallel situation in Pennsylvania in 1764 when the exasperated Scots-Irish dealt similarly with the Quaker Government in Philadelphia. Unfortunately the lesson of 1974, like that of 1764, appears to have been lost on British and Irish politicians. The temperament of the Scots-Irish would strongly suggest independence for Ulster as the best solution to the current troubles, but the practical problems are great. None of the small nation states created in modern times will serve as a model. On one hand, Israel, born out of an even more explosive situation than the Irish one, had the support of an immense, worldwide racial network during its first violent years; virtually all the support for a Scots-Irish nation would have come from within Northern Ireland. On the other hand Norway achieved its independence from Sweden in 1905 not only peacefully but with complete amity on both sides, a highly unlikely eventuality should Ulster become independent.

When independence was canvassed as an option in the 1970s there was little enthusiasm for it among ordinary Ulster people. There is, in fact, little belief in Northern Ireland that any purely political solution can succeed. Most people recognize that their problems lie much deeper than the structures of government – in a long history of distrust, in dissimilar cultures reinforced by religious beliefs from opposite ends of the Christian spectrum and in myths, totally outdated but so rigidly held that people are prepared to kill quite dispassionately for them.

The Emperor of Ice-Cream is a novel set in the Belfast blitz of 1941 in which the author Brian Moore explores the theme of Nationalist myths. It tells how the adolescent Gavin Burke emerges from the narrow intellectual confines of his family to a wider world where there are issues other than Catholic versus Protestant or Ireland's 'wrongs' at the hands of England. Moore's portrayal of Gavin's anti-Brit father, whose hero is Hitler, is a masterly interpretation of a certain type of Irish mind. The novel, which takes its title and underlying theme from a poem by the American Wallace Stevens, is an appeal to replace old fantasies with present realities. A line from the poem – 'Let be be the finale of seem' – offers a sentiment which Irish and Scots-Irish alike might well take to heart.

Popular Irish history has been created by 'novelists, fanatics, and politicians', but that does not make it any the less potent. It is widely accepted, for instance, that the population of the island consists of a broad base of Celtic people with a small minority of Anglo-Irish and a larger one of Scots-Irish. In fact, Ireland has been repeatedly settled by waves of invaders – Celts, Vikings, Normans, English, Scots – quite apart from the groups of traders who took up permanent residence around almost the entire periphery, from the mouth of the Foyle at Londonderry in a clockwise direction to Galway in the west. Writing in 1612, Sir John Davies said, 'There have been ... so many English colonies planted in Ireland as that if the people were numbered at this day by poll, such as are descended of the English race would be found to be more in number than the ancient natives.' This assessment was made well before the great Cromwellian Plantation which again altered the racial make-up of southern and central Ireland to the further detriment of the Celts. It would not be unreasonable to say that the Irish today are mostly English.

The racial position of the Ulster Scots is also worth examining. The population of their Scottish homeland was made up of remnants of the early Celtic inhabitants of the British Isles, of Anglo-Saxons from Europe, of another large Celtic group called Scots who had come in from Ireland and given Scotland its name, and some smaller groups such as Flemings from the Low Countries and Normans coming north after the conquest

The Locks at Edenderry: *the nineteenth-century linen village on the Belfast–Lisburn canal as seen through the 'innocent eye' of artist John Luke.*

of England. In any roster of Ulster Scots' surnames, the Celtic prefixes of 'Mac', 'Kil' and 'Kirk' dominate. It would appear that it is they and not the so-called 'native Irish' who are the truly Celtic people.

The greatest of the myths is that of the non-existence of the Ulster Scots as a separate people with a distinguished history and rich traditions. Lip service is paid by British and Irish politicians to the idea of a Protestant cultural identity, usually by a polite mention of the Twelfth of July as a folk festival; no attempt is made to probe beneath the cultural surface. How many people looking at the work of the Belfast artist John Luke would recognize in it a theme going back to the beginnings of the Scots-Irish race? In *The Locks at Edenderry* a young man hands his girl a bunch of flowers. In the distance people stroll leisurely along the canal banks, while white swans, instead of coal barges float on the water. The word Eden in the title provides the key. It is always Sunday in Luke's world, families walking their dogs through green, drumlin country in the warm afternoon; or evening after work as a father comes home to a white Ulster farmhouse set in formal idyllic landscape. Luke himself called it 'the eternal now', but it is in essence that curiously innocent Scots-Irish vision, the land of peace and plenty, often in the past expounded from Presbyterian pulpits and expressed in Biblical language.

The Ulster Scots have not been noted for their cultural output. The present crop of poets born in Northern Ireland, Seamus Heaney, Derek Mahon, Tom Paulin, Paul Muldoon, have made a considerable impact on the poetry of their time but ethnically and thematically they are dominated by an Irish rather than a Scots-Irish element. In the immediate past Louis MacNeice and W. R. Rodgers, while acknowledging the influence of their birthplace were more strongly attracted by the phoney romanticism of what passes as Irish culture. This comes out most clearly in MacNeice who, looking back to childhood, saw the twin poles of his home existence as the warm-hearted Catholic cook Annie with her fascinating stories of fairies and banshees and the hard-faced Protestant housekeeper Miss Craig obsessed with the twin virtues of cleanliness and godliness.

There has always been the additional problem created by the dual image of 'cultural Dublin', 'philistine Belfast', projected by the makers of aesthetic fashions in London. The sculptor F. E. McWilliam and the painter William Scott only achieved recognition when they left Northern Ireland for the mainland. Their contemporary Tom Carr, the finest watercolour artist alive today, has remained relatively unknown because he chose to live and paint in his native land.

The poet John Hewitt, who died in 1987, almost alone among twentieth-century Ulster writers broke through the hard crust of Ulster life to the reservoir of tradition on which the creative artist depends. Despite a lengthy exile in Coventry, where his job as an art curator took him, Hewitt worked ceaselessly interpreting in fresh and uncomplicated imagery the life of his own people. He believed that it was worth the effort to be 'rooted in honest history, in familiar folkways and knowledge'. He defined the present Ulster Scots dilemma more clearly than any politician, journalist or academic analyst. He saw the need for the Planter people to establish their identity in time as well as in place. 'A writer,' he said – and for the term 'writer' we can equally well substitute 'person' – 'must have ancestors. Not just of the blood, but of the emotions, of the quality and slant of mind. He must know where he comes from, otherwise how can he tell where he wishes to go?'

NOTES

Notes are related to their text by the page number on which the relevant text appears and by the first few words of the quotation (in quotation marks) or of the author's text or topic (without quotation marks) to which the note refers.

Full bibliographical details are only given in the notes when they do not appear in the bibliography.

The Public Record Office of Northern Ireland has been abbreviated to P.R.O.N.I.

Introduction

p. 2 'An Irish Scotch Presbyterian Rebellion'. Captain Johann Heinricks quoted in Leyburn.

p. 2 'formed the nucleus'. Dunaway.

p. 3 'A people who'. Blethen and Wood.

1 The Roots of a People

p. 4 'They christen without the cross'. *A Perfect Description of the People and Country of Scotland* (Leith, 1617).

p. 4 'John Tenender, session officer'. Perth Kirk Session Record, 1616, quoted in Chambers.

p. 5 'the first country to'. Leyburn.

p. 5 Abduction of women. Chambers.

p. 5 Bessie Tailiefeir 'branked'. Burgh Record of Canongate. Ibid.

p. 5 'kept like lions'. Ibid.

p. 5 'following the example'. Aberdeen Council Records, 1593. Ibid.

p. 5 On 15 October 1656, five people burned. Ibid.

p. 5 'Some women ta'en as witches'. Earl of Haddington's notes. Ibid.

p. 7 Actions against gipsies. P.H. Brown (ed,) *Register of the Privy Council of Scotland* (Edinburgh, 1877–1924).

p. 7 Punishment for incest. Ibid.

p. 7 Punishment of Alexander Blair. *Booke of the Universall Kirk of Scotland* (Edinburgh, 1839).

p. 7 High street violence. Chambers.

p. 7 Murder of Archbishop's cook. David Callender, *History of the Kirk of Scotland* (Woodrow Society).

p. 7 Execution of pirates. Robert Pitcairn, *Criminal Trials in Scotland* (Edinburgh, 1833).

p. 8 Execution of Francis Tennant. Chambers.

p. 8 Executions of John Dickson and Thomas Ross. Pitcairn, op. cit.

p. 8 'a traitor ... to the Church'. Rev. Robert Wodrow's *Analecta* quoted in Mathew.

p. 8 'given into the hands of Satan'. Excommunication formula quoted in Chambers.

p. 8 'the bigots of the iron time'. Sir Walter Scott, *The Lay of the Last Minstrel* in *The Poetical Works of Walter Scott* (London, 1892).

p. 8 Act of condemning 'minstrels'. Chambers.

p. 8 Poets hanged. Ibid.

p. 9 'within the compass'. Ibid.

p. 9 'cast ... out of their kindly possessions'. J. Donaldson, *Scotland, James V to James VII* (Edinburgh, 1965).

p. 9 'Scotland by reason of populousness'. *Royal Letters, Charters and Tracts 1621–1638.* D. Laing (ed.) (Edinburgh, 1867).

p. 9 'We spare none'. *Calendar of Irish State Papers* (London, 1860–1911).

p. 9 'Ireland is such'. *Calendar of State Papers,* relating to English affairs in Archives of Venice (London, 1864–1947).

p. 10 'The settling of religion'. James VI of Scotland to Arthur Chichester, *Calendar of Irish State Papers* (London, 1880).

p. 10 'The Scots are a middle temper'. *Calendar of Scottish State Papers* (London, 1858).

p. 11 Blennerhasset quoted in J.T. Gilbert, *A Contemporary History of Affairs in Ireland* (Dublin, 1897).

p. 13 'Every undertaker ... shall build'. Collection of orders and conditions to be observed by undertakers upon the plantation of the escheated lands in Ulster, quoted in Hill, *The Plantation of Ulster.*

p. 13 'Wee will give you'. James VI of Scotland to Arthur Chichester, *Calendar of Irish State Papers* (London, 1880).

p. 13 'Thomas Armstrang ... taen'. Pitcairn, op. cit.

p. 13 'Thom, Jok and Lancie Armestrangis'. P.H. Brown, op. cit.

p. 14 'it is almost become'. Ibid.

p. 14 'There are many Creaks'. George Monck, Irish Surveyor-General quoted in M. Perceval-Maxwell, *The Scottish Migration to Ulster in the Reign of James I.*

p. 14 'This was a small price'. Ibid.

p. 14 'If ever I live'. Border ballad.

p. 14 'Like the Homeric Greeks'. G.M. Trevelyan, *England under the Stuarts* (London, 1924).

2 Saints and Horse-Thieves

p. 16 'Make speed'. Thomas Blennerhasset, *A Direction for the Plantation of Ulster.* Quoted in Gilbert, op. cit.

p. 16 'scum .. fleeing from justice'. Adair.

p. 17 'Now, O Scotland'. Sermons by Samuel Rutherford, Glasgow. Quoted in Mathew.

p. 17 'A very near parallel'. *Diary of Johnston of Wariston,* Scottish History Society, (Edinburgh, 1896).

p. 20 'in three parishes'. Hill, *Montgomery Manuscripts.*

p. 20 'The wolf and the woodkerne'. Adair.

p. 22 'Art McGillechree'. Assize Records quoted in *Ulster Journal of Archeology,* Vol. II (Belfast, 1854).

p. 22 'such men for strict walking'. Adair.

p. 22 'Thou fool ... thou must'. Blair.

p. 22 'I met unexpectedly'. Ibid.

p. 22 'That same night'. Ibid.
p. 24 'his hearers fell'. A. Stewart, 'The History of the Church of Ireland', published as appendix to Adair.
p. 29 'I rather lay downe'. Wodrow MSS Collection, Vol. 25, No. 22, National Library of Scotland.
p. 29 'were it not for the Scottish'. Pynnar Survey quoted in Hill, *The Plantation of Ulster*.
p. 29 'The Scots are twenty to one'. Report of Surveyor-General, 1637. Harleian MS. 2138, British Museum.
p. 29 'It were good'. *Calendar of Irish State Papers*.
p. 31 'runninge up and downe'. *Calendar of Irish State Papers*.
p. 31 'like Nomades'. Fynes Moryson, 'The Commonwealth of Ireland' in *Illustrations of Irish History and Topography* (London, 1904).
p. 31 'sleep under the canopy'. Ibid.
p. 33 'Why should night dreams'. Andrew Bonnar (ed.) *Letters of Samuel Rutherford*, (Edinburgh, 1894).
p. 33 'The most inhumane'. *Newes from Londonderry in Ireland*, anonymous pamphlet (London, 1642).
p. 34 'Neither violence, robbery or murder'. Rev. J. Good quoted in Stewart, *The Narrow Ground*.

3 The Sword of the Lord

p. 35 'God should be cried'. Adair.
p. 35 'Flying at the Captaine's ... bells'. Robert Baillie, *Letters and Journals* (Edinburgh, 1775).
p. 36 'Ane great army' and following quote. John Spalding, *Memorials of the Troubles in Scotland and England* (Aberdeen, 1851).
p. 36 'repeated dreams'. 'Letters of Sir Thomas Hope 1627–46', in *Miscellany of the Scottish History Society*, Vol. 1 (1893).
p. 36 'They found it necessary'. Adair.
p. 36 'no favourers of religion'. Ibid.
p. 37 Monro's punitive expeditions. 'A True Relation of the proceedings of the Scottish Armie' quoted in D. Stevenson.
p. 37 'The people were very hungry' and following quotes. Adair.
p. 37 'Wretched dyet'. 'Transactions of the Scottish Army in Ireland', MSS, National Library of Scotland.
p. 37 'Righteous Hand of God'. Adair.
p. 38 'Well scene at Benbourb'. 'Transactions of the Scottish Army in Ireland', op. cit.
p. 38 'Were so fat'. Adair.
p. 38 'Oppression and insolence'. Blair.
p. 38 'tempestuous nights'. 'Transactions of the Scottish Army in Ireland', op. cit.
p. 38 'being neighbourly admitted'. John Milton, *Prose Works* (London, 1853).
p. 38 'God's wonderful Providence'. Adair.
p. 38 'the blockish presbyters'. John Milton, op. cit.
p. 38 'There came a dark cloud'. Adair.
p. 39 'they did visit'. Ibid.
p. 39 'unreasonable liberty'. Quoted in J. Stevenson.
p. 39 'the wild glen. Gamble.
p. 41 'there was scarcely'. Macaulay, *History of England* (London, 1848).
p. 41 'that all our Irishmen'. The Comber letter in Stewart, *The Narrow Ground*.
p. 41 'they scrupled not'. Thomas Witherow, *Derry and Enniskillen in 1689* (Belfast, 1876).
p. 41 'never let poor woman's son'. Diary of John Hunter quoted in Macrory.
p. 41 'The bonfires shone'. Macaulay, op. cit.
p. 44 'stript immediately'. Rev. George Storey, quoted in Macrory.
p. 44 'vast numbers of them'. 'A Discourse concerning Ireland, 1697' quoted in J. Stevenson.
p. 46 'Some die in the wayside'. Robert Sibbald, *Provision for the Poor in Time of Dearth and Scarcity* (Edinburgh, 1699).
p. 46 'our prelates are violent'. Wodrow MSS Collection, Vol. 20, No. 124.
p. 46 'We are surprised'. Petition of the Presbyterian Ministers and People, Wodrow MSS Collection, Fol. 51, No. 48.
p. 46 'at the boldness of the dissenters'. J. Stevenson.
p. 46 'toleration of all religions'. Sermons by Samuel Rutherford, Glasgow, quoted in Mathew.
p. 46 'the Prospect of establishing'. *The Conduct of Dissenters*, pamphlet of 1712 quoted in J. Stevenson.
p. 46 'assuming and insolent behaviour'. Ibid.
p. 46 'May the Lord'. Country tradition, source unknown.
p. 46 'his bag of oatmeal'. J. M. Barkley, 'The Presbyterian Minister in Eighteenth Century Ireland' in J. L. M. Haine.
p. 47 'in fair or foul weather'. Diary of Rev. John Kennedy quoted in J. Stevenson.
p. 47 'Jamie Allen ... firing', 'I was for some time'. Diary of John Scott. Ibid.
p. 48 'This bound minister'. J. M. Barkley in Haine.
p. 48 'Scotch Presbyterians'. Boulter letters.
p. 50 'a zealous, worthy preacher'. Adair.
p. 51 'Teach us to be contented'. Quoted in J. Stevenson.

4 A New Glimpse of Zion

p. 52 'This stern and virile people'. President Theodore Roosevelt, 'The Winning of the West', *The Works of Theodore Roosevelt* (National Edition, New York, 1925).
p. 52 'Brethren, let us depart'. Author's reconstruction from McGregor's notes quoted in Bolton.
p. 53 A petition signed by these immigrants shows. Bolton.
p. 55 'This country abounds'. Letters of Robert Parke quoted in Ford.
p. 55 'The whole North'. Letter of Archbishop Boulter. Ibid.
p. 56 'Just imported'. *Charleston Gazette*, 7 December 1734 quoted in E. McCracken *South Carolina under Royal Government* (New York, 1899).
p. 56 'Procure ... four lusty servants'. A. C. Myers, 'Immigration of Irish Quakers into Pennsylvania 1682–1750', quoted in Dickson.
p. 56 'As many of my friends'. Letter of Robert Smillie to the *Belfast Newsletter* (*Belfast Newsletter* files, Belfast Public Library).
p. 58 'We had a South-west Wind'. Letter of John Smillie quoted in the *Belfast Newsletter* (*Belfast Newsletter* files, Belfast Public Library).
p. 60 'the children could not walk'. James Magraw letter quoted in *The Shippensburg Story 1730–*

1970, Shippensburg Historical Society (Shippensburg, Pa., 1970).
p. 65 'the inhabitants of this country'. *Diary of David McClure* (New York, 1899).
p. 67 'savage backwoodsmen ... possessing all the vices'. William Strickland, *Observations on the Agriculture of the United States* (London, 1801).
p. 68 'Sweet water'. Magraw letter, op. cit.
p. 69 'If you had come home'. Kilgore Manuscript Westmoreland County Historical Society, Greensburgh, Pa., n.d.
p. 70 'with tools and one year's provisions'. *Witherspoon Family Chronicle*, Williamsburg County Historical Society, 1697.
p. 70 'had but one door and no windows'. Letter of Samuel Houston, MSS in Virginia Historical Society, Richmond.
p. 70 'They have bread'. Robert G. Albion (ed.) *The Diary of Philip Fithian*, (Princeton, 1924).
p. 71 'The "backwoods" life'. Estyn Evans, 'The Scotch Irish: Their cultural Adaption in the American Old West' in Green, *Essays in Scotch-Irish History*.
p. 72 'With a little corn'. Houston letter, Virginia Historical Society, Richmond.

5 Blood on the Buckskin

p. 73 'During the late and present Indian War'. Scots-Irish Remonstrance to the Pennsylvania Assembly, 1764, quoted in Dunaway.
p. 73 'Troublesome settlers to the Government'. James Logan, Colonial Secretary, on the Scots-Irish, 1730, quoted in J. H. Finley, *The Coming of the Scot* (New York, 1940).
p. 73 'I thought it might be prudent'. Letter of James Logan, Pennsylvania MSS, official correspondence, Historical Society of Pennsylvania, 1720.
p. 74 'Jean McCullough did enter' and following quotes. Diary of James McCullough (Private Collection).
p. 75 'Unwilling to quit'. McClure, op. cit.
p. 75 'Such people, if kindly used'. Logan letter, Pennsylvania MSS, Historical Society of Pennsylvania.
p. 75 'they propose to gain'. Ibid.
p. 78 Story of John Armstrong quoted in Flower.
p. 78 'a very great number'. Report of William Webb, MSS, Land Office, Harrisburg.
p. 79 Paxton massacre. Dunbar.
p. 80 'This rash act'. Houston letter, op. cit.
p. 80 'The express came softly'. Joseph Doddridge, *Notes on the Settlement and Indian Wars* (Wellsburgh, Virginia, 1824).
p. 80 'a scandal to our nation'. Diary of John Craig, Augusta Stone Church Museum, Virginia.
p. 83 McClure, op. cit.
p. 86 Trial of Robert Huey. *Inquisition at Hanna's Town*, Westmoreland County Historical Society (Greensburg, Pa., 1978).
p. 86 Elizabeth Brownlee's story. *A Captive's Tale*, A. L. Warren (ed.) Westmoreland County Historical Society (Greensburg, Pa., 1977).

6 God-Provoking Democrats

p. 88 'Call it not an American Rebellion'. Captain Johann Heinricks, German mercenary serving with the British, *c.* 1780, quoted in Leyburn.
p. 88 'Hi! Uncle Sam!'. Ballad of the American Revolution.
p. 88 'Play-Fair System'. W. H. Egle, *History of the Commonwealth of Pennsylvania* (Harrisburg, 1876).
p. 88 Material on Francis Hutcheson Barkley, and in W. R. Scott, *Francis Hutcheson* (Cambridge, 1900).
p. 93 'consummation of that sublime movement'. Proceedings of Third Scotch-Irish Congress, Nashville, 1891.
p. 94 'Give me liberty', and following quotes. Patrick Henry to the Virginia Assembly 23 May 1775, quoted in Charles Van Doren and Robert McHenry, *Webster's Guide to American History*.
p. 94 Alexander Chesney case. Alexander Chesney MSS, P.R.O.N.I.
p. 98 Ephraim Blaine. Anna A. Hays, *Col. Ephraim Blaine*, Hamilton Library Association (Carlisle, 1935).
p. 99 'We travelled this day'. Lawson.
p. 99 'Married women have been ravished', 'Some of their wives'. Woodmason.
p. 102 'Itinerant Presbyterian preachers'. Ibid.
p. 104 Rev. William Martin episode. 'The Roles of the Scots and Scotch-Irish in the Southern Campaigns of the War of American Independence', Bobby Moss, doctorate thesis, University of St Andrews.
p. 104–6 War in Carolina. Ibid.

7 In Search of America

p. 107 'The gifts of fortune'. Alexis de Tocqueville, *Democracy in America* (Cincinatti, 1851).
p. 107 'Isolationism ... a commonwealth'. Woodrow Wilson, *The Papers of Woodrow Wilson*, R. S. Link (ed.) (Princeton, 1966–85).
p. 107 'Stand at the Cumberland Gap'. F. J. Turner, *The Significance of the Frontier in American History* (Wisconsin, 1893), full text in J. S. Commager, *Living Ideas in America* (New York, 1951).
p. 108 'this perennial rebirth'. Ibid.
p. 108 'The true point of view'. Ibid.
p. 108 Quotations from Woodmason.
p. 109 John McElrath and Rev. William Richardson quoted in Moss, op. cit.
p. 112 Timber Ridge settlement. Quoted in Houston letter, op. cit.
p. 112 'a fish caught here'. Journal of Col. John May, quoted in Buck.
p. 112 'It was a characteristically Scotch-Irish community'. Dunaway.
p. 113 'We were provided with three horses'. Memoir of a 1784 migration from Carlisle, Pa. to Ohio, quoted in T. D. Clark.
p. 113 'Last night was a jovial one', quoted in Buck.
p. 113 'delights chiefly in company'. Ibid.
p. 113 'Every year after seeding time'. Ibid.
p. 114 'lower orders'. Ibid.
p. 114 Whiskey Rebellion. Baldwin.
p. 115 'the ruin of Christ's Government' and following quotes. Diary of John Craig, Augusta Stone Church Museum, Virginia.
p. 117 Quotations from Woodmason.

p. 119 Quotes concerning George Croghan. See Crist and T. D. Clark.
p. 122 'From the heart of these settlements'. T. D. Clark.
p. 122 'the number of horned cattle'. André Michaux writing in 1802. Ibid.
p. 122 Patton story. Letter of James Patton, privately published by Patton family (North Carolina, 1973).

8 Whiskey in the White House

p. 124 'The most roaring, rollicking'. Contemporary view of Andrew Jackson, quoted in James.
p. 124 'The stage is set'. Woodrow Wilson, op. cit.
p. 124 Andrew Jackson. James.
p. 125 'Kick this damned treaty'. George Gibbs, *Memoirs of the Administrations of Washington and Adams* (New York, 1846).
p. 125 'If some measures'. Harrison Gray Otis quoted in S. E. Morrison, *Life and Letters of Harrison Gray Otis* (New York, 1913).
p. 130 'was carefully crafted'. David Noel Doyle in interview with the author.
p. 134 'If the Nullies don't go back'. J. A. Woodburn.
p. 134 'Our fate as a people.' C. N. Wilson.
p. 134 McWhiney and Jameson, *Attack and Die*.
p. 135 'Yankees were cleaner'. Ibid.
p. 140 'You shall not crucify'. William Jennings Bryan, first used in a speech to Democratic Convention 1896. Quoted in Van Doren and McHenry, op. cit.
p. 141 'Woodrow Wilson and His Presbyterian Heritage' in Green, *Essays in Scotch-Irish History*.
p. 143 'The stern Covenanter tradition'. Ibid.
p. 143 'Christianity came into the world'. Lecture of 1909. Ibid.
p. 143 'Government of the people'. Lincoln's Gettysburg address.

9 Mountain Men and Millionaires

p. 145 'The half-civilized'. Billington, *The American Frontiersman*.
p. 145 'Without prudent children'. Thomas Mellon, *Thomas Mellon and His Times* (privately printed, Pittsburgh, 1885).
p. 147 John Colter. See Mattes and Chittenden.
p. 150 Osborne Russell, *Journal of a Trapper*.
p. 150 'For seven days'. Chittenden.
p. 150 'a reversion to the primitive', 'half-civilized, half-savage'. Billington, *The American Frontiersman*.
p. 151 'A son of Erin', and following quote. Russell.
p. 151 'Gotta larn'. Billington.
p. 154 'a class largely trained', and following quotes. Thomas Mellon, op. cit.
p. 154 'A place to bury'. Quoted in Koskoff.
p. 156 'Make no friends', and following quotes. Thomas Mellon, op. cit.
p. 156 'Cromwell was the only ruler'. Ibid.
p. 157 'the air very salubrious'. 'Journal of André Michaux', quoted in R. G. Thwaites, *Early Western Travels 1748–1846* (New York, 1904–7).
p. 157 'The masters of Pittsburgh'. James Parton, article in *Atlantic Monthly*, 1868, quoted in R. Lubove (ed.) *Pittsburgh* (New York, 1976).
p. 157 'There is no interruption'. M. Chevalier, quoted in Thwaites, op. cit.
p. 159 'The Mellons fixed up Rolling Rock'. Quoted by a Ligonier resident in conversation with the author.
p. 160 'He wrote songs'. Dean Root, Curator of the Stephen Foster Centre, University of Pittsburgh, in an interview with the author.
p. 165 'There is a strong tradition'., Jan Davidson in an interview with the author.
p. 166 'like a streak of greased lightning'. Quoted in D. J. Boorstin, *The Americans: The National Experience* (London, 1965).
p. 166 'petrified birds'. Interview with Bridger *c.* 1956, quoted in Chittenden.
p. 166 William Lynwood Montell, *Ghosts Along the Cumberland* (Knoxville, Tenn., 1975).
p. 167 Arnold J. Toynbee, *A Study of History* (London, 1934).
p. 167 'If the Scotch-Irish'. Estyn Evans, 'Cultural Relics of the Ulster-Scots in the Old West of North America', *Ulster Folklife*, 11 (1965).
p. 167 'Their successes when re-examined'. Denis Clark in an interview with the author.

10 Hearts of Ulster

p. 169 '... a brotherhood of affection'. From the oath of United Irishmen, quoted in Chart.
p. 169 'On Saturday last'. Files of the *Belfast Newsletter*, Belfast Public Library, 19 May 1772.
p. 169 'Betwixt landlord and rector'. Quoted in Connell, *Irish Peasant Society*.
p. 171 'the hanging of father and son'. Letter of John Alexander to Lord Donegall's agent quoted in Donnelly.
p. 171 'heavy oppression'. *Belfast Newsletter*, 4 January 1771.
p. 171 'filled at least two miles'. Donnelly.
p. 171 'One of their usual punishments'. Quoted in Connell, *Irish Peasant Society*.
p. 173 'The spirit of emigrating'. Young.
p. 173 'Friend Thomas'. Letter from Thomas Wright, Bucks County, Pennsylvania, to Thomas Greer, Dungannon. Greer MSS quoted in Crawford and Trainor.
p. 173 'No sooner did we enter'. 'John Wesley's Journal' quoted in Crawford, *Domestic Industry in Ireland*.
p. 173 'And joining they hunt'. Young.
p. 173 'From Monaghan to Carrickfergus'. Willes MSS quoted in Crawford and Trainor.
p. 178 Francis Hutcheson quotes. Barkley and Scott.
p. 178 'daft boy'. Quoted in Barkley, 'Francis Hutcheson'.
p. 179 'Nothing satisfies them'. Young.
p. 179 'The Protestant gentleman'. *Belfast Newsletter*, 21 July 1775.
p. 179 Yankee Club of Stewartstown. *Belfast Mercury*, 5 October, 1784.
p. 179 'A society having much'. Chart.
p. 182 'great levellers and republicans'. Rutland MSS, quoted in Stewart, *The Narrow Ground*.
p. 183 'Seamus ... sell your things'. Quoted in Connell, *Irish Peasant Society*.
p. 183 'Out of 230 or 240'. *Belfast Newsletter*, 7 October 1834.
p. 183 'If another shot'. De Latocnaye.

p. 184 'I die in the true faith'. F. J. Bigger, *William Orr* (Dublin, 1906).

p. 184 'I saw Samuel Bones'. MSS of Rev. Robert Magill quoted in R. M. Young, *Ulster in '98* (Belfast, n.d.).

p. 185 'Visions were affirmed'. McSkimin.

p. 185 'May the skin'. McSkimin.

p. 185 'thought it no more'. Confession of James Beaghan, Wexford rebel, reproduced in *Erin Go Bragh*, P.R.O.N.I.

p. 186 'Some hid ...', and following quotes. *Works* of James Orr (Belfast, 1935).

p. 187 'The awful spectacle ...'. Magill quoted in R. M. Young, op. cit.

p. 187 'Dear Father ...'. Letter of John Patton, 11 June 1798, P.R.O.N.I.

p. 187 'ungenerous advantage'. J. B. Woodburn.

p. 187 'Hanging and flogging'. Letter of Thomas Lane, 9 June 1798, P.R.O.N.I.

11 Cockpit City

p. 189 'a party of about seventy men'. Report of British officer on Belfast riot, 1864, quoted in Moore.

p. 189 '... while rioters do not mind'. Ibid.

p. 189 'This jewel that houses'. Ballad to a traditional refrain, M. J. Craig.

p. 190 'This day's dinner', and following quote. Poorhouse Records 1810, quoted in Strain.

p. 190 'For thirty-five years'. T. W. Moody, 'Higher Education' in Moody and Beckett.

p. 194 'hearty, thriving'. W. M. Thackeray, *The Irish Sketch-book* (London, 1843).

p. 194 'The profits of the York Street concern'. Hugh McCall quoted in Bardon.

p. 194 Old people in the 1950s. Interviews carried out by the author.

p. 195 'Our country is not'. *Belfast Newsletter*, 1 July 1894.

p. 195 'She is forty years old'. Medical report for factory district of Belfast, 1877.

p. 195 'It is but a false'. *Belfast Newsletter*, 27 October 1854.

p. 196 'Between the divided churches ...' Speech at Hillsborough, County Down, quoted in Bardon.

p. 201 'Call that clearance'. Moore.

p. 201 'Some of our more bellicose'. Ibid.

p. 201 'Pope's prisons'. Sermon published in 'Report on the Belfast Riots' (Dublin, 1857).

p. 201 'the close connection'. Moore.

p. 203 'imbued with an ethic'. Messenger.

p. 203 'Two or even three families'. O'Hanlon.

p. 203 'frantic shouts', 'whiskey drinking'. Ibid.

p. 203 'Forty five out of', and following quotes. Malcolm, *The Sanitary State of Belfast*.

p. 205 'never lifted its factory hat'. Quoted in 'Tether that held me to the hare', BBC radio documentary on W. R. Rodgers, 8 July 1979.

p. 207 'The men worked heartily'. *Belfast Newsletter* files, 21 October 1910.

12 The Sash Across the Sea

p. 208 'Here am I a loyal Orangeman'. Traditional Orange ballad.

p. 208 Norman Ritchie in an interview with the author.

p. 208 'As soon as any member'. Quoted in Senior.

p. 209 'received for the Orangemen'. Ibid.

p. 209 'a numerous and very troublesomely disposed'. Ibid.

p. 209 'A great number of our Brethren'. Proceedings of the Provincial Orange Lodge of Manitoba quoted in Houston and Smyth.

p. 211 'the liberty of freeborn subjects'. Quoted in Bruce Proudfoot, 'Irish Settlers in Alberta', *Studies in Irish Folklife*, Vol. 15/16, 1970.

p. 212 'The work and the isolation'. 'The Settlement of Mono Township', *The Canadian Geographer*, 19 (1975).

p. 212 'hilly and swampy'. Ibid.

p. 213 Details of life in Mono, anecdotes etc. Gordon and Bill Richardson and other Mono inhabitants in an interview with the author.

p. 213 'people like deep snow'. Carrothers Correspondence, 1839–70, Linenhall Library, Belfast.

p. 216 'so many persons'. Letters of Jane White, 1841–60, P.R.O.N.I.

p. 217 'send me 4'. Carrothers Correspondence, op. cit.

p. 217 'Do you know'. Robb family correspondence, 1862–78, P.R.O.N.I.

p. 217 'An oldish kind of lady'. Letter of John Miller, Hamilton, Ontario, 1857, P.R.O.N.I.

p. 217 'a storm arose'. Benson.

p. 220 'riding the goat'. Reported Orange initiation service.

p. 220 'We could stir up'. Norman Ritchie in an interview with the author.

p. 220 'Woe betide this city'. Quoted in Senior.

p. 220 'I never liked'. Letters of Jane White, op. cit.

13 Promised Lands Down Under

p. 222 'Rank and title have no charms'. G. Butler Earp, *The Gold Colonies of Australia* (London, 1852).

p. 222 Patrick O'Farrell, *Letters from Irish Australia 1825–1929* (Sydney and Belfast, 1984).

p. 223 Allen, *Bush and Backwoods*.

p. 223 'I am surprised'. Letters of Alexander Boyce, 1838–9, P.R.O.N.I.

p. 224 'all United Irishmen'. Quoted in A. G. L. Shaw, *Convicts and the Colonies*.

p. 224 Letters of Samuel Shaw, John Sayers, Bessie Macready, Oliver McSparran and Journal of Elizabeth Anketell, P.R.O.N.I.

p. 226 'screaming and praying'. Quoted in O'Farrell.

p. 227 'Our young men'. Diary of Voyage to Australia, 1858, Rev William Bates, P.R.O.N.I.

p. 227 Letter of Daniel Gardner, 1875, P.R.O.N.I.

p. 227 Log kept on board the ship *Prince of Seas* bound for Melbourne, 1861, Charles Elliot, P.R.O.N.I.

p. 229 Letters of Noah Dalway, 1854–7, P.R.O.N.I.

p. 229 Letters of J. S. Nicholson, 1861–1927, P.R.O.N.I.

p. 229 Lawrence letters, 1825–80, P.R.O.N.I.

p. 230 Getty papers, 1853–9, P.R.O.N.I.

p. 230 Letter of George McLean, 1870, P.R.O.N.I.

p. 230 Life of Andrew George Scott, see Calderwood.
p. 232 Allen, *Bush and Backwoods.*
p. 233 Correspondence of Joseph McGaw, P.R.O.N.I.
p. 236 'Not one of them'. Letter of George Adams, 1849, part of Adams correspondence, P.R.O.N.I.
p. 236 William Cherry, Letters to parents, 1866–8, P.R.O.N.I.
p. 236 Milliken correspondence, 1884–7, P.R.O.N.I.
p. 237 Letter of Frank Robb, 1878, P.R.O.N.I.
p. 237 Crawford correspondence, 1881–4, P.R.O.N.I.
p. 239 'Oh that the Orangemen'. Quoted in *The Journal of the Australian Historical Society,* No. 55 (Sydney, 1969).
p. 239 'Maxwell' correspondence, P.R.O.N.I. The author here maintains the pseudonym under which extracts appear in O'Farrell.
p. 240 'you Orange dog'. Anonymous letter to John Gray, Kiama, McCaffrey Papers, University of Wollongong.
p. 240 'The climate is everything'. Letter of Rev. John Mark, Kati-Kati, 1877. G. V. Stewart.
p. 240 'Not clerks'. Ibid.
p. 241 'Two generals'. Report by electric telegraph from *Bay of Plenty Times,* 1879, quoted in Kati-Kati Centenary leaflet.
p. 243 'dreams of freehold'. W. J. Gardner, 'The Rise of W. F. Massey, 1891–1912', *Political Science,* Vol. 13, 1961.

14 Contracts and Covenants

p. 244 'The dark eleventh hour'. Rudyard Kipling, '1912', in *Verse Inclusive* (London, 1911).
p. 244 'gradually creeping up'. Connell, 'The Colonization of Waste Land in Ireland'.
p. 245 'The bare country studded thickly'. A. C. Lyall, *Life of the Marquis of Dufferin and Ava* (London, 1905).
p. 245 'Everything was suddenly changed'. J. G. Kohl, *Travels in Ireland* (London, 1844).
p. 246 'From a state of primeval barreness'. *Belfast Telegraph,* 29 January 1850.
p. 246 Brian Walker, *Sentry Hill: An Ulster Farm and its Family* (Belfast, 1981).
p. 247 'Every field had a name'. Ibid.
p. 247 'the whole country'. Report of the Revenue Commissioners, 1823.
p. 247 Details of illicit distillation and unlicenced drinking taken from the Reports of the Commissioners of Excise, 1823, 1824 and 1834, quoted in Connell, *Irish Peasant Society.*
p. 248 Details of ether drinking are taken from the *Lancet* (1902), the *British Medical Journal, The Times* (1871–91), the *Medical Press and Circular* (1870) and are quoted in Connell, Ibid.
p. 249 Details of the Battle of Garvagh including ballad, see Aiken McClelland, 'The Battle of Garvagh', *Ulster Folklife,* Vol. 19 (1973).
p. 250 '38 men armed'. Pynnar Survey quoted in Hill, *The Plantation of Ulster.*
p. 250 'armed with scythes'. MSS in Trinity College Dublin, quoted in Gillespie.
p. 251 'felt as if enveloped'. Walker, op. cit.
p. 251 Effects of Revival in various parts of Ulster. See Carson.
p. 252 'I cannot understand'. Quoted in the doctorate thesis of J. R. B. McMinn, Queen's University, Belfast, 1979.
p. 252 'For thirty years'. The *Northern Whig,* Vol. 13, July 1867, *Northern Whig* files, Belfast Public Library.
p. 252 'The working class of Belfast'. *Weekly Northern Whig,* 21 May 1870.
p. 253 'the invasion of Ulster'. Buckland.
p. 253 'Lots were drawn'. Moore.
p. 254 'the Orange card', and following quotes. *Belfast Newsletter,* 24 February 1886.
p. 254 'When the Ulster settlements'. MacKnight.
p. 255 'Protestant Ideology and Politics', Frank Wright, in *Archives Européennes de Sociologie,* XIV, 2, pp 213–80 (1973).
p. 255 'Did not contemplate'. *Belfast Newsletter,* 17 May 1886.
p. 257 'I vowed that if ever'. Armour.
p. 257 'the prancing colonels'. Ibid.
p. 258 'relying on the God'. Quoted in Stewart, *The Ulster Crisis.*
p. 258 'No one for a moment'. Quoted in St John Ervine, *Craigavon, Ulsterman* (London, 1949).
p. 259 'I am responsible'. Quoted in Stewart, *The Ulster Crisis.*
p. 259 'There was certainly nothing'. Ibid.
p. 259 Fred H. Crawford, *Guns for Ulster* (Belfast, 1947).
p. 261 'soon . . . was as completely at home'. Quoted in Stewart, *The Ulster Crisis.*
p. 262 'come and try conclusions'. Ibid.
p. 263 'The parishes of Fermanagh' W. S. Churchill, 'The World Crisis'. Ibid.
p. 263 'with rifles sloped'. Stewart, *The Ulster Crisis.*
p. 263 'One of the finest displays', 'I would rather be an Ulsterman'. Ibid.
p. 267 'It is hard to say'. Lady Gregory, quoted in Horace Plunkett, *Ireland in the New Century* (Dublin, 1982).

Postscript

p. 270 'not to employ Roman Catholics'. News report quoted in David Harkness, *Northern Ireland Since 1920* (Dublin, 1983).
p. 272 Brian Moore, *The Emperor of Ice Cream* (London, 1965).
p. 272 Wallace Stevens's poem, 'The Emperor of Ice Cream', *Faber Book of Modern Verse* (London, 1940).
p. 272 'There have been'. Sir John Davies, *Historical Tracts,* G. Chalmers (ed.) (London, 1986).
p. 275 'he must have ancestors'. John Hewitt, *The Bitter Gourd* (Belfast, 1945).

BIBLIOGRAPHY

Adair, Rev. Patrick, *A True Narrative of the Rise and Progress of the Presbyterian Church in Ireland (1623–1670)* (Belfast, 1866)

Akenson, D. H., *Between Two Revolutions: Islandmagee, County Antrim, 1798–1920* (Ontario, 1979)

Akenson, D. H. and Crawford, W. H., *Local Poets and Social History: James Orr, Bard of Ballycarry* (Belfast, 1977)

Allen, H. C., *Bush and Backwoods: a comparison of the frontier in Australia and the United States* (Sydney, 1959)

Armour, W. S., *Armour of Ballymoney* (London, 1934)

Armstrong, William A., *The Armstrong Borderland* (Galashiels, 1960)

Baldwin, Leland D., *Whiskey Rebels: The Story of a Frontier Uprising* (Pittsburgh, 1939)

Bardon, Jonathan, *Belfast: An Illustrated History* (Belfast, 1982)

Barkley, J. M., *A Short History of the Presbyterian Church in Ireland* (Belfast, 1959)

Barkley, J. M., 'Frances Hutcheson (1694–1746)', *The Bulletin of the Presbyterian Historical Society of Ireland*, No. 14 (March 1985)

Bellam, Michael, 'The Irish in New Zealand', *Familia: The Ulster Genealogical Review*, 2, 1 (1985), pp 41–3

Benn, George, *The History of the Town of Belfast* (Belfast, 1823)

Benson, Wilson, *Life and Adventures of Wilson Benson, Written by Himself* (Toronto, 1876)

Billington, R. A., *Westward Expansion: A History of the American Frontier* (New York, 1967, 3rd edn.)

Billington, R. A., *The American Frontiersman*, an inaugural lecture (Oxford, 1954)

Blair, Robert, *Memoirs of the Life of Mr Robert Blair* (Belfast, 1844, original edn. 1754)

Blethen, Tyler and Wood, Curtis, *From Ulster to Carolina: The Migration of the Scotch-Irish to Southwestern North Carolina* (Western Carolina University, 1983)

Blum, John Morton, *Woodrow Wilson and the Politics of Morality* (Boston, 1956)

Bolton, Charles Knowles, *The Scotch-Irish Pioneers in Ulster and America* (Boston, 1910)

Borland, Robert, *Border Raids and Reivers* (Dalbeattie, 1898)

Boulter, Hugh, *Letters Written by Hugh Boulter, Lord Primate of Ireland*, M. Wall (ed.) (Oxford, 1769–70)

Brett, C. E. B., *Buildings of Belfast, 1700–1914* (Belfast, 1985, revised edn.)

Buck, S. J. and Buck, E. H., *The Planting of Civilisation in Western Pennsylvania* (Pittsburgh, 1939)

Buckland, Patrick, *Irish Unionism 2: Ulster Unionism and the Origins of Northern Ireland 1886–1922* (Dublin, 1973)

Burrell, S. A., 'The Apocalyptic Vision of the Early Covenanters', *The Scottish Historical Review*, XLIII, 135 (April 1964), pp 1–24

Bush, Ernest E. (ed.), *The Katikati Story, Tauranga Historical Society Journal*, centennial souvenir issue (March, 1975)

Calderwood, G., *Captain Moonlite: Bushranger* (London, 1971)

Caldwell, H. G., *Andrew Malcolm of Belfast, 1818–1856: Physician and Historian* (Belfast, 1977)

Calendar of State Papers for Ireland, 1603–1625 (London, 1872–80)

Campbell, T. D., *Francis Hutcheson: 'Father' of the Scottish Enlightenment*

Carnmoney Presbyterian Church, 'Minutes of Meetings of Session', 1686 to 1748, Presbyterian Historical Society, Belfast

Carrothers, Edward Norman (ed.), *Irish Emigrants' Letters from Canada, 1839–1870* (Belfast, 1951). Letters of Joseph and Nathaniel Carrothers

Carson, John T., *God's River in Spate: The Story of the Religious Awakening of Ulster in 1859* (Belfast, 1958)

Chambers, Robert, *Domestic Annals of Scotland* (Edinburgh, 1859)

Chart, D. A., *The Drennan Letters* (Belfast, 1931)

Chittenden, Hiram Martin, *The Yellowstone National Park* (Norman, Okla., 1964)

Clark, Thomas D., *Frontier America: The Story of the Westward Movement* (New York, 1959)

Clark, Wallace, *Linen on the Green: An Irish Mill Village, 1730–1982* (Hythe, Kent, 1982)

Commager, Henry Steele, *Documents of American History* (New York, 1963, seventh edn.)

Connell, K. H., *Irish Peasant Society* (Oxford, 1968)

Connell, K. H., 'The Colonization of Waste Land in Ireland, 1780–1845', *Economic History Review*, 2nd series, iii (1), 1950, pp 44–71

Crawford, W. H., *Domestic Industry in Ireland* (Dublin, 1972)

Crawford, W. H., 'The Market Book of Thomas Greer, A Dungannon Linendraper, 1758–59', *Ulster Folklife*, 13 (1967), pp 54–60

Crawford, W. H., 'The Origins of the Linen Industry in North Armagh and the Lagan Valley', *Ulster Folklife*, 17 (1971), pp 42–51

Crawford, W. H. and Trainor, B. (eds.), *Aspects of Irish Social History, 1750–1800* (Belfast, 1978)

Crist, Robert Grant, *George Croghan of Pennsboro* (Pennsylvania, 1965)

Davis, R. P., *Irish Issues in New Zealand Politics, 1868–1922* (Dunedin, 1974)

De Latocnaye, Chevalier, *A Frenchman's Walk Through Ireland, 1796–7* (Belfast, 1917)

Dexter, Franklin B. (ed.), *Diary of David McClure, Doctor of Divinity, 1748–1820* (New York, 1899)

Dickson, R. J., *Ulster Emigration to Colonial America, 1718–1775* (London, 1966)

Dinsmore, John Walker, *The Scotch-Irish in America* (Chicago, 1906)

Donnelly, James S., 'Hearts of Oak, Hearts of Steel', *Studia Hibernica*, 21 (1981), pp 7–73

Doyle, David Noel, *Ireland, Irishmen and Revolutionary America, 1760–1820* (Dublin, 1981)

Draper, Lyman C., *King's Mountain and Its Heroes: History of the Battle of King's Mountain, October 7th, 1780* (Cincinnati, 1881)

Dunaway, Wayland F., *The Scotch-Irish of Colonial Pennsylvania* (Chapel Hill, N.C., 1944)

Dunbar, John R. (ed.), *The Paxton Papers* (The Hague, 1957)

Eachard, L., *An Exact Description of Ireland* (London, 1691)

Evans, E. Estyn, 'Cultural Relics of the Ulster-Scots in the Old West of North America', *Ulster Folklife*, 11 (1965), pp 33–8

Evans, E. Estyn, 'The Scotch-Irish in the New World', *Journal of the Royal Society of Antiquaries of Ireland*, 95 (1965), pp 39–49

Flower, Milton E., *John Armstrong, First Citizen of Carlisle* (Carlisle, Pa., 1971)

Foote, Rev. William Henry, *Sketches of North Carolina, Historical and Biographical* (New York, 1846)

Ford, Henry Jones, *The Scotch-Irish in America* (Princeton, 1915)

Fraser, George MacDonald, *The Steel Bonnets* (London, 1971)

Gamble, J., *A View of Society and Manners, in the North of Ireland, in the Summer and Autumn of 1812* (London, 1813)

Gardner, W. J., 'The Rise of W. F. Massey, 1891–1912', *Political Science*, 13, 1 (1961), p 3

Geary, F., 'The Rise and Fall of the Belfast Cotton Industry: Some Problems', *Irish Economic and Social History*, VIII (1981), pp 30–49

Gillespie, Raymond, *Colonial Ulster* (Cork, 1985)

Green, E. R. R., *The Lagan Valley, 1800–50: A Local History of the Industrial Revolution* (London, 1949)

Green, E. R. R., *Essays in Scotch-Irish History* (London, 1969)

Green, E. R. R., 'The Scotch-Irish and the Coming of the Revolution in North Carolina', *Irish Historical Studies*, VII, 26 (September 1950), pp 77–86

Gribbon, Sybil, *Edwardian Belfast: A Social Profile* (Belfast, 1982)

Hafen, Leroy R. (ed.), *The Mountain Men and the Fur Trade of the Far West* (Glendale, Calif., 1965. 4 vols.)

Haine, J. L. M., *Challenge and Conflict: Essays in Irish Presbyterian History and Doctrine* (Antrim, 1981)

Hamilton, W. T., *My Sixty Years on the Plains: Trapping, Trading and Indian Fighting* (Norman, Okla., 1960)

Hanna, Charles A., *The Scotch-Irish or the Scot in North Britain, North Ireland, and North America* (New York, 1902. 2 vols.)

Harris, R. C., Roulston, P. and de Freitas, C., 'The Settlement of Mono Township', *The Canadian Geographer*, 19 (1975), pp 1–17

Hays, Anna A., *Colonel Ephraim Blaine, Commissary General of the Revolutionary Army* (Carlisle, Pa., 1935)

Hickson, Mary, *Ireland in the Seventeenth Century or the Irish Massacres of 1641–2* (London, 1884. 2 vols.)

Hill, George, *The Plantation of Ulster* (Belfast, 1877)

Hill, George (ed.), *The Montgomery Manuscripts* (Belfast, 1869)

Hindle, Brooke, 'The March of the Paxton Boys', *William and Mary Quarterly*, Third Series, III, 4 (October 1946), pp 461–86

Holmes, Finlay, *Our Irish Presbyterian Heritage* (Belfast, 1985)

Hoover, Herbert, *The Ordeal of Woodrow Wilson* (London, 1958)

Houston, C. J. and Smyth, W. J., *The Sash Canada Wore* (Toronto, 1980)

Houston, Samuel. Letter of 1837 in MSS of Virginia Historical Society, Richmond, Va.

Hutchison, William T., *Cyrus Hall McCormick* (New York, 1930 and 1935. 2 vols.)

Inglis, K. S., *The Australian Colonists* (Melbourne, 1974)

James, Marquis, *The Life of Andrew Jackson* (New York, 1938)

Kaufman, Jean Troxell, *Inquisition at Hanna's Town: Excerpts from Donegal Presbytery Minutes, Book IV, 1770–1777, Concerning Western Pennsylvania,* (Greensburg, Pa., 1978)

Klett, Guy Soulliard, *Presbyterians in Colonial Pennsylvania* (Philadelphia, 1937)

Koskoff, David E., *The Mellons* (New York, 1978)

Latner, Richard B., *The Presidency of Andrew Jackson: White House Politics, 1829–1837* (Athens, Ga., 1979)

Lawson, John, *History of North Carolina, Containing the Exact Description and Natural History of That Country* (London, 1714)

Lemon, James T., *The Best Poor Man's Country: A geographical study of early southeastern Pennsylvania* (Baltimore, Md., 1972)

Leyburn, James G., *The Scotch-Irish: A Social History* (Chapel Hill, N.C., 1962)

Loughridge, Adam, *The Covenanters in Ireland* (Belfast, 1984)

Lyons, F. S. L., 'The Irish unionist party and the devolution crisis of 1904–5', *Irish Historical Studies*, VI, 21 (March 1948), pp 1–22

Lyons, F. S. L., *Ireland Since the Famine* (London, 1971)

Macrory, Patrick, *The Siege of Derry* (London, 1980)

Maguire, W. A., 'Lord Donegall and the Hearts of Steel', *Irish Historical Studies*, XXI, 84 (September, 1979), pp 351–76

Malcolm, A. G., *Report on the sanitary state of Belfast, read, adopted and ordered at the Town Meeting held 2nd March 1848* (Belfast, 1848)

Malcolm, A. G., *The Sanitary State of Belfast with Suggestions for its Improvement* (Belfast, 1852)

Mannion, John J., *Irish Settlements in Eastern Canada* (Toronto, 1974)

Mathew, David, *Scotland Under Charles the First* (London, 1955)

Mattes, Merrill J., *Colter's Hell and Jackson's Hole* (Yellowstone, Wyo., 1980)

McClelland, Aiken, 'The Battle of Garvagh', *Ulster Folklife*, 19 (1973)

McCourt, Desmond, 'County Derry and New England: The Scotch-Irish migration of 1718', *County Londonderry Handbook* (Londonderry, 1964), pp 87–101

MacKnight, Thomas, *Ulster as it is, or twenty-eight years' experience as an Irish editor* (London, 1896 2 vols.)

McMinn, J. R. B., 'Liberalism in North Antrim, 1900–14', in *Irish Historical Studies*, xxiii, 89 (May 1982), pp 17–29

McSkimin, Samuel, *Annals of Ulster* (Belfast, 1906)

McWhiney, Grady and Jameson, Perry D., *Attack and Die* (Tuscaloosa, Ala., 1984)

Miller, David W., 'Presbyterianism and "Modernization" in Ulster', *Past and Present*, 80 (1978), pp 66–90

Miller, David W., Queen's Rebels: *Ulster Loyalism in Historical Perspective* (Dublin, 1978)

Miller, Kerby A., *Emigrants and Exiles: Ireland and the Irish Exodus to North America* (Oxford and New York, 1985)

Mitchel, N. C., 'Katikati: An Ulster Settlement in New Zealand', *Ulster Folklife*, 15/16 (1970), pp 203–15

Montgomery, Eric, *The Scotch-Irish in America's History* (Belfast, 1965)

Moody, T. W. and Beckett, J. C. (eds.), *Ulster Since 1800, Second Series: A Social Survey* (London, 1957)

Moore, F. Frankfort, *The Truth about Ulster* (London, 1914)

Morton, Grenfell, 'Ulster Emigrants to Australia, 1850–1890', *Ulster Folklife*, 18 (1972), pp 111–20

Moss, Bobby G., *The Patriots at the Cowpens* (Greenville, S.C., 1985)

Moss, Bobby G., 'Rev. William Martin and the Revolution', *Selected Proceedings of the Scotch-Irish Heritage Festival at Winthrop, I*, Jack Weaver (ed.) (Baton Rouge, La., 1981)

O'Farrell, Patrick, *Letters from Irish Australia, 1825–1929* (Sydney and Belfast, 1984)

O'Hanlon, Rev. W. M., *Walks Among the Poor of Belfast, and Suggestions for their Improvement* (Belfast, 1853)

Paisley, Ian R. K., *The 'Fifty Nine' Revival: An Authentic History of the Great Ulster Awakening of 1859* (Belfast, 1958)

Pakenham, Thomas, *The Year of Liberty* (London, 1969)

Porter, Rev. James, *Billy Bluff and Squire Firebrand* (Belfast, 1879)

Powell, J. M. and Williams, M. (eds.), *Australian Space, Australian Time* (Melbourne, 1975)

Public Record Office of Northern Ireland:

Duke of Newcastle, T722: Duke of Newcastle to Primate Boulter, 2 February 1731.

Anketell, T1769/3: Journal kept by Elizabeth Anketell during a voyage to Australia, December 1865–April 1866.

Boyce, T3650/2: Letter from Alexander Boyce, Wollongong, N.S.W. to his wife in Belfast, 25 January 1838.

Brisbane, D207/67/58: Letter from Thomas Brisbane to friend in Cork, 24 February 1823.

Cherry, D1560: Letters from William Cherry, near Melbourne, Australia, to his parents in Belfast, 1866–8.

Chesney, D2260: Captain Alexander Chesney's Account of his Life, 1795.

Dempsey, T1935/1: Letter from James Dempsey on board an emigrant ship, 18 October 1838.

Gardner, D1099/7 and 9: Letters of Daniel Gardner, Melbourne, Australia to his wife Rosey in Ireland, October and November 1875.

Justice of N.W. Circuit, T659 (1445): Report of Justice of N.W. Circuit into the causes of emigration, 11 June 1729.

Katikati (New Zealand), various documents on microfilm (No. 70, Reels 1 and 2): Notes on Katikati Special Settlement, including Te Puke.

Macready, D1757/2/4, 5 and 6: Three letters from Elizabeth Macready, Christchurch, New Zealand to her cousins, 1878 and 1881.

Miller, D2630/2/7: Letter of John Miller, Hamilton, Ontario, to Susan Maguire, Drumalane, Co. Down, March 1857.

Monche, T615/3: Report of Charles Monche, Surveyor General, on progress of plantation, 16 September 1637.

Robb, T1454/5/17: Letter from Frank Robb, Tooma, N.S.W., to his brother John, 19 December 1878.

Robb, T1454: Robb Family Letters; correspondence between Co. Down and New South Wales, New York and British Columbia.

Scott, T2609/5: Mrs C. Scott, Kingston, Upper Canada to Miss Maria Scott, 6 Lower Crescent, Clifton, Bristol, England, 2 August 1834 (?)

T2609/11: Mrs J. Scott, Picton, Bay of Quinte (?), Canada to Mrs Anne Scott, Willsborough, Londonderry, 8 September 1838.

Shaw, T1923/1: 'An Account of a Voyage to Australia in a Sailing Vessel in the Years 1877–78' by Samuel Shaw, 6 February 1878.

Stewart, D2092/1/3: Ezek. Stewart to Michael Ward, re the causes of emigration, 25 March 1729.

Walker, T2018: Walker and Lowry Family papers, Canada (also USA).

White, D1195/3: Letters of Jane White, Goderich, Ontario.

Purdon, C. D., *Longevity of Flax and Factory Operatives* (Belfast, 1875)

Purdon, C. D., *The Sanitary State of the Belfast Factory District, during ten years (1864–1873 inclusive)* (Belfast, 1877)

Patton, Helen and Patton, George (eds.), *Letter of James Patton, one of the first residents of Asheville, North Carolina, to his children* (March, 1839. Republished Philadelphia, 1970)

Perceval-Maxwell, M., *The Scottish Migration to Ulster in the Reign of James I* (London, 1973)
Perry, T. M., *Australia's First Frontier: the spread of settlement in New South Wales, 1788–1829* (Melbourne, 1963)
Pitcairn, Robert, *Criminal Trials in Scotland from 1488 to 1624* (Edinburgh, 1833)
Ramsey, Robert W., *Carolina Cradle: Settlement of the Northwest Carolina Frontier, 1747–1762* (Chapel Hill, N.C., 1964)
Reid, James Seaton, *History of the Presbyterian Church in Ireland* (London, 1853)
Reid, Richard and Johnson, Keith, *The Irish Australians* (Sydney and Belfast, 1984)
Robinson, Philip, *The Plantation of Ulster: British Settlement in an Irish Landscape, 1600–1670* (Dublin, 1984)
Roebuck, Peter (ed.), *Plantation to Partition* (Belfast, 1981)
Russell, Osborne, *Journal of a Trapper*, Aubrey L. Haines (ed.) (London, 1969)
Saunders, Leslie H., *The Story of Orangeism: its origin and history for more than a century and a quarter in Canada, particularly in Ontario West* (Toronto, 1941)
Savage, D. C., 'The Origins of the Ulster Unionist Party, 1885–6', *Irish Historical Studies*, XII, 47 (March 1961), pp 185–208
The Scotch-Irish Society of America, *Proceedings of the (First) Scotch-Irish Congress* (Cincinnati, 1889)
The Scotch-Irish Society of America, *Proceedings and Addresses of the Second Congress* (Cincinnati, 1890)
The Scotch-Irish Society of America, *Proceedings and Addresses of the Third Congress of Louisville, KY, May 14 to 17, 1891* (Nashville, Tenn., 1891)
The Scotch-Irish Society of America, *Proceedings and Addresses of the Fourth Congress* (Nashville, Tenn., 1892)
Scott, Ernest (ed.), *Australian Discovery by Land* (London, 1929)
Scott, W. R., *Francis Hutcheson: His Life, Teaching and Position in the History of Philosophy* (Cambridge, 1900)
Senior, Hereward, *Orangeism: The Canadian Phase* (Toronto, 1972)
Smout, T. C., *A History of the Scottish People, 1560–1830* (London, 1969)
Smyth, William J., 'The Irish in Mid Nineteenth-Century Ontario', *Ulster Folklife*, 23 (1977)
Stevenson, David, *Scottish Covenanters and Irish Confederates: Scottish-Irish Relations in the Mid Seventeenth Century* (Belfast, 1981)
Stevenson, J., *Two Centuries of Life in Down, 1600–1800* (Belfast, 1920)
Stewart, A. T. Q., *The Ulster Crisis* (London, 1967)
Stewart, A. T. Q., *The Narrow Ground: Aspects of Ulster, 1609–1969* (London, 1977)
Stewart, George Vesey, *Notes on the Stewart Special Settlement No. 4, Bay of Plenty, New Zealand* (London, 1883)
Strain, R. W. M., *Belfast and its Charitable Society* (London, 1961)
Temple, Sir John, *The Irish Rebellion* (London and Dublin, 1646)
Ulster-American Folk Park, Omagh, Northern Ireland:
Scotch-Irish Congress, reports of proceedings for ten years, 1889–1901.
Theses histories of Antrim (New Hampshire), Ulster County (New York), Susquehanna County, Crawford County.
Biographies of Daniel Boone and Davy Crockett.
Other material on: artefacts, dress, furniture, folklore, crafts, agriculture and passenger lists.
Journals in the collection: *Appalachian Journal, Early American Life, North Carolina Folklore Journal, Pennsylvania Folklore, Pennsylvania Heritage, Pennsylvania Folklife, Western Pennsylvania Historical Magazine.*
Ulster Folk and Transport Museum, 'Illustrations of the Irish Linen Industry in 1783 by William Hincks', *Ulster Folklife*, 23 (1977), pp 1–32
Unstead, R. J. and Henderson, W. F., *Pioneer Home Life in Australia* (London, n.d.)
Walker, Rev. George, *A True Account of the Siege of Londonderry* (London, 1689, 2nd edn.)
Ward, Russel, *The Australian Legend* (Melbourne, 1965)
Warren, Anna L., *A Captive's Tale: The Story of Elizabeth Brownlee Guthrie*, Westmoreland County Historical Society (Greensburg, Pa., 1977)
Wilson, Clyde N., *The Papers of John Calhoun* (Columbia, S.C., 1980)
Wilson, Howard McKnight, *The Tinkling Spring, Headwater of Freedom* (Fisherville, Va., 1954)
Woodburn, James Albert, 'The Scotch-Irish Presbyterians in Monroe County, Indiana', *Indiana Historical Society Publications*, IV, 8 (1910), pp 437–522
Woodburn, J. B., *The Ulster Scot* (London, 1914)
Woodmason, Charles, *The Carolina Backcountry on the Eve of the Revolution*, edited with an introduction by Richard J. Hooker (Chapel Hill, N.C., 1953)
Wright, J. E. and Wright, Doris, *Pioneer Life in Western Pennsylvania* (Pittsburgh, Pa., 1940)
Young, Arthur, *A Tour in Ireland* (Cambridge, 1925)

ILLUSTRATION ACKNOWLEDGMENTS

The author and publishers would like to thank the individuals, museums and other institutions listed below for kind permission to reproduce the illustrations in this book, and in many instances making available original material to be photographed:

Amon Carter Museum, Fort Worth: p. *63*, 146, 148 (*above and below*), 161
Archives of Ontario, Toronto: p. 219 (*below*)
Belfast City Hall: p. 264 (*above and below*)
Belfast Harbour Office: p. 12 (*above*)
Canadian National Railways: 210 (*above*)
Carnegie Library, Pittsburgh: p. 155 (*below*)
In the collection of the Corcoran Gallery of Art, Gift of W. W. Corcoran: p. 138
City of Edinburgh Museum and Art Gallery: p. 19
Filson Club, Kentucky: p. 116 (*above and below*), 121 (*above*)
Great Smoky Mountains National Park: p. 81, (*below*), 84–5
Harriton House Collection: p. 100 (*below*)
Historical Society of Philadelphia: p. 59 (*above*), 90
Historical Society of Western Pennsylvania, Pittsburgh: p. 121 (*below*), *164* (*above and below*)
Hunterian Art Gallery, Glasgow: p. 176
Hulton Picture Library, p. 235 (*above*)
Illustrated London News: p. 256 (*above*) 260
King's Mountain National Military Park, South Carolina: *p. 61* (*above and below*)
Lancaster County Historical Society: p. 77 (*below*)
Library of Congress: p. *62*, 91, 97 (*above and below*), 100 (*above*), 101, 121 (*above*), 129 (*above and below*), 137, 139, 142 (*above and below*)
Linenhall Library,Belfast: p. 54
Lady Macnaghten: *p. 26*
Courtesy of the Mitchell Library, Sydney Holtermann Collection: p. 228 (*above and below*)
National Galleries of Scotland: p. 6 (*below*)
National Gallery of Ireland: p. 202
National Library of Australia, Nan Kivell Collection: p. 225 (*above*), 234, 235 (*below*)
National Library of Ireland: p. 170
New Orleans Museum of Art: p. 131
R. W. Norton Gallery, London: *p. 64*
Peter Newark Western Americana: p. 76, 118
Private Collection: p. 273
Public Archives of Ottawa: p. 215 (*above and below*)
Science Museum, London: p. 152 (*above*)
Courtesy of Simcoe County Archives, Ontario: p. 219 (*above*)
Stephen Foster Memorial Centre, Pittsburgh: p. 158 (*above and below*)
Texas State Library: p. 132 (*above and below*)
Thomas Gilcrease Institute of American History and Art, Tulsa: *pp. 162–3*
Trinity College Library, Dublin: *p. 25*
Ulster American Folk Park, Omagh: p. 152 (*below*)
Ulster Folk and Transport Museum: *p. 197* (*above and below*), *198*, 225 (*below*), 265
Ulster Museum: p. 175 (*above and below*), 180 (*above and below*), 181, 192 (*below*), 193, *199* (*above and below*), *200* (*above and below*), 204 (*above and below*), 206, 256 (*below*)
West Point Museum Collections, United States Military Museum: p. 77 (*above*)
Yale University Library: p. 149

Photographs onfollowing pages were taken by Kenneth McNally: endpapers, p. 2, 12 (*below*), *27*, *28*, 30 (*above and below*), 42, 43, 57, 59 (*below*), 66 (*above and below*), 81 (*above*), 82 (*above and below*), 103 (*above and below*), 126, 155 (*above*), 175 (*above*), 192 (*above*), 206, 268 (*above and below*), 269

Numbers in *italic* indicate colour illustrations.

INDEX

Page numbers in *italic* indicate illustrations.